THE

ISTHMUS

OF

TEHUANTEPEC:

BEING THE RESULTS OF A SURVEY FOR A RAILROAD TO CONNECT THE
ATLANTIC AND PACIFIC OCEANS, MADE BY THE

SCIENTIFIC COMMISSION

UNDER THE DIRECTION OF

MAJOR J. G. BARNARD,

U. S. ENGINEERS.

WITH A RÉSUMÉ OF THE

GEOLOGY, CLIMATE, LOCAL GEOGRAPHY, PRODUCTIVE INDUSTRY,
FAUNA AND FLORA, OF THAT REGION.

Illustrated with numerous Maps and Engravings.

ARRANGED AND PREPARED FOR THE

TEHUANTEPEC RAILROAD COMPANY OF NEW ORLEANS,

BY

J. J. WILLIAMS,

PRINCIPAL ASSISTANT ENGINEER.

NEW YORK:
D. APPLETON & COMPANY, 200 BROADWAY.

M DCCC LII.

Entered according to Act of Congress, in the year 1852, by B. FALLON, Secretary of the Tehuantepec Railroad Company of New Orleans, in the Clerk's Office of the District Court for the Eastern District of Louisiana.

PREFACE.

IN presenting to the public the results of the recent survey of the Isthmus of Tehuantepec, I cannot restrain the expression of regret that these results, foreshadowing as they do an enterprise calculated to effect a great commercial revolution, and fraught with so many mutual benefits to the United States and to Mexico, are not set forth by abler hands than my own. It is nevertheless satisfactory to me, that the work has received the endorsement of the Engineer-in-Chief, under whose instructions and personal supervision all the operations of the different parties were conducted, from the commencement to the close of the survey. Under these circumstances I trust to be exculpated from the charge of personal vanity in appending herewith the letter of Major Barnard, whose prolonged stay on the Isthmus precluded the issue of these pages over his own signature.

NEW YORK, FEB. 1st, 1852.

DEAR SIR :—

Returning home after a much more protracted absence than I had at first reason to anticipate, it is a source of gratification to me to find myself relieved by you from the task of collating from the official reports of the Engineering and Hydrographic Parties, such portions of them as are desirable for the public, whose attention has already been attracted to the undertaking by the course of events connected with it, and in whose mind a deep and steadfast interest has been awakened by the great national hopes, of which I cannot but think our humble labors are the precursors.

Within three years a new era has dawned upon us, and with the acquisition of California and the settlement of Oregon, the energies of men's minds have been diverted from the old and circuitous channels of trade to other and shorter ones, which, while they are destined to bind us

PREFACE.

more closely together as a nation, promise likewise to give us in return for their opening all the varied treasures of the Eastern World. A few years only will elapse ere we shall witness every part of the Pacific whitened by the sails of our ships, and every wave in its broad expanse bearing to distant lands, hitherto unknown to us, except by name, the people and the commodities of our country. That this publication, setting forth as it does the advantages of one of those great inter-oceanic routes, must contribute in no small degree to such results, I cannot doubt; and in returning the work to you after a careful examination, it affords me pleasure to lighten, if I can, the burden of your responsibility, by giving it my unqualified approval as a faithful record of operations, to which all of us, I am sure, must look back with feelings of pride and mutual congratulation.

Under other circumstances than these, such expressions might well be considered out of place; but when I reflect on the difficulties that assailed us in the offset of our work, and find in the end that it is one of those rare cases wherein the most sanguine hopes have been changed to realities, my privilege to congratulate can hardly be questioned.

If I may be permitted to judge by the amount of labor executed during the limited time of the survey, it would not be difficult to imagine how much more it might have been extended, but for the termination put to it by the Mexican authorities. Nevertheless, with the existence of good harbors at each terminus, and the survey of an entire length of line, favorable in its character, and of facile grades (although we have reason to believe that further explorations would give other lines much more advantageous and preferable for permanent location, which might supersede the one already run), sufficient is established to demonstrate beyond all doubt the practicability of the project in a complete and satisfactory manner — a result to which the liberality and active co-operation of the Managing Committee of New Orleans has contributed greatly. And while it is to be regretted that Mexico, through an unwise course of policy, has thwarted the designs of those who, in the pursuit of their interests (based upon her plighted faith and invited by her passports), would have aided her tottering government, and extended the influence of her people; yet it is a satisfaction that so much has been accomplished by the surveying party in so short a time.

I am, dear sir, very truly yours,

J. G. BARNARD, *Chief Engineer.*

J. J. WILLIAMS, Esq., Prin. Ass't Engineer.

PREFACE. 5

In the preparation of this work for the press (called forth now by the exigencies of the New Orleans Company), I have endeavored to avoid all gratuitous expressions of opinion, both with regard to the project itself and its relation to other routes. Throughout, my desire has been to give a plain history of the survey, and a correct account of the results obtained by it; knowing full well how much more trustworthy are the conclusions of the mass than of the individual, whose mind is naturally biased by a personal identity with the events and circumstances upon which he passes judgment.

With reference to the subject-matter of Part II., no apology is requisite. We have many interesting details of the history of Mexico from the earliest periods to the present day; but there is much with regard to her local Geography, Climate, and Natural Resources, which yet remains to be written. And in the establishment of a great national highway across the Isthmus of Tehuantepec, a portion of the Mexican territory on which the hopes of her conqueror were centered, something is necessary to be known beyond the mere arithmetical results of instrumental observations. I have therefore devoted a part of this report to an exposition of the geology, climate, and productions of the Isthmus, accompanied by some brief notes on the character, customs, and habitations of the people who constitute a remnant of the old Mexican race, whose thrilling and dramatic history (through the eloquent writings of Prescott) has become as familiar to us as "household words."

All parts of the work are illustrated with sketches of the natural scenery of the Isthmus. These are faithful representations, and give a better idea of the country than any written detailed description.

For convenient reference the maps have been bound in a separate book by themselves, and embrace all the results of the recent survey, together with those obtained by the officers of Commodore Perry's Squadron, in 1847-8.

In the APPENDIX will be found the documents of the grant of Señor Don José de Garay (upon whose privileges the undertaking was necessarily predicated), with such other papers as it may be desirable for the public to peruse. From these they will be enabled to judge to what extent the faith of Mexico has been plighted, and how far the Tehuantepec Railroad Company of New Orleans have been justified in the outlay they have made.

For many valuable suggestions, and for much of the details embraced in the statistical part of the work, I am indebted to Mr. John McLeod Murphy of the Navy, and to Mr. J. C. Avery, 1st Assistant Engineer.

My acknowledgments are likewise due to Dr. Antisell, of New York, for the assistance rendered me in preparing the articles on Geology and Climate.

J. J. WILLIAMS.

NEW YORK, FEB. 10, 1852.

CONTENTS.

PART I.

ENGINEERING REPORTS.

	PAGE.
Landing of the Expedition at Minatitlan	11
Major Barnard's Instructions	11
General Topographical View of the Isthmus	13
Cortes' Examination of the Coatzacoalcos Bar	23
Disposition of the Railroad parties	23
General Description of Route	25
Reconnaissance to Mt. Encantada.	29
Report on the Line North of the Dividing Ridge	38
Reconnaissance of the Country east of Coatzacoalcos River	51
Table of Grades from Jaltepec River to Pacific Plains	54
Tangents, Curvature, etc., Middle Division	56
Comparative Table of Grades, Curvature, etc.	56
Railroad Distances across the Isthmus of Tehuantepec	57
Native Labor	58
Ibid. (Letter of J. C. Trautwine, Esq.)	59
Material for Construction	60
Estimated Cost of Construction	61
Summary of Cost of Construction	66
Superstructure	67
Equipment	67
Station Buildings	68
Auxiliary Carriage-Road	68
Distance by ditto and Coatzacoalcos River	72
Estimated Cost of Auxiliary Road	73
Income of ditto	74
General Summary of Total Cost	77
Comparative Cost of Principal Roads in the United States	78
Comparative Cost of Principal Roads in England	78
Proposed Lines	78
Mountain Passes	81

HYDROGRAPHIC REPORTS.

	PAGE.
Survey of the Coatzacoalcos	83
Major Barnard's Instructions	83
Lieut. Leigh's Chart	84
Manner of Conducting Survey	85
Head of Ship Navigation	85
Capacity for Shoal-water Navigation	88
Effect of Rains	88
Formation of Coatzacoalcos Bar	90
Reconnaissance of the Rio del Corte	92
Vegetable Productions	92
Geological Character of Mountains	94
Scenery on Rio del Corte	95
Tributaries	96
Rapid of Alto Mayor	97
Height of Water in Rio del Corte	98
Survey of Uspanapa River	99
Vegetation of River Banks	100
El Rompido	101
Arroyo de los Urgells	102
River Tancochapa	102
Hacienda of San José	102
Rancho Maria del Carmen	102
Capacity of River for Navigation	104

PACIFIC PORTS.

Survey of Ventosa by Mr. Trastour	104
Temperature of the Pacific Coast	110
Mr. Temple's Report on Ventosa	111

GENERAL SUMMARY.

Practicability of the Road	112
Expenses of Construction	113
Equipment	114
Formation of the Coatzacoalcos Bar	114
Sailing directions for the Coatzacoalcos Bar	115
Capacity of Rivers for Navigation	116
Improvement of the Harbor of Ventosa	116
Letter of Capt. Mott of the Steamer "Gold Hunter"	117

CONTENTS.

REVENUE AND INCOME.
	PAGE.
Comparison of Distances by Panama, Nicaragua, and Tehuantepec Routes	120
Extract of Letter from Hon. Geo. M. Dallas	121
Table of Passengers, Freight, and Gold, between Atlantic States and California, by different Routes	121
Comparison of Harbors of the Isthmus Routes	123
Extent of Whale Fishery in the Pacific	123
Requirements of California	126
Report of Naval Committee on Steamers between San Francisco and China	128
Effects of Winds and Currents on Sailing Ships	129
Value of Imports into Great Britain from Asia and the Pacific Ocean	130
The Canadian Railway Project	131
Comparison of Time between England and China, via Panama, Suez, and Tehuantepec	131
Advantages of Tehuantepec Route to U. S. Government	133
Supply of Coal for Pacific Steamers	134
Mr. Buchanan's Instructions to Mr. Trist with reference to Purchase of Tehuantepec Route	135
Statement of American Trade with Asia and Pacific	136
Nicaragua Ship Canal	137
Emigration to California	138
Extent and Value of the Garay Grant	140
Way Trade	140
Value of Isthmus Productions	142
Australian Emigration	144
General Review	145

PART II.

GEOLOGY AND MINERALOGY.
Character of the Pacific Slope	150
Dividing Ridge	151
Middle Division	153
Atlantic Plains	154
Discovery of Gold on the Isthmus	156
Iron Ore	158
Cinnabar Ore	159
Obsidian	159
Petroleum	159
Salt	160
Stability of the Isthmus	161

CLIMATE.
Disposition of Mountains, etc.	162
Humidity of Atmosphere	164
Prevailing Winds	165
Rainy Season	166
Temperature	167
Sanitary Condition of the Isthmus	170
Precautions to be Observed	171
Epidemics	171
Report of Dr. Kovaleski	173

VEGETABLE PRODUCTIONS.
Distribution of Plants on the Isthmus	180
Influence of Temperature on Vegetation	181
Valuable Timbers	183
India-rubber Tree	183
Ixtle (Bromelia Pita)	184
Maize, Sugar, Tobacco, etc.	185
Theobroma Cacao	187
Vegetable Dyes	189
Vegetable Gums and Balsams	191
Fruits	192
Durability of Timber	194
Botanical Tables	197

ANIMALS.
Domestic Animals	201
Wild Animals	205
Birds	208
Reptiles	210
Fish	212
Insects	212
Mollusca	216

INHABITANTS.
European Population	217
Creoles	217
Mestizos	218
Indians	219
Aztecs and Agualulcos	219
General Appearance	219
Characteristics	220
Subsistence	221
Dress	221
Degradation	222
Doña Marina	224
Mijes	224
General Character	225
Zoques	225

CONTENTS.

	PAGE.
Zapotecos	226
Intellectual Capacities	226
Juchitecos	227
Huaves	227
Mulattoes, Zambos, Negroes	228

TOWNS, PRODUCTIVE INDUSTRY, ETC.

San Cristoval Ishuatlan	229
Santiago Moloacan	230
Hacienda of San Antonio	231
San Francisco Sanapa	231
Hacienda of San José del Carmen	232
Indian Relics	232
Gold Dust	232
Cacao Trade with Tobasco	233
Mina-titlan	233
Cosuliacaque	234
Longevity of Natives	235
Otiapa	235
San Juan Chinameca	235
Coffee Plantation	236
Jaltipan	236
Hill of Malinche	236
Native Women	236
Family of Mutes	237
Salubrity of Jaltipan	237
Tesistepec	237
Hacienda of Almagro	237
Hidalgo-titlan, or Almagres	237
San Martin Acayucam	238
Extent of Trade	239
Neighboring Towns	239
Mal Paso	239
Boca del Monte	240
Beauty of Scenery	241
San Juan Guichicovi	241
Church, Tradition, etc.	242
Iron Ore	242
Santa Maria Petapa	243
Church, Paintings, etc.	243

	PAGE.
Santo Domingo	243
Description of Cave	244
El Barrio de la Soledad	244
La Chivela	244
Santiago	244
Tarifa	245
Rancho Agua Escondida	245
San Miguel Chimalapa	245
Singular Custom of the Zoques	246
Road between San Miguel and Santa Maria Chimalapa	246
Santa Maria	246
Balsas on Rio del Corte	247
Ruins of Chimalapilla	247
Family of Albinos	247
Cerro of Guié-vixia	248
Scenery from the Summit of Dividing Ridge	248
Guichilona	248
San Gerónimo	248
Mineral Spring in Chivela Pass	249
Santo Domingo Chihuitan	249
Sugar Mill of Santa Cruz	249
Itztaltepec	249
El Espinal	250
Juchatan	250
Church	250
Productive Industry	250
Tehuantepec	251
Parroquia	251
College	251
Plaza and Market Place	252
Manufactured Articles	252
Municipal Government	252
Trade	253
View from Cerro del Tigre	253
Ruins of Guiéngola	253
Other Settlements on Pacific Plains	255
Huilotepec	255

ILLUSTRATIONS.

TEHUANTEPEC, from Cerro del Tigre. *Frontispiece.*	
MINA-TITLAN	21
CHIVELA, showing entrance to the Pass on the left	26
TABLE-LANDS near El Barrio	42
AMATE PICADURA	47
CAMP SANDILLA (Brazo Mistan)	87
PIEDRA LAGARTA (Rio del Corte)	95
CERRO MORRO (Ventosa)	104

VENTOSA, looking north	116
MAPS, showing inter-oceanic routes	146
GEOLOGICAL SECTION	149
VIEW IN THE MASAHUA PASS	152
THERMAL CURVES	167
MAKING TORTILLAS	221
CHURCH AT ISHUATLAN	230
CHURCH AT EL BARRIO	244
CERRO GUIÉ-VIXIA	248

PART I.

ENGINEERING REPORTS.

On the 25th of December, 1850, the steamer Alabama, having on board the corps of Engineers destined for the survey of a route for a railroad across the Isthmus of Tehuantepec, entered the Coatzacoalcos River, and on the same day arrived at Mina-titlan, a town situated at the head of present ship navigation, twenty miles from the mouth of the river. The engineering party consisted of fifty-four persons, placed under the immediate direction of Major J. G. Barnard, of the U. S. Engineers. Another party, under Mr. P. E. Trastour, had previously been sent down by the company, for the purpose of exploring the harbors on the Pacific coast, and were at that time employed in making a survey of the harbor of *Ventosa*.

On arriving at Mina-titlan, the parties were immediately organized for the commencement of active operations in the field; and pursuant to Major Barnard's instructions, a party under Mr. W. G. Temple, U. S. N., commenced a survey of the Coatzacoalcos River, at Mina-titlan;* and another under Mr. J. C. Avery was directed to make a reconnaissance to Mt. Encantada, situated on the west bank of the Coatzacoalcos, about forty miles southwesterly from Mina-titlan, on the route of the proposed survey. At the same time I received Major Barnard's instructions, from which the following is an extract:

"You will get your party through as rapidly as possible to some cen-

---

* Between this point and the Bar, a survey had been made by Com. Perry, in 1847, the maps of which accompany this Report.

tral point, and I think *Chivela* will be the best. There, you will start your survey of the dividing ridge—perhaps *Chivela* first, *Masahua* next, and *Tarifa* last. Having found the best Pass, run your line down to the Pacific, assuming *La Ventosa* as the terminus.

"If Tarifa be the best Pass, start from that. In both cases you will be able to judge of the practicability of connecting with the lagoons, should the *Boca Barra* be selected.

"It might prove that not much length would be saved on account of the rapidity of descent. Keep your grades below forty feet, if possible; and tunnel, if necessary and practicable.

"If Boca del Monte appears to be a good starting point, Mr. Avery might commence there, and run towards you; if not, bring him up to you, and let him run a line back, more to the eastward. I shall be able to communicate with you before you get to work.

"Establish your bench marks so as to be referred to without doubt by future surveys.

"We must leave out of mind entirely the idea of locating the road; a demonstration of *practicability* and *probable cost* is the utmost that we can hope to obtain.

"As the parties are full in juniors, use them (instead of confining them to carrying instruments) as much as possible in *lateral reconnaissances*, directing them to penetrate a certain distance each side of your line, and give you the topography, &c., of the country.

"Your journals should be full as to the survey, and the topographical and geological features and vegetable growth of the country. Note what productions are valuable articles of commerce; what timbers are useful for construction; what building stone, &c., is available; and endeavor to ascertain if mines and precious metals are likely to be found.

"It is enjoined upon all individuals attached to the survey, to conduct themselves with the utmost decorum in their intercourse with the natives; to interfere with them as little as possible, to pay respect to civil and religious authorities and ceremonies, and in particular to refrain from trespassing on private property, taking fruits, &c., &c. Chiefs of parties will be held responsible for the good conduct of their respective parties, and will discharge any individul whose conduct does not conform to the stipulations contained in the articles he has signed.

"You will pay particular attention to the use of firearms. They are issued exclusively for personal defence, or rather more for moral effect than for any anticipated necessity for their use. They should, therefore, not be resorted to, even should a quarrel occur, without the utmost caution, as more evil might arise from their imprudent use than from being without them."

Before entering upon the details of our surveys, or the manner of operating the parties in the field, it seems proper to give a *general topographical view* of the Isthmus.

ENGINEERING REPORTS. 13

The Isthmus of Tehuantepec is that portion of the Mexican territory which lies between the Gulf of Mexico and the Pacific Ocean, where the two seas approach the nearest to each other; and comprises the eastern portions of the states of Vera Cruz and Oaxaca.

From the mouth of the Coatzacoalcos, which discharges itself into the Gulf in 18° 8' 20" north latitude, and 94° 32' 50" longitude west (from Greenwich), to the harbor of Ventosa on the Pacific, situated in 16° 11' 45" north latitude and 95° 15' 40" west longitude, the distance in a direct line is $143\frac{1}{2}$ miles. The coast-lines on either side have a general direction nearly east and west.

In considering the Isthmus with reference to its general topographical features, it may properly be said to comprise three main divisions, more or less distinct in their general characteristics; the first, embracing that portion extending from the Gulf to the base of the Cordillera, and which may be called the *Atlantic plains;* the second, comprising the more elevated or *mountainous districts* in the central parts, and the third, including the level country bordering the ocean on the south, and known as the *Pacific plains.*

The first division comprises a belt of country of some forty or fifty miles in breadth, lying contiguous to the Gulf-coast, and made up of extensive alluvial basins of exceeding richness and fertility, through which the drainage of the northern slope of the Cordillera discharges itself into the Gulf.

The principal of these hydrographic basins is that of the Coatzacoalcos, which occupies the central portion of this division, and has a general direction of N. N. E by S. S. W. It is separated from the basin of the Tonala and Tancochapa rivers on the east, and the San Juan on the west, by a moderately elevated plateau or table-land, furrowed by numerous small streams, and generally covered with dense forests. These tablelands, with few exceptions, are not elevated more than two or three hundred feet above the sea-level.

Conspicuous to the west of the Coatzacoalcos are the peaks of San Martin and Pelon, mountains of considerable magnitude, and constituting the most striking topographical features of this division of the Isthmus. They occupy an angle in the coast, which at the Barrilla turns to the north, making nearly a right angle with the coast-line to the east, and gradually curving to the west for a distance of 20 or 30 miles, when it again assumes an east and west direction. The mountains referred to terminate a long range of hills extending to the west, and gradually decreasing in height till they subside to the level of the plain country bordering the San Juan River on the east; the whole being known as the Tuxtla range. Between this mountain chain and the Jaltepec River, the only highland breaking the general uniformity of the surface of the country, is the Encantada Mountain, five miles to the west of the Coatzacoalcos, and thirty miles from the Gulf. This mountain has an elevation of about eight hundred feet above the surrounding plains, and its base extends nearly two miles in a direction W. N. W. by E. S. E. Thirty-seven miles eastward of this range is Mt. Tecuanapa, surrounded by extensive plains, and having an elevation of 1200 or 1500 feet above the level of the Gulf. The country bordering the Uspanapa River on the east, and distant ten or twelve miles to the north of Tecuanapa, is considerably broken and divided by elevated ridges or ranges of hills, with an extreme elevation of four or five hundred feet above the sea-level; and about midway between the Coatzacoalcos and the Tonala rivers, at a distance of eight or ten miles from the Gulf, are the Cerros of St. Vincent and Acalapa, which, though styled "mountains," consist of but moderately elevated broken ranges of hills.

With the few exceptions here referred to, the entire country embraced in the northern division (as seen from the highlands immediately south of the Jaltepec River) presents the appearance of a broad plain, entirely covered with dense forests.

The second or middle division may be said to extend from the Jaltepec River on the north to within twenty or twenty-five miles of the Pacific coast, comprising a strip of country through the central portions of the Isthmus, of some forty miles in breadth on the west, and gradually widening out towards the east to sixty or seventy miles. This division presents a great diversity of feature. The immense chain of the Cordillera, which, under different denominations, extends, almost without interruption, the entire length of the two Americas, traverses the country from east to west; but instead of those lofty volcanic peaks, which constitute so striking a feature of extensive portions of this gigantic chain of mountains, there is a sudden depression of the range in its passage across this Isthmus, the continuity of the chain being nearly broken at a point directly in the line of shortest communication between the two oceans. The Cordillera here approaches very near the Pacific coast, and its southern slope terminating suddenly, extends in nearly a right line for a considerable distance in an east and west direction. But on the north side, the base of the mountain range, commencing at the point of greatest depression, forms an extended curve to the northeast on one side, and to the northwest on the other, having the concave side turned towards the north. The section of country lying to the south of the Jaltepec and Chalchijapa rivers, and circumscribed on the east, south, and west by the above mountain range, is made up of elevated table-lands, more or less broken and divided by low irregular spurs from the main Cordillera. To the east and west we find a confused mass of mountains, which, though attaining to but a moderate elevation, cover a large extent of country, particularly on the east, where they fill nearly one-half the breadth of the Isthmus. The table-lands above mentioned comprise an area of about 1400 square miles, and are watered by the Jumuapa, Sarabia, Malatengo, Almoloya, and Chichihua rivers, all tributaries to the Coatzacoalcos, and streams of small importance, by reason both of their limited length and the comparatively small volume of their waters. The first four take their rise in the mountains to the west, and the last drains a portion of the mountainous districts to the east. These streams present through nearly half their length the character of mere torrents, and their currents are generally rapid throughout their entire course. In their passage through the table-lands, they are generally bordered by a greater or lesser breadth of rich alluvial bottoms.

The elevated spurs and ridges referred to, and which traverse the country generally in an east and west direction, offer the principal obstacles to the construction of a railroad across this portion of the Isthmus. The Jaltepec and Jumuapa rivers are separated by a chain of highlands, constituting a spur from the Cordillera on the west, and extending easterly to the Coatzacoalcos; branching from this main ridge, are numerous lateral spurs, which, decreasing in width and height, gradually subside to the level of the river-bottoms. We also find the country bordering the Sarabia River considerably elevated and broken, from its confluence with the Coatzacoalcos to a point about two miles westward of Boca del Monte; and three miles S. W. of this latter place is a high range of hills, known as the mountain of Sarabia.

Further to the south are the hills of Xochiapa, which originally seem to have formed a connected chain, joining the mountain range to the east and west, but have been cut through or divided by the Malatengo, Almoloya, and Chichihua rivers; thus opening *natural* passages through a range of hills, which otherwise would seem to have offered an almost insuperable obstacle to the construction of a railroad. Between this range and the Summit Pass, the country is made up of elevated rolling plains, which are divided by low ranges of hills into three divisions, known respectively as the plains of Xochiapa, Chivela, and Tarifa, which generally present a very smooth surface, but more or less undulating, and nearly destitute of heavy timber, except on the margins of the principal streams. They gradually become more elevated as we approach the Summit Pass, and also present a more uniform level surface. They are bounded on the south by the cerros Prieto, Masahuita, and Espinosa, all of which terminate in rugged limestone peaks, at an elevation of from 1500 to 2000 feet above the Pacific; and form the only connecting links between the high mountain chain extending westwardly through the State of Oaxaca, and the Cordillera of Guatimala on the east.

By a narrow opening or gap in these mountains, we descend suddenly from the elevated table-lands to the Pacific plains, which form the third or southern division. These plains average about twenty miles in breadth, from the base of the mountains to the Pacific coast, and descend on the meridians to the lagoons, at an inclintion varying from ten to fifteen feet in the mile; thus forming, as it were, an immense inclined plane, with its side next the mountains, about two hundred and fifty feet above the Pacific. Under these circumstances they present a remarkably smooth, even surface, with a uniform, gentle slope towards the sea. In some instances there are occasional isolated hills, which, rising abruptly, form a prominent feature in the topography of this part of the country. The plains are traversed by eight rivers, which discharge the drainage of the southern slope into the sea. Seven of these rivers empty into the lagoons, which are connected with the sea by a narrow outlet, called the Boca Barra: the eighth, or Tehuantepec River, comes from a northwesterly direction, and passing through the city of the same name, discharges itself directly into the sea at the Bay of Ventosa.

The most important of the streams referred to, as respects length and the volume of their waters, are the Ostuta and Chicapa on the east, and the Tehuantepec on the west. The first two named rivers have their source in the highest parts of the Sierra to the east of San Miguel Chimalapa. It is said of them that they always rise and fall simultaneously, the slightest change in one stream being accompanied by a corresponding variation in the other—a fact which has originated the belief that they have a common source in a lake supposed to be on the summit of the mountains to the east; though the true reason is no doubt to be found in the fact that they both proceed from the highest points of the Sierra, and through the upper part of their course are in close proximity to each other. These streams derive their chief importance as being the source from which a sufficient supply of water may probably be obtained for the summit-level of a ship-canal. The plan proposed by Mr. Moro for obtaining this supply was, " to open a trench that would lead the waters of the Ostuta to the valley of the Chicapa; and another, which, beginning a little above the ' Ultimo Rancho,' would direct the waters thus collected to the table-lands of Tarifa, following the brows of the hills to the north of the valley watered by the upper Chicapa and the Monetza." The average depth of water in the Chicapa (at San Miguel Chimalapa), from June to October inclusive, is seven feet, and a section of the stream in the driest part of the season gives one foot by twenty-five feet, with a very rapid current. The waters of the Ostuta are at least three times as abundant as those of the Chicapa. The elevated mountain peaks near the source of these streams are almost constantly enveloped in clouds, which may account for their remarkably uniform flow of water throughout the entire year.

Most of the rivers watering the southern slope have a comparatively limited extent, and before reaching the plains present the character of mere mountain torrents. In the dry season many of the smaller ones become completely absorbed, or lose themselves in the sands of the plains; even the Rio de los Perros, a stream of some magnitude in the rainy season, exhibits a dry channel below El Espinal for six months in the year, viz., from December to July; while near the mountains it always carries a considerable volume of water.

All of these streams, as they issue from the mountains, are remarkably pure and limpid, even in times of flood, thereby indicating the rocky nature of the districts which they drain. In their descent towards the plains they offer almost unlimited sources of water-power, which at many points may be made available for sawing lumber or for other purposes.

The lagoons, which receive most of the drainage of the southern slope, extend a distance of nearly forty miles along the coast, and comprise an area of more than 200 square miles; they are divided by a narrow peninsula of land into two principal divisions, known as the upper and lower lagoons. Though of considerable extent, they are generally shallow, and no doubt annually becoming more so from the sediment brought down by the numerous rivers which discharge into them.

The bay of Ventosa is formed by an indentation in the coast, and the projection of the Cerro Moro on the west. The Tehuantepec River discharges itself near this point. The bay is partially sheltered from the north winds by low ranges of hills from three to four miles distant. A short distance to the westward are two similar indentations of the coast, known respectively as Salina Cruz and Salina del Marques.*

---

* For a detailed description of Ventosa, vide page 104.

Of the streams watering the northern slope of the Isthmus, the most important by far is the Coatzacoalcos,* by reason both of the comparatively large extent of country, for the drainage of which it is the outlet, and also as furnishing the natural channel through which the projected communication between the two oceans may, in part, be effected. This river takes its rise in the unexplored part of the Sierra to the east of Santa Maria Chimalapa. About thirteen miles above this village, the Chimalapilla falls into the Coatzacoalcos on its right bank. This was the highest point explored by the commission; but the Indians ascend it on rafts thirty or forty miles further beyond. On the same side, and one mile below the Chimalapilla, is the confluence of the Rio del Pinal; thence to a point nine miles below Santa Maria the course of the river is southwest, and thence to the confluence of the Malatengo, a distance of thirty-six miles, it runs in a northwesterly direction. Between the Pinal and Malatengo, it receives the waters of the Milagro, Iscuilapa, and Coyoltepec rivers on its left bank. The Malatengo, which also enters the Coatzacoalcos on the left, drains the elevated table-lands of Xochiapa, Chivela, and Tarifa, as well as a portion of the mountain districts to the east and west of them. Its principal tributaries are the Chichihua and Almoloya; the latter takes its course through the plains of Chivela, and derives its chief importance as probably furnishing the most feasible route by which the railroad may be carried to these plains from the north.

The rivers Sarabia, Jumuapa, and Jaltepec (or de los Mijes) enter the Coatzacoalcos on the left bank, and next to them the Chalchijapa on the right. The first two descend from the Sierra of Santa Maria Guinenagate; and although the Sarabia carries a considerable volume of water, it is not navigable on account

---

* Many disputes have arisen with regard to the orthography of this name. In the official dispatches of Hernan Cortes to the Emperor Charles V. he writes it in no less than six different ways, viz., "*Mazamalco*," "*Quacalco*," "*Cuacuacalco*," "*Cuicicacalco*," "*Guazacualco*," and "*Guazaqualco*." The veteran soldier Bernal Diaz del Castillo, who resided more than thirty years in the province, calls it "*Cuacasualco*." De Solis, on the other hand, writes it "*Guazacoalco*," and the Abbé Clavigero, who, from his extensive knowledge of the languages of Mexico, is perhaps the best authority, writes it after this manner, viz., "*Coatzacualco*."

of its course being too precipitous, and having near its mouth a fall which impedes the entrance of canoes; but the Jumuapa can be ascended in the rainy season to a point known as the Paso de la Puerta, from which there is a good mule-road to San Juan Guichicovi. The Jaltepec River has its source in the Sierra of the Mijes, situated in the district of Villa Alta, and is navigable for canoes all the year round to a spot called Tutla, about fifty miles from its mouth. This river is nearly as large as the Coatzacoalcos above the confluence of the two streams, and is the most important tributary on the west. The Chalchijapa is also a considerable stream, and the Indians ascend it for five days with rafts, and then cross by land to the village of Santa Maria Chimalapa. Between the confluence of the Chalchijapa and the point of La Horqueta, where the river divides into two branches, the small streams Colorado, Naranjo, Peñas Blancas, and Cuapinoloya join the river by its left bank, and the Churriagao by the right. The general course of the Coatzacoalcos from the confluence of the Malatengo to that of the Jumuapa, is from south to north: it then runs northwest until it meets the Jaltepec, and thence to the bar its general course is northeast.

The length from the mouth of the Malatengo to the Sarabia is 19 miles; from the Sarabia to the Jumuapa, 14; from the Jumuapa to the Jaltepec, 10; from the Jaltepec to the Chalchijapa, 14; and thence to the Horqueta, 38—being 95 miles between the Malatengo and that point.

Above the confluence of the Jaltepec, the country on either side of the Coatzacoalcos is more or less broken and hilly, and the banks of the stream often rocky and precipitous; but below this point the margins are comparatively low, and the surface level for some distance back from the river. Between the Jaltepec and the Horqueta, there are a few spots called *cerritos*, or hillocks, composed of beds of clay, from 40 to 60 feet in height. The banks of the river, however, seldom exceed 10 or 15 feet, and are sometimes so low as to be covered in times of flood.

At the Horqueta, as has been said, the river branches—the western arm being called the Brazo Mistan, and the eastern the Brazo Apotzongo: these branches unite after having formed the island of Tacamichapa. The Mistan receives the waters of the rivers Tatagapa and Monzapa ; the former draining the country to the west of Mt. Encantada, and the latter having its source to the southwest of Tesistepec. The Monzapa has a depth of 15 feet at its mouth, and in the rainy season is navigable for canoes to a considerable distance. Seven miles below the island of Tacamichapa, the Coatzacoalcos receives the waters of the Coachapa River on the east. The source of this stream is unknown, but it has been ascended in canoes for twelve days, the time usually occupied in going from the bar of the Coatzacoalcos to the Pass of Sarabia; schooners have also sailed up it for a distance of several miles. The cross-ties used on the railroad at Vera Cruz were manufactured from timber obtained from the banks of this stream.

Four miles below the debouche of the Coachapa, but on the opposite shore, is the village of Mina-titlan; and three miles below this, the river Uspanapa joins the Coatzacoalcos by its right bank.

Half way between the river Coachapa and Mina-titlan is situated, on the left bank, in front of an islet, the common entrance to the creeks Tocajalpa, Ojosapa, and Cuamecatan.

The Uspanapa is the most considerable of all the numerous tributaries of the Coatzacoalcos, and is in some respects even superior to the latter stream for purposes of navigation, carrying a sufficient depth of water to float large vessels to a greater distance from the Gulf, and also being less tortuous. The Indians assert that it has been ascended in canoes for twenty-five days; but it was probably never explored to its source. The mountains near the head-waters of this stream have the reputation of being rich in gold and silver mines. A great extent of country bordering the Uspanapa and Coachapa rivers is subject to periodic inundation. Below the Uspanapa, near a spot named Paso Nuevo, through which runs the high-road leading to Tobasco, the river San Antonio joins the Coatzacoalcos, proceeding from some marshes nineteen miles above its mouth; and one mile lower down, on the opposite bank, it receives the waters of the Tacoteno River. Finally, at twelve miles below the Uspanapa, and five miles from the bar, on the left, is the confluence of the river Tierra

Nueva, or the Calzadas, this being the channel through which the Coatzacoalcos receives the waters of the river Huasuntan, a considerable stream draining an extensive alluvial basin to the south of the Tuxtla range of mountains. This river also connects with the sea by a narrow channel at La Barrilla. The strip of land intercepted between the river Tierra Nueva and the Gulf coast, and extending from the bar of the Coatzacoalcos to the Barrilla, near the base of Mt. Pelon, is made up on the Gulf side by a chain of sand-hills, leaving a considerable margin of low land on the river side. These sand-hills are elevated from fifty to one hundred feet above tide-water, and border all this part of the coast.

The banks of the river below Mina-titlan are very low and frequently flooded. The mouth of the Coatzacoalcos, the geographical position of which has been given, is one hundred and fifteen miles west from the river Grijalva or Tobasco, and about one hundred and ten miles from Vera Cruz. Its width is about fifteen hundred feet, and its depth varies in different places. A transversal section of the river, over the bar, shows it to be slightly swelled in the middle and hollowed out towards the two banks of the river; the hollow on the right forming the eastern, and the other the western pass. The greatest depth of the latter is close to the bank on which the fort is built. This pass is a straight channel, of easy entrance, and always the same, by reason of the nature of the material composing the bar. It has a width of three hundred and fifty feet and a depth of thirteen feet, which, however, is diminished to twelve and a half in the month of May. The tides are not strong on this part of the Mexican coast; but in case of heavy northerly winds, the waters of the river are backed up, giving a sensible increase of depth on the bar. The eastern channel is about one hundred feet in width, and its depth varies from eleven to twelve feet.

As soon as the bar is crossed, and the ascent of the river commenced, it widens and deepens, and at seven miles from the Gulf the lead shows a depth of forty feet, which is preserved for some distance. The least depth in the channel below Mina-titlan is twelve feet, and this may be carried nearly to the island of Tacamichapa. The superior advantages offered by this stream as a safe and convenient harbor for ships, early attracted the attention of the Spanish conquerors. Cortes, in his official dispatches to the Emperor Charles V., speaks of the importance of this river, as furnishing the best harbor to be found on the Gulf coast of Mexico. In giving the results of a survey of the river, made by his order, he says: "They found two fathoms and a half of water at its entrance, in the shallowest part, and ascending twelve leagues, the least they found was five or six fathoms."

These soundings were made in the year 1520, and give about the same depth over the bar at the mouth of the river which we now find. This is an important fact, as proving that the material of which the bar is formed does not change its position, and giving promise that any work for deepening the channel at this point will afford permanent results.

In compliance with Major Barnard's instructions, and as soon as arrangements could be made for our departure, I ascended the river with the party under my immediate charge to Paso Sarabia, from whence we proceeded on horses and mules, via San Juan Guichicovi and El Barrio, to La Chivela, a Hacienda directly at the entrance to the Pass of the same name. Here we established our head-quarters, and after making a reconnaissance of Chivela and Masahua Passes, in company with Major Barnard, it was determined to commence at once the survey through Masahua, as Chivela was then considered more difficult, while that of Tarifa was too far to the east.*

Having completed this survey down to the plains of the Pa-

---

* It was the intention to have made a regular survey of Chivela Pass, as well as down the Rio Almoloya, so as to enable us to compare the relative cost of the two routes; that is, the Rio Malatengo and Masahua Pass route, with the Rio Almoloya and Chivela Pass route, as also a combination of both. This would have been done had not the further progress of the survey been arrested by the Mexican authorities just as the party were commencing the line through Chivela. And it is to be regretted that while the parties were on the ground, with ample provisions and time, these routes could not have been surveyed, inasmuch as it will hereafter involve considerable additional expense in the re-equipment of parties for this purpose.

cific, we continued the line in the vicinity of the Rio Verde to its entrance in the lagoons; after which we all returned to the Hacienda of Chivela, where the party was divided. One division was directed to run out the carriage-road through Chivela Pass; the stream descending from its summit; an experimental line to the west of Torrenta de Chivela, and a line from the foot of this Pass via San Geronimo, Comitancillo, and Tehuantepec, to Ventosa.

The other division received orders to commence at Chivela (the starting point), and run in a northwesterly direction over the plains towards El Barrio, via the Pass of Nisi Conejo (through the Majada range), on to the plains of Xochiapa, where they would connect with the line from Boca del Monte, at which point Mr. Avery had been directed to commence after completing his reconnaissance from Mina-titlan to the Encantada Mountain.

These two parties having connected their lines of survey on the plains of Xochiapa, the one under Mr. Avery returned to Boca del Monte, from whence they continued the survey, via the Paso de la Puerta, down to the Jaltepec River.

The party under my own immediate charge descended the Coatzacoalcos to the Jaltepec, and commenced at a point on the stream, near where the line of railroad will probably cross, in the event of locating west of the Coatzacoalcos. This crossing is about six miles in a direct line from the mouth of the Jaltepec, and about nine by the windings of the river. From thence we struck off on a course about N. 20° E., or a little to the west of Encantada Mountain, in order to meet the reconnaissance from Mina-titlan.

Mr. Avery having completed the line from Boca del Monte to the Jaltepec, was directed to descend the river to Mina-titlan and commence a compass line at that point and run on towards Tesistepec, or until he should meet the other party coming down from the Jaltepec River. The two parties joined just north of the Encantada Mountain, and thus was completed a base line of operations for all future surveys, *from ship navigation on the Atlantic to ship navigation on the Pacific.*

From the topography of the country it will be seen that the

part traversed by the survey is naturally divided into three sections, each of which possesses its own peculiar characteristics.

The *first* of these embraces that belt of country which lies between the parallel of Mina-titlan and the Jaltepec River. The line traversing it is $62\frac{1}{4}$ miles in length.

The *second*, which extends from the Jaltepec to the base of the mountains on the Pacific plains, reaches $68\frac{3}{4}$ miles.

The *third*, from the base of the mountains to La Ventosa, comprises 35 miles. Making a total length of line of 166 miles. This, it must be recollected, runs by way of Masahua Pass; but there is a great probability of reducing this distance from ten to fifteen miles on the final location. The *air*-line between Mina-titlan and Ventosa is 130 miles.

General Description of Route.

Leaving Mina-titlan, the line bears off in a southwesterly direction, passing from one to two miles to the left of the towns of Cosuliacaque, Jaltipan, Tesistepec, and the Hacienda of Almagro, curving eastwardly to a point about three-fourths of a mile west of the Encantada Mountain (keeping generally out of reach of the line of overflow), and passing through one of the most beautiful and productive portions of the Isthmus. From the Encantada, the line enters a dense forest, in which it continues, on the same character of profile for thirty miles to the Jaltepec River. For the whole distance from Mina-titlan to that river, we encountered no streams requiring more than fifty feet waterway. The grades upon this portion of the road will be remarkably light, and the alignment good; the material to be moved mostly sand, gravel, and clay, and in a few places sandstone rock.

Leaving the Jaltepec, the line, still continuing in the forest, advances in a southerly direction, but soon ascending on a grade of sixty feet to the mile, reaches the summit which divides the waters of the Jaltepec from those of the Jumuapa.

From the summit the line descends on an average grade of twenty-five feet to the mile, till it reaches the level of the river-bottoms, keeping to the left of the dividing ridge, which separates the waters of the eastern and western tributaries of the Jumuapa, and along the crest of which, a *picadura* for the carriage road has already been cut. Continuing its course, it finally reaches Paso de la Puerta. Soon after leaving this place it skirts the open fields, or savannas, belonging to San Juan Guichicovi, and passing these, which are somewhat broken, it continues to the Rio Sarabia. Thence, the line extends two miles to the eastern base of Cerro Sarabia, from whence it continues in a southerly direction to the Malatengo over the plains of Boca del Monte; thence leaving Cerro Tigre about one mile to the left, it reaches the deep gorge in the hills of Xochiapa through which the Malatengo runs. Ascending on a sixty feet grade, it continues its sinuous course up the banks of this stream; and finally, leaving it on the southern side of the hills, it again ascends on a grade of sixty feet to the plains of Xochiapa, crossing which and advancing, it is brought to the summit of Nisi Conejo, on a grade of sixty feet to the mile.

This pass opens on to the plains of Xochiapa, and divides a range of limestone mountains, whose western extremity is called *Cerro Majada*. It commences near El Barrio, and runs in a southeasterly direction about six miles, where it is finally arrested by the Rio Almoloya. This range forms the southwestern limit of what are termed the plains of Xochiapa.

From the summit of Nisi Conejo the line continues in a southeasterly direction, descending on a grade of sixty feet to the mile, to the level of the plains of Chivela; thence it continues its course to the Hacienda of that name at the entrance of Chivela Pass.

The entrance from these plains to the Pass of Masahua is three miles distant, from a point 2000 feet north of the Hacienda, and bears S. 74° E. From this initial point the line ascends the valley of a stream winding among the bare hills, on a general direction a little east of south, nearly one mile and three-quarters to the summit, which is 125 feet above the plains of Chivela; 115 feet above the *bench mark* at the Hacienda of that name, and 843 feet above the Pacific Ocean. Here it is proposed to make a thorough cut of about 2500 feet, with an average depth of 40 feet, the grade line at the deepest point being 63 feet below the surface. This would reduce the summit at grade to only 60 feet above the plains of Chivela, and 793 feet above the Pacific.

From the surface indications, there is reason to believe that the material in this cut will be found almost entirely composed of talcose and clay slates—rocks which generally disintegrate on exposure to the atmosphere, and are very easily blasted in their more solid state. It is very probable that from five to twenty feet of the surface can be readily removed with the pick and shovel—the remainder by blasting.

Descending from the summit on a sixty-feet grade, the general course of the line is nearly south, and continues on the right of the valley of the *Summit Arroyo*, till it reaches *Danta Pass*, where the valley opens between the ends of two high mountains into that of the " *Torrente de Masahua.*" The mountain on the right is called " *Masahuita ;*" that on the left, " *Cerro de Espinosa.*"

From the summit to Masahuita, we encounter a succession of ridges or sharp spurs of the main range. These will be difficult to turn without heavy cutting and filling, or making four or five short tunnels ; which last, for the sake of alignment and want of more extended surveys, I have estimated upon, although they may, in all probability, be avoided, by throwing the line a little further to the east. These tunnels occur about a mile below the summit, and in the aggregate will be nearly half a mile long, contiguous to each other, and separated only by steep intervening ravines, which serve as natural shafts. A very favorable feature about these tunnels is, that they will admit of being worked at not less than ten different points at the same time, and without the necessity of raising any of the material.

There is but little choice of ground across the spurs ; for, by throwing the line to the right, we at once encounter the main ridge, which is too high, and by laying it to the left, it as suddenly drops into the valley, the bottom of which is nearly 150 feet below the grade line.

The material on the line, from the summit to Masahua, is mostly composed, like that of the summit itself, of talcose and clay slates, with the exception that they partake more of a shaly character. From ten to twenty feet of the earth next to the surface can probably be moved with the pick and shovel, and rattled down into the ravines below. Nearly the whole of the slate formation is more or less traversed in various directions by small veins of quartz.

It will be seen by the profile of the Masahua Pass, that the lowest declivity of the valley, with reference to grade, is at a point two miles from the summit, from which it increases from zero to 150 feet; thence decreasing to zero again, where the line enters the plains.

Just before reaching Cerro Masahuita, we encounter a deep ravine, running parallel with the northern base of the mountain. The fill here for 700 feet will average 80 feet in depth: this cannot be avoided in running through Danta Pass. It may, however, be entirely obviated by running the line back of the mountain, and coming into the valley of "Torrente de Masahua" by the "Arroyo de Molino." At this point I have estimated for a wooden bridge, with stone abutments and piers. From this fill the line sweeps around the end of "Masahuita" on a radius of 1000 feet; thence taking a westerly course along the southern slope of the mountain to the "Arroyo de Molino," which it crosses on a fill of 65 feet; thence on to the southern slope of "Cerro Barnard" to Arroyo de Juan, crossing on an elevation of 55 feet; thence continuing along the southern base of Cerro Prieto, it reaches the Camino Real, descending through Chivela Pass, where the line crosses to the opposite bank of Torrente de Masahua, and continues in the vicinity of this stream till it reaches a point opposite the extreme end of the bare hills called Cerro de la Martar, and, after recrossing what is now called Rio Verde, it passes by the Rancho de la Martar, over the plains to San Geronimo, Comitancillo, Tehuantepec, and lastly, to the harbor of Ventosa.

This is the line surveyed west of the Coatzacoalcos, by way of the dividing ridge between the Jaltepec and Jumuapa, the Malatengo and the Pass of Masahua; but it will not probably be the final location, as a better route undoubtedly exists east of the Coatzacoalcos, via the Almoloya and the Pass of Chivela. The reason for not surveying this line will be found in another place.

There seems to be but two favorable localities for railroad crossings over the Tehuantepec River—one at the city of Tehuantepec itself, and the other just below Huilotepec: the former is by far the best.

If the line should be located by way of Tehuantepec, it ought to pass between Cerro de San Diego and the ridge of *Cerro Xunirahui*. In this case it would necessarily cross the San Jone.

Should it be thought advisable to run the line from the mouth of the Pass of Chivela,* by the most direct route to Ventosa, instead of by the towns just mentioned, it would go to Huilotepec, and then either cross the river Tehuantepec to the lower base of *San Diego*, and so sweep round under the Cerro Morro; or, without crossing the river, keep its left bank to the sea. It is, however, better to cross the river, and run down near the base of Cerro Morro close to the site of the proposed breakwater, for by extending the breakwater from the end of Cerro Morro fifteen hundred or two thousand feet, it would afford ample protection to the wharves at this terminus of the road.

The material on the Pacific plains is sand, gravel, red and yellow clay. The embankments over this portion of the route will not average more than two or three feet in height, and may be thrown up directly from the sides.

The following extracts from *the report of Mr. J. C. Avery* embrace the details of the operations of the party under his charge, and a particular description of the line *north of the dividing ridge:*

"In compliance with instructions, I occupied a portion of the time that we were waiting canoe transportation, in making a reconnaissance of the country to the west of the Coatzacoalcos River, from Mina-titlan to Mt. Encantada. In order to obtain some data on which to base an estimate of the probable length and cost of a railroad to connect those points, I provided

---

* The entrance to the Masahua and Chivela Passes from the plains of the Pacific is a point common to both.

myself with a compass and quadrant, by means of which a connected survey was made of the route traversed as far as Tesistepec; the relative position of Mt. Encantada being approximately determined by triangulation, taking the distance between Jaltipan and Tesistepec as a base-line.

Leaving Mina-titlan on the 3d of January in company with Messrs. Davidge and Baldwin, and taking the mule-road leading to Tesistepec, via Otiapa and Chinameca, we reached the village of Cosuliacaque, distant seven and a half miles from Mina-titlan, in a westerly direction. This is situated on the summit of an elevated broken ridge, which separates the head-waters of the Tacoteno River from a number of small streams discharging into the Coatzacoalcos above Mina-titlan. This portion of our route traversed a moderately elevated table-land or plateau but partially wooded, the trees being generally small and of little value.

A short distance to the left of the road, the ground uniformly descends to the level of the river-bottoms; but on the right we find broad, level savannas, alternating with occasional patches of timber, and extending many miles in a northerly and westerly direction. In the vicinity of the road the soil is light and sandy, the rock formation being a coarse ferruginous sandstone.

About one and a half miles from Cosuliacaque is a small place called Otiapa, and two and a half miles further on, is Chinameca, a neat village of some 1400 inhabitants.

Between Cosuliacaque and this place, the surface of the country is considerably undulating, and the soil gravel and sandy loam. We passed some heavy timber on this portion of the route, including the Uale, Macaya, Encina, Juasimo, Ceiba, Nanche, Cedro, &c.

From Chinameca to Jaltipan, a distance of five miles, the road traverses the summit of a sandy ridge, but sparsely covered with a stunted growth of trees and bushes.

On the right is an extensive alluvial basin, stretching as far as Mounts San Martin and Pelon, distant some twenty miles, and drained by the river Huasuntan and its tributaries, the Chacalapa and Osaluapa. The Chacalapa heads in a small lake situated about three miles south of Acayucam, and the Osaluapa takes its rise between San Martin and Pelon. As we approached Jaltipan, the soil changed from sand and gravel to a rich sandy loam, sustaining a dense growth of vegetation.

This village contains about 2300 inhabitants, and is built on a gentle rise of ground, the summit of which is occupied by a mound of earth built in honor of Malinche, Doña Marina, who was a native of this place. It is about forty feet in height, and one hundred feet in diameter at the base. From its summit we saw both Cosuliacaque and Tesistepec, and also had a fine view of the country for a considerable distance on all sides. As seen from this mound, the general appearance to the east, south, and southwest, is very uniform and level, but in the direction of Tesistepec, and more westerly, the surface is considerably broken, though at no point much elevated above the general level. This latter village is situated about nine miles southwesterly from Jaltipan. The route thence, for the first three miles, lies over a beautifully rolling country, with a rich soil, covered with a most luxuriant growth of vegetation, but presenting no large timber; advancing thence, it traverses, for a distance of two miles, a level bottom bordering the Apepeche Creek, and which is flooded in times of high water to a depth of five or six feet. Immediately on striking these bottom-lands the soil changes to a stiff plastic clay, of dark color, and unctuous to the touch. At the time of making our reconnaissance the ground was so much saturated with water, owing to the recent overflow, that we could with difficulty get our horses over it. In the rainy season the Apepeche Creek has some nine feet depth of water in the channel, and is navigated by the natives with canoes, but for two or three months in the year it is entirely dry. After leaving these bottoms, which are heavily timbered, we find no more large growth for a distance of five or six miles, but the overwhelming fertility of the soil is indicated by a reeking mass of vegetation which covers the whole face of the country, almost choking up the narrow mule-roads which traverse it.

As we approach Tesistepec the country becomes gradually higher and more rugged. This village is built on a broken sandstone ridge, elevated some two hundred feet above tide-water, and commanding a fine view of the surrounding country. The sandstone above referred to is of a grayish-white color, and about the weight and consistency of chalk; it is distinctly stratified, the prevailing strike being S. 15° W., and the dip 11° W. This formation extends from three to eight miles on all sides of Tesistepec, the soil found in connection with it being clay, of the same nature as that already described.

We were told by the natives that wherever this rock occurred the soil was much more productive than that of other portions of the country. The porosity of this sandstone is great, and the inhabitants are supplied with water from a large number of wells sunk to depths of thirty or forty feet into the substance of the rock.

The Hacienda of Almagro lies to the southwest of this place, distant about thirteen miles by the roads. Our route thence, for the first two miles, lay over high, broken ground; we then came down upon a level prairie, bordering a small sheet of water called Lake Otiapa. This lake is about three miles in length, by half a mile in width, and quite shallow; in the rainy season, however, its depth is increased six or eight feet by the back-water of the Coatzacoalcos.

Soon after leaving this lake we crossed the main branch of the Monzapa River, and at about three miles further, the most southern branch of the same stream: thence to the Hacienda of Almagro is a distance of some two miles. This is situated in a beautiful rolling prairie, of three or four miles in length, by one mile in width. Between Tesistepec and this place we found the timber much larger and of better quality than any we had before seen. The soil was generally a stiff clay, with occasional beds of sand. South of Lake Otiapa we found the surface of the country quite smooth and uniform, with the exception of a narrow ridge separating the two branches of the Monzapa, and which may be turned by keeping a little further to the east.

Mt. Encantada is distant from the Hacienda of Almagro about ten miles, in a southeasterly direction, and is situated in the midst of extensive *potreros*, which are flowed in times of high water to a depth of from three to twelve feet. The base of the mountain extends nearly two miles in a direction W. N. W. by E. S. E., and its summit is elevated from eight hundred to one thousand feet above the surrounding plains.

In order to obtain a better knowledge of the topography of the country, we made the ascent of the mountain, and found its summit a very favorable point for observation, commanding as it did, a view of nearly one-half the breadth of the Isthmus.

From observation and inquiry, we learned that all the country east of Encantada to the Coatzacoalcos was subject to overflow, with the exception of a few isolated points ; also for three or four miles both north and south, and westward to the extreme end of the mountain. In a southerly direction, all that portion of the country included between the Coatzacoalcos, and a line bearing S. 40° W. from our point of observation, presented a very even surface, for a distance of twenty or thirty miles; beyond which it was much more broken, the view being limited by a low range of hills, running in nearly an east and west direction. These highlands I have since ascertained to be the dividing ridge, separating the Jaltepec and Jumuapa rivers. To the west and northwest, the surface of the country becomes gradually higher and more broken, but not mountainous. The nearest highland seen to the east or southeast, I judged to be twenty-five or thirty miles distant.

There being no roads extending south of Mt. Encantada, we did not penetrate further in that direction.

The natives informed us that about two years since an attempt was made to cut a road through to Paso de la Puerta, under the direction of Señor Moro. They commenced near the Hacienda of Almagro, and after penetrating some distance in a southwesterly direction, struck what they supposed to be the head-waters of the San Juan River, and concluding they had missed their course, abandoned the work. The surface of the country in this direction was found to be very rough, being traversed by a multitude of ravines and intervening ridges: the road has since grown over with small timber, so as to render it impassable.

About eleven miles west from Jaltipan is the important town of Acayucam, containing some five thousand inhabitants. Three miles east of this place is the small village of Soconusco, and two miles south the village of Oluta. Paso San Juan is situated about twenty miles from Acayucam, in a direction W. S. W., and is accessible from the latter place by a good mule-road, traversing, for a great part of the distance, the dividing ridge separating the head-waters of the Monzapa from the Huasuntan.

From near Jaltipan, to a point two or three miles westward of Acayucam, the soil is a stiff clay; thence to Paso San Juan it is gravelly, with a formation of sandstone. This latter place is the port or outlet for most of the trade of Acayucam and the neighboring villages. The San Juan River at this point carries about the same volume of water as the Coatzacoalcos at Paso Sarabia, and is navigated by boats of considerable size.

The villages of Cosuliacaque, Otiapa, Chinameca, Jaltipan, and Tesistepec, are built on the summit of an irregular, broken ridge, which may be traced continuously from Mina-titlan to near the San Juan River, in the direction of the *Paso*.

These villages are generally located on the highest points of this ridge, and are elevated from one hundred and fifty to two hundred feet above the Coatzacoalcos River.

A large portion of the country comprised between the villages of Cosuliacaque, Jaltipan, and Tesistepec, on one side, and the Coatzacoalcos on the other, is subject to periodic overflow; the limit of flowage being, however, quite irregular. On either side of the Ocosoapa Creek, the highlands reach nearly to the Brazo Mistan; while between Jaltipan and Tesistepec, and also to the west of the latter place, the flowage extends eight or ten miles back from the river.

From all the information I have been able to obtain, I should judge that the best line for the location of the railroad would coincide nearly with the following general route, viz.:

Commencing at Mina-titlan, thence running to the left of the mule-road leading to Cosuliacaque, so as just to skirt the river-bottoms, and passing from one-half to one mile south of the latter village; thence to a point two or three miles south from Jaltipan; thence to near the south end of Lake Otiapa, and thence to a point near the western extremity of Mt. Encantada, passing from two to three miles eastward of the Hacienda of Almagro. Leaving the mountain on the left, the line would deflect considerably to the east, so as to avoid the more elevated grounds which bound the river bottoms on the west.

Of the feasibility of the route from Mina-titlan to a point considerably south of Mt. Encantada, within a reasonable cost, there can be no doubt; but a road terminating at any point on the Brazo Mistan is impracticable, without involving a large outlay and the risk of damage from the effects of high water. In fact, there are but three or four points on the Brazo Mistan which are above overflow, and these only small isolated knolls; while nearly all the country west, to within two or three miles of the Hacienda of Almagro, thence to Mt. Encantada, and for some distance further south, is subject to periodic inundation, the depth of the flowage being often ten or twelve feet.

The best route for the road, supposing its terminus to be at Mina-titlan, would evidently coincide nearly with a line limiting the overflow, where the course is sufficiently direct.

On the route above described, there will be no difficulty in obtaining a good alignment, with easy grades, for the entire distance. The maximum grade would not probably exceed 15 or 20 feet per mile. From Mina-titlan to a point near Cosuliacaque, the surface of the country is extremely favorable for the construction of the road, as also from near Tesistepec to Mt. Encantada. Between Cosuliacaque and the last-named village the ground is more uneven, but in no case will very heavy work be encountered in the construction of the road. There will be but little rock excavation on this portion of the route, and that mostly in a coarse, friable sandstone, that can be easily worked. The soil for the entire distance is either clay, sand, or gravel, furnishing a solid substratum on which to build.

The streams crossing the line of road are all small; between Mina-titlan and Tesistepec, the line proposed intersects them very near their source; and more to the south, the near vicinity of the San Juan River on the west accounts for the small amount of drainage passing the line.

As the configuration of the Gulf coast would seem to indicate that a good harbor might be formed at La Barrilla; and as, by making this point (instead of Mina-titlan) the terminus, the length of the railroad would be increased but two or three miles, thus making a saving of sixteen or eighteen miles in the total distance from sea to sea; I have paid some attention to the determination of the *practicability* of carrying the road directly to the Gulf at the point referred to. The topography of the country clearly indicates that the line laid down on the map (diverging from our present line of location at a point three miles south of Lake Otiapa, thence passing this lake on the west and following down the valley of the Chacalapa River) would not only be a feasible route, but one very favorable for the cheap construction of the road.

As regards building material, the country furnishes abundance of excellent timber, convenient to all parts of the work: there is an extensive limestone quarry within two or three miles of Jaltipan, from which may be obtained a good quality of lime, and fine building stone. Abundance of the best material for manufacturing brick is found on all parts of the line, and there is also no lack of sand for purposes of construction. A good limestone quarry is said to exist on the Coachapa River, at a point six or eight miles above its confluence with the Coatzacoalcos. This quarry would furnish stone convenient to any works that might be required at the terminus of the road, whether at Mina-titlan or any other point on the river.

It is not improbable that future explorations will demonstrate the existence of good quarries at numerous points on or near the route above described.

In case stone is not found convenient for the masonry of all parts of the line, the work being generally light, temporary wooden structures might be substituted till the track was laid, when materials could be transported to the work at a small expense. Every point on the proposed line is easily accessible from the mule-roads which traverse the country.

The total distance from Mina-titlan to Mt. Encantada by the travelled roads (via Otiapa and Chinameca) is about fifty-four miles, but by railroad it will not vary much from thirty-eight.

As regards the cost of construction on this portion of the route, the graduation and masonry of a single-track road, requiring the same amount and quality of work, would probably not cost in the United States more than ten or twelve thousand dollars per mile; to this estimate would have to be added from fifty to seventy-five per cent. to obtain the cost of doing the same work on the Isthmus.

Though the line described was not actually traced on the ground (our instrumental surveys being confined to the mule-roads), I am satisfied that the above is a liberal estimate for the cost of the work. A profile of the mule-road leading from Mina-titlan to Tesistepec (which may be considered the worst route that could be found through that part of the country), shows lighter work than is encountered on many roads in the United States, with a maximum grade of fifty feet per mile.

The entire country embraced in our reconnaissance, with the exception of a portion of the distance between Mina-titlan and Jaltipan, is remarkably fertile, producing an excellent quality of tobacco, cotton, rice, sugar-cane, maize, coffee, cacao, &c., &c. That part lying back from the river bottoms is beautifully rolling and well watered; the streams generally coursing over sandy or gravelly beds, and having a fair current. The bottom-lands lying to the west of the Coatzacoalcos, and subject to overflow, are of considerable extent and but partially wooded; those portions destitute of timber being called by the natives *potreros;* these are clothed with perpetual verdure, and furnish rich pasturage for immense herds of cattle, horses, and mules.

Bordering the potreros we generally find abundance of excellent timber. But in the vicinity of the road leading from Mina-titlan to Tesistepec, there is comparatively little, a fact which would seem to indicate that at some period, not very remote, a much larger portion of this country was under cultivation than at present. To the south of Tesistepec, the timber is generally of a large size and good quality; between the Hacienda of Almagro and Mt. Encantada, we met with considerable mahogany, as well as other valuable woods.

The inhabitants of this part of the Isthmus number about twenty-five thousand, and mostly live in compact villages, invariably located on the most elevated sections of the country. They are principally devoted to agriculture and the raising of cattle, horses, and mules, and though naturally indolent, are not more so than might be anticipated from the combined influences of climate and a soil remarkably productive, which, with little labor on the part of the inhabitants, supplies them with all the necessaries of life. In our intercourse with them, they invariably manifested a very friendly disposition, and a desire to render us all assistance, in gaining information of the country, in their power.

We were occupied with the reconnaissance some ten days, but were delayed till the 20th of the month before obtaining canoes with which to ascend the river.

In pursuance of instructions, we proceeded directly to Boca del Monte, at which point we arrived February 2d, having been delayed a week at Paso Sarabia, awaiting mule transportation. We immediately commenced operations in the field, starting our line of survey at a point about two miles west of Boca del Monte, and working to the south. From this point our surveys were extended to the plains of Xochiapa, and northerly to the Jaltepec River, a total distance of forty-one miles.

The southern portion of the route presents the following characteristics:

Commencing at the initial point above described, the line of survey follows down the valley of a small stream, draining the northern slope of the Sarabia Mountain, and has an average course of about S. 70° E., for a distance of two miles; thence, turning the eastern end of that mountain, it traverses a level prairie for a distance of two and a half miles to the crossing of the Malatengo River, with a course S. 5° 45′ E.; passing the river, the course thence is S. 7° 15′ W. for half a mile over an alluvial bottom; thence deflecting a few degrees to the right, the line traverses moderately elevated rolling ground for the distance of a mile, when it again strikes the river-bottoms, and deflecting to the right, bears S. 33° 45′ W. for one mile further, where the highland on the east comes down to the river, forming high, precipitous banks. For a distance of six and a half miles southward of this point, the line is confined to the immediate banks of the Malatengo River, by high hills on either side, the river having for this distance worn a deep, narrow channel through a range of hills varying in height from two to eight hundred feet above the bed of the stream. The width of this channel or gorge is from one to three hundred feet at the base, from which the banks rise directly, on slopes, varying from 20° to 90°.

The line, for about two miles above the confluence of the Pachine River, follows the east bank of the Malatengo, with an average direction of about S. 10° E.; then crossing the river (which here makes a short bend to the right), it follows the west bank for about a mile in a southeasterly direction; then crossing to the left bank, it commences curving to the right, making a total angle of 95° 15'; thence its course averages about S. 65° W. for a distance of one and three-fourths miles; then crossing to the right bank, and curving to the left, it runs in a southerly direction about three-fourths of a mile, to a point where the river makes a sharp bend to the right; crossing which, it follows up the valley of a small stream tributary to the Malatengo, and for two miles after leaving the river, has an average direction of about S. 20° E. A mile and a half further on, our line of survey connects with the line from Chivela, making a total length of seventeen miles.

From the point of beginning, near Mt. Sarabia, to the Malatengo River, the cost of construction will be very light, and the soil is admirably well adapted to the formation of a permanent road.

For the first two miles of this distance, the line is confined to nearly its present location by the mountain range on the right, and high, irregular ground to the left. The section of country lying between the Sarabia Mountain and Boca del Monte, and extending westward to within half a mile of the Sarabia River, is entirely destitute of timber, except a small growth bordering the principal streams, and is generally unfit for cultivation, except in the valleys; the formation of these plains is sandstone, underlying a thick deposit of drift: this is generally disposed in long winding ridges, the slopes of which have the appearance of being scooped out into deep basin-shaped depressions, leaving corresponding elevations, the difference of level being often 50 or 100 feet.

The Sarabia Mountain consists of a high range of hills, extending about three miles in a direction W. N. W. by E. S. E., and terminated on the west by a sharp conical peak, elevated some ten or twelve hundred feet above the surrounding plains. Between this range and the Coatzacoalcos is a smooth, level plain, having an average breadth of two or three miles; being limited on the south by the Malatengo River, and on the north by an elevated, broken ridge, or chain of highlands, which, terminating at Mal Paso on the east, separate the waters of the Malatengo and Sarabia rivers. This plain country alternates with woods and prairie; the latter furnishing abundance of excellent pasturage.

The first crossing of the Malatengo will require a bridge of 175 feet span, with an elevation at grade of thirty or thirty-five feet above the bed of the stream; the foundations will rest on coarse gravel. The left bank of the river at this point is bordered by rich alluvial bottoms, which extend to within half a mile of the confluence of the Pachine River, and vary in width from one-fourth to three-fourths of a mile: these are covered with a dense growth of tangled vines and underbrush, which it is impossible to penetrate without the use of a *machéte;* and are limited on the east by elevated ground, the summit of which forms a continuous ridge, running nearly parallel with the Malatengo, and joining the hills of Xochiapa to the south.

The rock formation to the east of the Malatengo, and opposite the confluence of the Pachine River, is a compact limestone of a slaty structure, and traversed by numerous veins of calcareous spar. This stone would constitute a good building material, and also burn to quicklime. It extends a distance of about one mile on the line of survey.

There is a considerable interval of bottom-land on the west of the Malatengo, extending as far south as the Pachine River, beyond which the ground becomes much more elevated, forming rocky, precipitous banks on either side of the Malatengo for a distance of six miles. The excavations for this distance will be wholly in rock. The formation at the surface is sandstone of a loose friable texture, which, as we descend, gradually becomes more close and fine-grained, and in the bed of the river is found very compact: the lower beds have generally a dark purple color, probably due to the presence of a small quantity of iron. This rock will furnish abundance of excellent building stone, and also a valuable gritstone for purposes of grinding and polishing.

In following up the valley of the Malatengo, the direction of the line of survey necessarily coincides very nearly with the course of the river: for about one half this distance the road will have a very good alignment, but for two or three miles there is considerable curvature, the minimum radius being one thousand feet.

In order to secure as good an alignment as possible, we are obliged to make four crossings of the river, requiring one bridge of 125 feet span, one of 150 feet, and two of 175. The elevation of the abutments will vary from 35 to 50 feet, and will rest on solid rock. All the stone required for their masonry can be obtained from the excavations, or may be quarried within a few feet of the work. There will also be required a bridge of 50 feet span at the crossing of the Xuchiapa Creek. Commencing at the confluence of the above creek, the bed of the Malatengo breaks down suddenly, forming a succession of falls and rapids for a distance of two miles; the greatest fall in one mile being 90 feet, and the total for two consecutive miles, 141 feet. The maximum grade on this part of the route is 60 feet per mile, and the greatest elevation of the grade-line above the bed of the river 55 feet. The extreme rise of water in the channel of the river is from 15 to 20 feet, depending upon the width of the channel and the rapidity of the current. The banks of the stream are sparsely covered with a growth of trees and underbrush, embracing three or four varieties of timber of good quality, and in sufficient quantity to answer all purposes of construction.

We found the survey of this portion of the route very laborious, owing to the precipitous nature of the ground. After running a base-line through, accurate cross-sections were taken at intervals of 100 feet, and for the entire width to be occupied by the road; by which means we are enabled to make a very close estimate of the amount of work required in its construction. The cost will here be somewhat increased by the difficulty of getting to and from the work. There can, however, be a good mule-road opened along the immediate banks of the river, for the entire distance, and at a small expense. This road would be available for bringing provisions and materials of all kinds to the work, except for two or three months in the rainy season, when it would have to be abandoned on account of high water.

The natural scenery of this part of the route is wild and romantic; at the point of passing the summit of the Xochiapa hills, the banks of the river rise abruptly to a height of six or eight hundred feet, and the channel is nearly choked up with huge rocks that have fallen from the banks as they have been undermined by the action of the water. Intersecting the main channel, are deep, narrow ravines, through which, in the rainy season, the drainage of the neighboring hills is discharged in foaming torrents.

Our surveys and observations establish the fact that this is the only practicable route west of the valley of the Almoloya River, by which a railroad can be constructed across this part of the Isthmus.

We ran a line a short distance up the Xuchiapa Creek, but found the ascent much too rapid to be overcome with a grade of sixty feet per mile.

From the point of leaving the Malatengo River to the termination of our survey going south, the excavations will be entirely in a compact gravel, consisting of rounded quartz and sandstone pebbles. For the first two miles of this distance the ground is quite undulating, and will require a grade of sixty feet per mile, and rather expensive work, to overcome the ascent from the river; the surface of the country then becomes much more uniform and level.

The plains of Xochiapa are bounded on the north by the range of hills of the same name, and extend about six miles to the south, and four or five miles in an east and west direction. They are drained by the Malatengo and its tributaries, and are almost entirely destitute of timber; they generally present a very smooth surface, but more or less undulating, the soil being gravelly, and unfit for tillage, except in the valleys bordering the streams, but afford fine pasturage, and we find scattered over them numerous herds of cattle, horses, and mules.

ENGINEERING REPORTS.

Our surveys of this portion of the route were completed March 24th, when we commenced running northerly from Mt. Sarabia.

The line of survey crosses the elevated ground separating the valleys of the Malatengo and Sarabia rivers, with a maximum grade of fifty feet per mile, and light work; advancing thence, it runs in a southwesterly direction a distance of one and a half miles, to the crossing of the Sarabia; then curving to the right, its course is N. 18° W. for a distance of five miles; thence it is continued for about three miles in a direction N. 11° W.; advancing thence, and curving to the right, the course is N. 10° E. for a distance of four and a half miles; then curving to the left, it is continued about four miles in a direction N. 23° W., and in about one mile further, is brought upon the ridge which separates the waters of the Jumuapa and Jaltepec rivers; thence the course of the line averages about N. 16° E. for a distance of some five miles, to the crossing of the Jaltepec River, making a total distance, from the terminus of our survey to the south, of forty-one miles.

The crossing of the Sarabia River will require a bridge of one hundred and seventy-five feet span, with an elevation just sufficient to clear high water, the extreme rise of which is about eighteen feet. The stream has here a rapid current, and a hard gravelly bed. The river-bottoms at this point are about three-fourths of a mile in width, and with the exception of a few patches under cultivation, are heavily timbered. The country lying immediately north of the Sarabia River, for an extent of about four miles square, is entirely destitute of timber, and beautifully rolling (being very similar in character to the plains of Xochiapa): though quite undulating, they are at no point elevated more than one hundred and twenty feet above the level of the Sarabia River. These prairies furnish pasturage for large droves of horses and mules.

There is an elevated ridge of ground, extending from near the point of crossing the Sarabia to the Paso de la Puerta, the summit of which is traversed for a great portion of the distance by the mule-road leading from Boca del Monte and San Juan Guichicovi to the Paso. Our line of survey lies to the east of this, and for nearly the entire distance to the Jumuapa River, traverses a heavy rolling country, requiring for the construction of the road a considerable amount of excavation and embankment. The line passes the open plains above mentioned on the east, and is timbered for nearly the entire distance between the Sarabia and Jumuapa rivers. The excavations on this portion of the route will be mostly in a gravelly clay. There is no rock at the surface, but in the beds of some of the creeks we find a soft argillaceous sandstone, and in one or two instances a conglomerate or pudding-stone, united with a calcareous cement.

At the points of crossing the Sarabia and Jumuapa rivers, we find the former elevated one hundred and fifty feet above the latter; and in descending towards the Jumuapa, a grade of sixty feet per mile is required for a distance of nearly two miles. This latter stream can be passed with a bridge of one hundred and fifty feet span, with the same elevation as at the Sarabia. The foundations of the abutments will probably require piling, or other artificial support.

We found some difficulty in selecting a good route for the road between the Jumuapa and Jaltepec rivers, owing to the irregular formation of the ground, and the fact that this portion of the country is entirely covered with a dense forest, which renders it difficult of observing its topography. The principal obstacle is found in crossing the summit of an elevated ridge, or chain of highlands, separating the valleys of the above-named streams. These highlands terminate at Suchil, on the east, and running nearly parallel with the Jaltepec River, join the Cordillera to the west, their summits being distant from the Jaltepec from three to four miles, and elevated from 250 to 600 feet above the stream. This main dividing ridge is intersected by a secondary ridge, extending from a point near Paso de la Puerta to the Rancho Amate, the crest of which is traversed by a picadura throughout its entire length. There is also a road traversing the summit of the main dividing ridge, from its intersection with this picadura to Suchil. Of these roads, the former may be termed the Amate Picadura, and the latter the Suchil Picadura.

From the summit the ground descends rapidly towards the

Jaltepec, in some cases leaving a considerable interval of bottom-lands on the south side of this river. Between the summit and the river-bottoms the surface is very rough, being traversed by a multitude of deep, narrow ravines, separated by sharp spurs from the main ridge.

The general appearance of the country to the east of the Amate Picadura and southward of the summit, is nearly level. On a closer inspection, however, we find it traversed by numerous ravines and intervening ridges, having a general direction nearly east and west, or at right angles to the line of survey. The country to the west of this picadura is drained by two or three principal streams, having a southerly direction, and discharging into the Jumuapa, below the Paso de la Puerta. These streams are separated by high spurs or ridges, joining the summit ridge on the north, and extending a considerable distance to the south. The intervening valleys are narrow towards the summit, but gradually widen out as they approach the Jumuapa.

In starting our survey northerly from this river we had the choice of two general routes; one to the east of the Amate Picadura, and the other to the west, following up the valley of a large creek running nearly parallel with this road. With the limited knowledge we then had of the country, the latter appeared the more feasible route, as we could take advantage of two considerable creeks; one discharging into the Jumuapa, and the other into the Jaltepec, and having a general direction nearly coincident with the proposed line of survey. But after gaining the summit from the south with a maximum grade of sixty feet per mile, and but moderately heavy work, we found the descent towards the Jaltepec too rapid to be overcome without increasing the maximum grade, or involving a heavy expense. In the mean time we discovered a depression in the summit at a distance of one and a half miles to the east of our first line; and finding this impracticable, we immediately commenced operations from the new summit, which proved to be 120 feet lower than the first, and elevated but 200 feet above the Jumuapa river, and 260 feet above the Jaltepec. From this point to the crossing of the latter stream the line is very direct, and the maximum grade sixty feet per mile: for two or three miles of this distance the line encounters a succession of deep ravines and intervening spurs, involving rather heavy cutting.

To the south, the descent is much more gradual, and the character of the work similar to that between the Sarabia and Jumuapa rivers.

The excavations on that portion of the line extending from the Jumuapa to the Jaltepec river will be mostly in a gravelly clay soil, that can be easily worked; there will, however, be considerable rock excavation at the crossing of the main dividing ridge. The formation at this point is a compact, earthy limestone, overlying a coarse conglomerate or pudding-stone: this latter is mainly composed of rounded flint, and hornstone pebbles and boulders united with a calcareous cement. The limestone formation is most abundant near the intersection of the Amate and Suchil picaduras, where it extends two or three miles in a north and south direction. The stone has a porous structure, but is quite hard, and is found in compact beds of considerable thickness, the plane of stratification being nearly horizontal. In connection with this rock we find extensive beds of fossil madrepore.

On the northern slope of the highlands separating the Jumuapa and Jaltepec rivers, the pudding-stone constitutes nearly the entire rock-formation; this is everywhere covered with a rich mould, sustaining a luxuriant growth of vegetation.

The country lying between the rivers mentioned, presents many interesting features. The streams, in some instances, have tunnelled through hills of solid limestone, and at other points have worn out extensive caverns in this rock, ornamented with beautiful stalactites, and which furnish secure retreats for the wild beasts abounding here.

This rock also frequently forms sharp, rugged peaks, rising to a height of two or three hundred feet above the level of the intervening valleys. The summits of the long, narrow ridges which constitute the most striking feature in the topography of this part of the country, are often very sharp, sometimes having a width of only three or four feet at top, and descending abruptly on either side to a depth of two or three hundred feet.

The summit of the main dividing ridge commands a magnificent view of the country to the north, which presents the appearance of a vast plain stretching northerly to the Gulf, and in an east and west direction as far as the eye can reach. The only highlands seen in this direction are the Encantada range, and in the extreme distance the peaks of San Martin and Pelon. Looking south, the view extends to the Pass of Chivela, and is limited on the right and left by the high ranges of the Cordillera; thus embracing a great extent of country, presenting a very diversified and picturesque appearance.

Between the Jumuapa and Jaltepec rivers the entire country is densely wooded. These forests are truly magnificent; exhibiting an almost endless variety of trees, variegated with foliage of every hue, and entwined and interwoven with innumerable vines, which, climbing to the tops of the tallest trees, arch and trellis the winding picaduras, so as almost completely to intercept the direct rays of the sun. Some of these vines are more than a foot in diameter, and contain large quantities of pure, sweet water, furnishing a welcome beverage to the thirsty traveller; others, as the vanilla, load the air with their delicious fragrance; and others, again, are covered with flowers of various hues. The trees grow to an immense size, presenting many varieties which are valuable, either for the timber they furnish, the gums, oils, and balsams they distil, the medicinal properties they possess, or the fruits and flowers they bear. We find here the india-rubber tree in great abundance, also the Mahogany, Lignum-vitæ, Acacia, Achote, Mamey-zapote, Tamarindo, Cuapinol, Fern-tree, the huge Ceiba, the grotesque Palo-Amate, a great variety of Palms, &c., &c.

This portion of the country is also well watered, the larger streams furnishing an abundant supply through the driest part of the season. The waters of the streams seem literally alive with fish, and the forests abound in game of all descriptions.

In making a final location of the railroad between the plains of Xochiapa and the Jaltepec River (provided the route to the west of the Coatzacoalcos is determined upon), there are a number of points which I think would be important to examine, with a view of obtaining a better location than at present.

It will be borne in mind, that the time in which we were actually engaged on this survey was extremely short, considering the complicated nature of the country and the limited knowledge we had of it previous to commencing operations; consequently we were obliged to confine our instrumental surveys mainly to one route, even where others seemed to offer equal facilities for the location of the road.

Between the Jumuapa and Jaltepec rivers, we have accurately traced with a compass, the courses of many of the principal streams, together with the summits of the main ridges; making a total of more than fifty miles of compass-lines through this part of the country, in addition to our transit-lines. In this way we ran out the main dividing ridge from Suchil to a point four and a quarter miles west of our line of location, accurately noting its principal features for the entire distance. The result was, that we found but one point to the west of our present line, at which it was possible to obtain a better location across these highlands; and this at the extreme limit of our examinations to the west. We here find a considerable depression in the summit of the ridge, from which a broad valley extends to the south, being drained by a branch of the Tortugas Creek. This valley widens as it approaches the Jumuapa; and at the junction of the creek with this river, we find a large interval of level bottom-land, extending three or four miles westerly. The practicability of this route can easily be determined by an examination of the ground for a short distance on either side of the Jaltepec summit. It will be more circuitous than our present line, but may possess advantages that will more than compensate for the loss in distance.

To the east of the line of survey the dividing ridge is considerably broken, and varies in height from 200 to 500 feet above the level of the Jaltepec River. There are three or four depressions of the summit in this direction, which seem to offer facilities for obtaining as good, or a better location.

In case the road is located to the plains of Xochiapa, via the valley of the Malatengo, it is not improbable a better route may be found, by diverging from the present line, near the confluence of the Pachine and Malatengo rivers, thence running to the west of Mount Sarabia, striking the Sarabia River some distance above the present crossing, and thence, by nearly a straight course, to the Jumuapa, keeping to the west of the mule-road leading to Paso de la Puerta. This line, in connection with the one proposed up the valley of the Tortugas Creek, would form a pretty direct route.

I am, however, of opinion that decidedly the best route by which to pass the Xochiapa hills to the plains of Chivela, will be found through the valley of the Almoloya River.

There exists no impediment to running a straight line from the confluence of the Almoloya and Malatengo Rivers, to intersect the existing line of location near Mount Sarabia.

As regards the supply of material necessary for purposes of construction on the line of the road, little more need be said. On all those portions of the work, which, from the nature of the ground, are most difficult of access, are found abundance of good building stone immediately at hand; and where it is necessary to haul it any distance, the surface of the country is uniformly favorable for its cheap transportation. The road for the greater portion of the distance lies through forests capable of supplying timber of any size and quality. On the uplands we find two species of live-oak, which are extremely hard and durable, and generally of a convenient size to be manufactured into railroad sleepers. Every thing required for the sustenance of man or beast can be grown on the line of the road. Bordering the Malatengo, Sarabia, Jumuapa, and Jaltepec rivers there is a great extent of rich bottom-lands, which, with little labor, could be brought under cultivation. On the first three mentioned rivers the inhabitants of San Juan Guichicovi have extensive *milpas*, or cultivated fields. On the prairies are large droves of horses, mules, and cattle; the latter are generally very large and fine, and will be of great service in the transportation of the earth and other materials required in the construction of the road.

In conducting the above surveys, we had occasion to employ considerable native help, principally from San Juan Guichicovi.

These were occupied mainly in transporting baggage, provisions, &c., and in cutting paths through the woods to expedite our operations: in this latter business they were very expert, using their *machétes* with great dexterity and effect.

In order that you may be able to judge of the degree of confidence that may be placed in the results given, I deem it important to state, that on commencing operations in the field, it was strictly enjoined on each member of the party to use the utmost care in obtaining accurate results in every part of the work; and we have availed ourselves of every means in our power to guard against errors. The line on which the estimates were based, was traced for the entire distance with a transit by means of backsights, the magnetic bearing being noted at every change as a test of the correctness of the deflections. We find on working out the courses of the line, by the deflections as actually measured in the field, that the total error in the distance of forty-one miles amounts to but one degree and thirty minutes, the most of which occurs in the last four or five miles run; so that by making the slight correction indicated by the needle, the line may be considered practically perfect.

About ten miles of the line, including the roughest portions, were accurately cross-sectioned with a spirit-level, and the topography carefully sketched for the entire distance; the character of material to be excavated, as well as could be judged from surface indications, was also noted. In running the levels, the readings of the rod at every change were recorded by the rod-man, independent of the leveller, so as to guard against the possibility of error. In our estimates of the amount of material to be moved in the construction of the road, we have taken into account the cross-section of the ground, wherever it was sufficiently sloping to essentially vary the result; and in determining the amount of water-way necessary to pass the streams intersecting the line of road, we have allowed about double the space that would be deemed necessary for streams draining the same area of country in the United States.

For the entire distance from the Jaltepec River to the plains of Xochiapa, the line of survey crosses but two streams which do not offer a sufficiently good foundation to build upon, without the necessity of reversed arches, or other artificial support. In a majority of cases the foundations of bridge and culvert masonry will rest on solid rock. By reference to the maps, it will be seen that the alignment is remarkably favorable, with the exception of a short distance through the valley of the Malatengo, and even there the minimum radius of curvature is greater than on many of the principal roads in the United States.

It will also be seen, by the profile, that for a great portion of the distance, we encountered a succession of cuts and fills, which, though amounting to a considerable quantity in the aggregate, do not give very heavy work at any one point. This should be considered a favorable feature in the route, inasmuch as the opportunity thus afforded for the division of labor will greatly facilitate the early completion of the road.

We completed our surveys to the south of the Jaltepec River on the 25th of May, and arrived at Mina-titlan on the 28th. Being detained here a few days, awaiting the arrival of the parties from the southern division of the Isthmus, we improved the time in running a compass line from Mina-titlan to the Hacienda of Almagro, where it joined the line through from the Jaltepec, thus making a connected instrumental survey from Mina-titlan to the bay of Ventosa. This line being accurately traced with a compass and chain, afforded us a good base from which to determine a number of important points by triangulation. We used for this purpose the distances between Cosuliacaque and Jaltipan, and also between the latter place and Tesistepec, from each of which points we had an extensive view of the country in all directions.

While a portion of the party were engaged as above, Messrs. Murphy, Smith, and myself made a reconnaissance of the country to the east of the Coatzacoalcos, bordering the Uspanapa and Tancochapa rivers with a view of obtaining sufficient data to enable us to map correctly a portion of the Isthmus that was previously but little known. Taking with us a transit, we proceeded directly to the Hacienda of San José del Carmen, situated on the west bank of the Tancochapa River, 20 miles from the Gulf. From Mina-titlan to a point on the Arroyo de los Urgells, about seven miles above its confluence with the Uspanapa, we availed ourselves of canoe navigation. Leaving this point, our route thence to the Hacienda of San José, a distance of 7 miles, lay over a gently undulating country beautifully diversified with woods and prairie. The timber bordering the arroyo, and extending some distance easterly, is very fine, comprising many valuable woods.

About a mile westward of the Hacienda we crossed a high, rolling prairie, elevated 150 or 200 feet above the level of the Tancochapa River. From this point the ground descends very gradually to the south and west, but towards the Tancochapa it falls rapidly to the level of the river-bottom. On this elevation, which commands an extensive view of the country, we measured off two base-lines—one of half a mile, and the other of a mile in length—from which we determined by triangulation the relative position of all the principal mountain ranges, as well as numerous other points. The location of our base-lines with reference to the line of survey to the west of the Coatzacoalcos, was obtained by measuring the angle subtended by a line joining Mts. Tecuanapa and San Martin, the position of which was afterwards accurately determined by observations made at Cosuliacaque, Jaltipan, and Tesistepec.

The following are some of the results of observations made from this point (designated on the map as Station "A"). The nearest highland in a southeasterly direction we found to be distant from 22 to 30 miles, the mountain ranges being limited on the left by a line bearing about S. 60° E. from Station "A." To the left of this line, and east of the Tancochapa and Tonala rivers, the country presents the appearance of a vast level plain. We could distinctly trace, meandering through this plain, the courses of the Tancochapa and Sanapa rivers, by the peculiar foliage of the trees on their banks; the former from the Hacienda of San José to its confluence with the Tonala, and the latter from the town of San Francisco to the same point. The country bordering the Sanapa River on the south is gently undulating, and well adapted for cultivation; on the north it is more level, but extremely rich and fertile, and generally above overflow. There are a number of fine Haciendas on this river. Most of the land bordering the Tonala and Tancochapa rivers, below the Hacienda of San José, is subject to periodic inundation. For a distance of six or eight miles south and west of Station "A" the country presents a very smooth, uniform surface; beyond which it is traversed by elevated ridges or ranges of hills, varying in height from three to five hundred feet above the sea-level. With the exception of Tecuanapa, the nearest mountains in a southerly direction are from 30 to 40 miles distant.

On our return to Mina-titlan we took the road to Paso Nuevo, via Moloacan and Ishuatlan. From the Hacienda of San José to the Cerro Acalapa the surface of the country is gently undulating, and alternates with woods and prairie, the soil generally consisting of a light sandy loam. From the Cerro Acalapa to the Gulf there is a continuous chain of highlands separating the basins of the Coatzacoalcos and Tonala rivers. Between these and the Coatzacoalcos we find a considerable interval of low land, which, however, decreases in width as we approach the mouth of the river; at which point, as well as at Paso Nuevo, the highlands extend to the banks of the stream. This latter place is the only point between the mouth of the river and Mina-titlan above overflow.

With regard to the practicability of constructing a railroad on the east side of the Coatzacoalcos I may here state, that the road can be located from Paso Nuevo to a point on the Uspanapa, near the confluence of the Arroyo de Mexcalapa, over very favorable ground as regards both alignment and grades; thence to the mouth of the Malatengo River, the route as laid down on the map would encounter no highlands of sufficient elevation to offer any serious obstacle to the construction of the road. The distance would, however, be greater than by the line to the west of the Coatzacoalcos; and the comparatively large amount of drainage necessarily passing the line of road, requiring expensive constructions, with the risk of damage from the effects of floods, would seem to be conclusive in favor of the western route, notwithstanding the superior advantages offered at Paso Nuevo for a harbor, and as a terminus for the road.

Finally, I cannot omit saying that in obtaining the results herein communicated, I have been greatly aided by Messrs. C. C. Smith and D. J. Johns, respectively, in charge of the Transit and Level parties."

Having thus given a detailed description of the whole line, it is proper to refer to some of its principal characteristics, and the cost of the road.

The following tables show the length, rise and fall, and rate per mile of every grade, as also the total ascent and descent at each successive change, over the middle division, embraced between the Atlantic and Pacific plains.

TABLE OF GRADES *from Jaltepec River to Pacific Plains.*

Division II., Sections 1 to 11 inclusive.

Stations of 100 Feet.		Length.	Elevation above Pacific.	Total rise of each Grade.	Total fall of each Grade.	Total Ascent.	Total Descent.	Grade per Mile.	
From	To.							Ascend'g.	Descen'g.
Feet.		Feet.	Feet.	Feet.	Feet.	Feet.	Feet.	Feet.	Feet.
0	...	...	115	...	...	...	...	...	...
0	20	2000	115	...	...	...	...	Level.	Level.
20	74	5400	160	45	...	45	...	44	...
74	127	5300	175	15	...	60	...	15	...
127	230	10,300	292	117	...	177	...	60	...
230	407	17,700	230	...	62	...	62	...	18½
407	476	6900	194	...	36	...	98	...	27⅓
476	503	2700	218	24	...	201	...	47	...
503	527	2400	205	...	13	...	111	...	28½
527	539	1200	215	10	...	211	...	44	...
539	584	4500	170	...	45	...	156	...	53
584	610	2600	155	...	15	...	171	...	30½
610	655	4500	155	...	...	...	...	Level.	Level.
655	705	5000	197	42	...	253	...	44½	...
705	723	1800	200	3	...	256	...	9	...
723	778	5500	232	32	...	288	...	30½	...
778	884	10,600	352	120	...	408	...	60	...
884	915	3100	338	...	14	...	185	...	24
915	933	1800	338	...	...	...	...	Level.	Level.
933	987	5400	307	...	31	...	216	...	30
987	1020	3300	325	18	...	426	...	29	...
1020	1070	5000	310	...	15	...	231	...	16
1070	1095	2500	323	13	...	439	...	27½	...
1095	1126	3100	305	...	18	...	249	...	30½
1126	1137	1100	305	...	...	...	...	Level.	Level.
1137	1180	4300	340	35	...	474	...	43	...

ENGINEERING REPORTS.

Division III., Sections 12 to 22 inclusive.

Stations of 100 Feet.		Length.	Elevation above Pacific.	Total rise of each Grade.	Total fall of each Grade.	Total Ascent.	Total Descent.	Grade per Mile.	
								Ascend'g.	Descen'g.
From	To.	Feet.	Feet.	Feet.	Feet.	Feet.	Feet.	Feet.	Feet.
1180	1215	3500	315	...	25	...	274	...	37½
1215	1240	2500	340	25	...	499	...	53	...
1240	1290	5000	295	...	45	...	319	...	47½
1290	1340	5000	280	...	15	...	334	...	16
1340	1350	1000	286	6	...	505	...	31½	...
1350	1405	5500	286	...	...	...	...	Level.	Level.
1405	1450	4500	300	14	...	519	...	16½	...
1450	1474	2400	287	...	13	...	347	...	28½
1474	1490	1600	287	...	...	...	...	Level.	Level.
1490	1540	5000	330	43	...	562	...	45½	...
1540	1570	3000	295	...	35	...	382	...	61½
1570	1590	2000	307	12	...	574	...	32	...
1590	1660	7000	315	8	...	582	...	6	...
1660	1720	6000	348	33	...	615	...	29	...
1720	1864	14,400	512	164	...	779	...	60	...
1864	1900	3600	512	...	...	...	...	Level.	Level.
1900	1947	4700	550	38	...	817	...	42½	...
1947	1963	1600	555	5	...	822	...	16¼	...
1963	2103	14,000	723	168	...	990	...	63*	...
2103	2139	3600	714	...	9	...	391	...	13

Division IV., Sections 23 to 33 inclusive.

Stations.		Length.	Elevation above Pacific.	Total rise of each Grade.	Total fall of each Grade.	Total Ascent.	Total Descent.	Grade per Mile.	
								Ascend'g.	Descen'g.
From	To.	Feet.	Feet.	Feet.	Feet.	Feet.	Feet.	Feet.	Feet.
2139	2177	3800	754	40	...	1030	...	55	...
2177	2238	6100	783	29	...	1059	...	25	...
2238	2300	6200	795	12	...	1071	...	10	...
2300	2350	5000	855	60	...	1131	...	63	...
2350	2445	9500	745	...	110	...	501	...	61
2445	2472	2700	723	...	22	...	523	...	43
2472	2502	3000	741	18	...	1149	...	32	...
2502	2621	11,900	683	...	58	...	581	...	26
2621	2753	13,200	770	87	...	1236	...	35	...
2753	2810	5700	708	...	62	...	643	...	58
2810	2863	5300	688	...	20	...	663	...	20
2863	2914	5100	712	24	...	1260	...	25	...
2914	2960	4600	707	...	5	...	668	...	6
2960	2980	2000	714	7	...	1267	...	18½	...
2980	3051	7100	793	79	...	1346	...	59	Summit.*
3051	3299	24,800	490	...	303	...	971	...	64·4*
3299	3490	19,100	302	...	188	...	1159	...	52
3490	3526	3600	272	...	30	...	1189	...	44
3526	3600	7400	240	...	32	...	1221	...	23
3600	3630	3000	240	...	...	...	...	Level.	Level.

* Will not exceed sixty.

Tangents, Curvature, &c., over Middle Division.

Total length of tangent lines,	47 miles.
" curved "	21.7 "
Length of line,	68.7 "
Degrees of curvature right,	1734°.23'
" " left,	1656°.25'
Total degrees of curvature,	3390°.48'
Total ascent, from Jaltepec to Pacific plains,	1346 feet.
" descent, " " "	1221 "
Elevation of summit to be overcome above Pacific plains,	593 "
Equated distance for mean of total ascent and descent,	48.6 miles.
Equated distance for curvature,	2.2 "
Total length of line equated for grades and curvature,	119.5 miles.

This shows the length of a straight and level road, which, with a given engine and train of cars, would require the same amount of power in passing over it, as the same given engine and train would consume in passing over all the grades and curves on the line as actually surveyed.

It should be borne in mind, that these calculations are made only on the most difficult part of the line, between the Jaltepec River and the base of the mountains on the Pacific plains. On the portion of the route from Mina-titlan to the Jaltepec, and from the base of the mountains to Ventosa, there are no engineering difficulties to be met with.

As the maximum grade approaching the summit, on either slope of the dividing ridge, will be sixty feet to the mile, the same weight of maximum train would have to be made up from each terminus.

Comparative Table of Grades, Curvatures, and Tunnelling.

Name of Road.	Maximum Grade per mile.	Minimum radius of Curvature.	Length of Tunnels.
	Feet.		
Baltimore and Ohio,	116	880	2 miles.
Baltimore and Susquehanna,	90		
Connecticut River,	32	882	
Boston and Worcester,	40	600	
Western,	84	882	A tunnel 4 miles long is now being built through Hoosac Mountain.
New York and Erie,	60	800	
Tehuantepec,	60	1000	½ mile.

ENGINEERING REPORTS. 57

The 116 feet grade on the Baltimore and Ohio Railroad is eight and a half miles long, and has a curve of 1000 feet radius. Upon this grade, an engine weighing twenty-four tons, built by Ross Winans, and with a tractive power of 15,160 lbs., has ascended with a train of sixteen loaded cars, weighing in the aggregate, exclusive of tender, 208 tons, and at a speed of from six to eight miles per hour.

The same engine ascended the same grade, with a passenger train weighing 118 tons, at the rate of seventeen miles per hour.

It may therefore be safely calculated that a similar twenty-four ton freight engine, will draw a train of twenty cars, weighing 122 tons, with 178 tons of freight, from Mina-titlan to Ventosa, or the return, over the grades of the line as now surveyed, and at an average speed of 20 miles per hour.

RAILROAD DISTANCES, *across the Isthmus of Tehuantepec, from ship navigation on the Atlantic to ship navigation on the Pacific.*

From Mina-titlan to Ventosa.	By line of survey.	By Air-lines.	Difference between air & develop'd lines.
	Miles.	Miles.	Miles
Mina-titlan to crossing of Jaltepec,	62·1	54·2	7·9
Jaltepec to Cerro Sarabia,..........	24·0	22·8	1·2
Cerro Sarabia to foot of Chivela Pass,*................................	45·1	30·6	14·5
Foot of Chivela Pass† to Ventosa,	35·0	23·6	11·4
Jaltepec to Rancho de la Martar,	69·1	53·8	15·3
Jaltepec to Ventosa,................	104·1	82·7	21·4
Mina-titlan to Ventosa,............	166·2	129·8	36·4
Mouth of river to Mina-titlan,.....	20·0	00·0	00·0
Mouth of river to Ventosa,........	186·2	143·5	42·7

From this table it is evident that passengers may, on the completion of the road, pass with perfect facility from one ocean to the other in the short space of *six hours*.

The excavations on the Tehuantepec Railroad will be made chiefly in the following materials: common earth, sand, gravel, clay, and loose and solid rock.

In calculating for the removal of these I have added from 50 to 100 per cent. to the usual prices in the United States. This estimate will be found on the safe side.

---

* Rancho de la Martar. † By way of the city of Tehuantepec.

The average haul per cubic yard per 100 feet, moved beyond the first hundred, has been put at 10 mills for earth and 15 for rock.

A considerable portion of the earth can be excavated by native labor. The Indians residing in the villages, could probably move, by the cubic yard, the portions of the road passing in their immediate vicinity; but remote from settlements or haciendas, it will be necessary to build ranchos for the accommodation of themselves and families, because when they have their wives and children around them and proper means for obtaining food, they can have no excuse for being absent. By making it a pleasure for them to work, they can be counted on with a good deal of certainty. The present total want of employment, the anxiety evinced to obtain it, the scarcity of money on the Isthmus, all combine in placing labor at a low rate easily attainable by the company. It would probably be necessary to work them in gangs, away from the foreign laborers, with one intelligent overseer to about every twenty men. They certainly could do the clearing and grubbing a good deal cheaper than foreign laborers—as the handling of the *machéte* is their principal *forte*.

The *Cura* of one of the towns near the line of railroad informed me that he could furnish and control from 500 to 1500 men, and wished to be apprized by letter when the company expected to commence work, in order that he might spread the information amongst the natives and make all necessary calculations for this object. About 500 of them, mostly Juchitecos, were employed on the carriage-road in Chivela Pass, under the direction of the engineers of Don José de Garay, where they had an opportunity of learning the use of the shovel, pick, and barrow, and are therefore not totally ignorant of the character of the work to be done.

The price of daily labor in the United States is nearly three times the price of native labor on the Isthmus, and allowing that a native will do only half the work of a foreigner, it can be safely calculated that what work is done by natives will not exceed in cost, but most likely fall short of that done by foreigners. The company can send down foreign laborers in their own vessels with great facility, as soon as a regular communication is established; besides, the inducements to colonize, and the probability of many seeking employment on the road—even at the expense of their own passage to the Isthmus, will throw an abundance of men into the country.

On the subject of the employment of native labor, I give an extract from a letter of J. C. Trautwine, Esq.

"Our usual payment to common native laborers on the canal between Carthagena and the Magdalena River, in the Republic of New Grenada, was three *reals* per working day—and to native superintendents of gangs, four *reals* per working day; this was considered good wages.

"They received indifferently the real of their country, and the ten-cent piece of the United States, both having the same current value in New Grenada. From these sums they provided their own subsistence, the cost of which varied from half a real to a real per day, provisions being abundant.

"They lived *chiefly* on plantains, yams, rice, cassava bread, and the jerked beef of their country; but to these they added corn, beans, dried fish, fruit, &c., when procurable.

"Where any large body of workmen was collected for some time, a small native village generally grew up at a few weeks' notice. In these many of the workmen lodged and purchased their supplies. Generally they breakfasted and dined in gangs, on the work; some of the wives acting as commissaries and cooks. The cooking was performed on the line of the work, and the men ate in the open air. In some few instances we built huts for them where circumstances rendered it necessary to do so.

"They were tasked every week, and generally averaged from three to six cubic yards per day (per man) removed, depending on the character of the soil, their own degree of training, &c. I am not sufficiently acquainted with the peculiarities of your work to advance any opinion respecting the advisability of employing foreign workmen, but from the experience I have had I should never think of relying upon any but the natives for forming the *great mass* of laborers. We found a system of light premiums, to those gangs who did more than their tasks, was productive of a very good result. It created a rivalry among the several parties as to who were the best workmen, and the lazy ones of each gang were kept moving by the others in order to secure the premiums.

"We removed much of the earth in carts, drawn by either horses or mules. We also used the small donkeys or '*burros*' of the country, for carrying earth out of the cuttings, in boxes holding about a cubic foot each: one being slung on each side. The bottoms of the boxes were hinged, for letting the earth drop out.

"This method answered very well, but the carts were better, generally speaking.

"In shallow cuts we also used wheelbarrows to advantage. With proper training the natives worked very well. I am confident they did more work than whites could have done in the same climate, and more cheaply.

"I hope the line of your route is not in the vicinity of the present route of travel; for although the natives when left to themselves, and treated with a proper degree of kindness and firmness, are tractable and willing to work; yet when brought into contact with a stream of travel, such as that which now flows to and from California, they become altogether depraved, as I fully experienced on the Isthmus of Panama."

Material for Construction.

Quarries.—Stone for purposes of construction is found on the route of the survey, in the hills between the Jaltepec and Jumuapa rivers; in the Cerro Sarabia, the hills of Xochiapa, the Majada range, the mountain passes, Cerros San Diego and Morro, and at numerous other points on the line of the road. These, mainly, consist of sandstone, granite, sienite, limestone, and marble.

Hydraulic lime.—It is said that hydraulic limestone is found in some portions of the States of Vera Cruz and Oaxaca, but I am not aware of its existence on the Isthmus of Tehuantepec. Its component parts, however, such as common limestone, clay, ferruginous clay, and shale, constitute some of the principal formations, and, I have little doubt, by a proper combination, would make an excellent artificial cement.

Common lime can be manufactured in immense quantities on most parts of the Isthmus, and at many points immediately on the line of the railroad, there being entire mountains composed mainly of limestone and marble.

Sand is found in the greatest quantities in all the principal streams on the plains, and in many places over the middle division.

Brick.—Good brick-clay is found in many parts, and is used for paving, and in the construction of houses at Tehuantepec and many other towns on the northern and southern divisions.

Timber of the best quality is also found convenient to nearly all parts of the work.

Estimated Cost of Construction.

In the event of the final location of the road west of the Coatzacoalcos River, it may be thought advisable to construct that portion from the Jaltepec to Ventosa previous to that from Mina-titlan to the Jaltepec. These portions, therefore, have been estimated separately.

The estimate is made for a single track, of six feet gage, with the requisite side-tracks and turn-outs, and on a road-bed of twenty-two feet wide in excavation, and sixteen feet in embankment, with slopes for cuttings of one and a half to one in earth, and one-fourth to one in rock; and for filling one and a half to one in earth, one to one in rock. These, however, on the construction of the road, will be subject to modification whereever the nature of the material requires it.

The estimated *quality* of the material is only approximate, but will generally be found near the truth.

The masonry for culverts are supposed to be of good, substantial, hammered rubble arches, laid dry. The bridge abutments and piers, with hammer-dressed beds and joints, also laid dry, and the bridge superstructure of wood.

I should not however recommend, in every case, the building of the bridge masonry before getting the road into operation— for the transportation by teams of the stone and material for these works, where the haul is considerable, would involve heavy expense and delay, owing to the entire absence of roads and the difficulty of getting to quarries. It would perhaps be better to substitute temporary trestle-work over the site of the bridges, as an abundance of timber is generally close at hand. In some places it may be expedient to substitute the same for those embankments which require a long haul, as otherwise too much time would be consumed in the building. For the same reason, and to get the road into operation as soon as possible, it may be advisable to build it on piles in some places north of the Jaltepec. In this way the road could be put in operation much sooner and at a less expense; for the saving of time and the cost of hauling material by teams would more than compensate for the expense of the trestles. The stone for the bridge masonry, which could be brought upon cars from some point on or near the road, might be put up without interfering with the regular trains. For the loss by delay, and loss of interest on the original investment, certainly makes it for the interest of the company to get their road into operation as soon as possible; and if it can be done any sooner by putting up temporary works at some points, so that the permanent ones may be built after the road is in operation, and at an expense sufficiently cheap to justify the building of these temporary works, it certainly seems proper that it should be done.

Estimate from Mina-titlan to the Jaltepec.

In order to arrive at a safe estimate of the cost of this portion of the road, which I have called the FIRST DIVISION, I have estimated one mile of the most difficult part, next to the Jaltepec, and taken it as an average of the whole, with the following result.

Clearing, grubbing, earth-work, masonry and bridging, per mile, including the crossing of the Jaltepec River, $19,043

Or sixty-two miles at $19,043...................... $1,180,666

In the same way I have estimated that portion of the road from the foot of the Pass, over the Pacific plains, to Ventosa, as follows:

FIFTH DIVISION.

Clearing and grubbing, earth-work, masonry and bridging, per mile, including the crossing of the Los Perros and Tehuantepec rivers,..................... $9,880.56

From Rancho de la Martar to Ventosa, *via* Tehuantepec—thirty-five miles at $9,880.56, ... $345,819.60

ENGINEERING REPORTS. 63

Division No. 2, commencing at Jaltepec River.

No. of Section.	Length of Section.	Total Excavation.	Total Embankment.	Average Haul.	Clay and Gravel.	Com. Earth and Sand.	Solid rock.	Masonry. Cubic perches of 25 feet.		Bridging, Lineal Ft.	Amount.
								Hammered Rubble.	Hammer Dressed.		
	Miles.	Cubic Yards.	Cubic Yards.	1 c. earth 1½ c. rock.	34 cts.	26 cts.	$1.50.	$7.00.	$11.00.	$40.00.	
1	2.237	141,518	242,296	600	184,900	40,000	17,396	623	...	...	$116,270 70
2	1.970	189,300	294,940	600	298,507	...	46,250	1,483	...	...	199,642 48
3	1.856	202,374	42,681	700	148,900	...	53,474	120	172	...	147,315 66
4	1.780	42,241	245,985	700	245,985	...	...	411	277	...	104,318 00
5	1.856	91,341	101,545	800	91,545	10,000	...	96	1,035	...	52,890 45
6	2.064	137,672	164,423	1000	164,423	...	...	649	...	...	75,244 89
7	2.008	53,449	155,072	700	55,072	70,000	...	468	1,124	216	68,708 80
8	1.989	237,070	168,283	1000	237,070	...	...	1,245	...	...	110,655 10
9	1.989	172,059	177,930	1600	177,930	...	...	1,191	...	...	95,522 70
10	1.932	155,259	132,137	1000	155,259	19,000	...	1,073	239	...	76,901 37
11	1.970	82,318	101,867	1100	82,867	...	...	538	...	...	45,807 48
	21,651	1,504,581	1,797,159		1,842,458	139,000	117,120	7,897	2,847	216	1,093,277 63

ENGINEERING REPORTS.

Division No. 3.

No. of Section.	Length of Section. Miles.	Total Excavation. Cubic Yards.	Total Embankment. Cubic Yards.	Average Haul. 1 c. earth, 1½ c. rock.	Clay and Gravel. 34 cts.	Com. Earth and Sand. 26 cts.	Clay. 30 cts.	Solid rock. $1.50.	Masonry: Cubic yards of 25 feet. Hammered Rubble. $7.00.	Hammer Dressed. $11.00.	Bridging. Lineal Ft. $40.00.	Amount.
12	1.789	90,518	83,238	1700	90,518	......	......	......	138	820	183	$62,565 00
13	2,121	29,233	61,255	500	29,255	22,000	10,000	......	394	......	......	23,874 90
14	2.576	44,506	72,556	1000	30,000	......	46,556	......	285	1,492	183	56,783 84
15	1.930	97,261	141,467	1100	120,467	40,000	......	......	365	......	......	69,960 48
16	1.989	62,022	66,810	700	24,441	......	......	51,363	806	......	......	97,085 57
17	1.989	106,984	81,272	900	......	......	......	106,984	317	2,445	221	211,268 08
18	2,121	129,031	61,461	500	......	......	......	129,031	328	1,867	216	232,761 36
19	2.292	186,788	223,515	700	204,835	......	35,326	35,326	1,308	3,293	316	196,121 34
20	2.102	196,724	120,558	1300	203,591	......	......	......	459	......	......	96,864 86
21	2.074	105,030	136,948	1400	91,299	......	45,649	......	896	1,845	48	91,026 60
22	1.875	81,467	173,824	1000	86,888	......	34,072	52,864	366	752	......	147,916 56
	22,858	1,129,564	1,222,904		881,294	62,000	136,277	375,568	5,662	12,514	1,167	1,286,228 59

ENGINEERING REPORTS.

Division No. 4, ending at Pacific Pleins.

No. of Section.	Length of Section.	Total Excavation.	Total Embankment.	Average Haul.	Clay and Gravel.	Com. Earth and Sand.	Clay.	Loose rock.	Solid rock.	Masonry. Cubic perches of 25 feet. Hammered Rubble.	Hammer Dressed.	Bridging. Lineal Ft.	Amount.
	Miles.	Cubic Yards.	Cubic Yards.	1 c. earth 1½ c. rock.	34 cts.	26 cts.	30 cts.	75 cts.	$1.50.	$7.00.	$11.00.	$40.00.	
23	1.969	109,686	34,302	300	46,694	......	46,695	......	16,297	174	......	......	$57,904 65
24	1.969	52,062	69,864	700	34,932	11,644	23,288	......	......	123	2,027	48	51,160 56
25	2.045	32,135	87,566	400	......	32,135	55,431	......	......	222	2,510	48	58,695 38
26	1.970	66,099	24,998	400	......	44,666	22,033	......	......	58	208	......	22,918 03
27	2.027	338	31,137	......	......	15,569	15,568	......	......	55	69	......	9,862 34
28	2.027	437	21,138	......	......	10,769	10,369	......	......	54	......	......	6,288 64
29	2.121	250,459	13,871	400	92,108	92,108	......	5,885	60,358	152	......	......	159,786 96
30	2.045	219,473	336,935	900	......	181,138	......	81,262	26,298	877	3,134	660	241,900 62
30 Tunnel.				500	......	......	......	......	48,237	......	......	......	244,079 22
31	1.894	186,562	168,870	300	70,944	70,944	......	28,191	16,484	604	......	......	96,841 38
32	2.121	367,215	252,588	700	100,022	150,034	......	89,727	27,432	406	3,732	78	254,021 24
33	4.053	199,912	243,015	600	......	200,298	......	31,234	11,483	514	2,739	565	162,973 15
	24.241	1,484,378	1,284,284		344,700	809,304	173,384	236,299	205,589	3,239	14,419	1,399	1,365,732 17

5

66 ENGINEERING REPORTS.

Summary of Cost of Clearing, Grubbing, Graduation, Masonry, and Bridging, from the Jaltepec River to Pacific Plains.

No. of Division.	Length of Division.	Total Excavation.	Total Embankment.	Clay and Gravel.	Com. Earth and Sand.	Clay.	Loose rock.	Solid rock.	Masonry. Cubic perches of 25 feet. Hammered Rubble.	Hammer Dressed.	Bridging, Lineal Ft.	Amount.
	Miles.	Cubic Yards.	Cubic Yards.									
2	21,651	1,504,581	1,797,159	1,842,458	139,000	......	......	117,120	7,897	2,847	216	1,093,277 63
3	22,858	1,129,564	1,222,904	881,294	62,000	136,277	......	375,568	5,662	12,514	1,167	1,286,228 59
4	24,241	1,484,378	1,284,284	344,700	809,304	173,384	236,299	206,589	3,239	14,419	1,399	1,365,732 17
68,750		4,118,523	4,304,347	3,068,452	1,010,304	309,661	236,299	699,277	16,798	29,780	2,752	3,745,238 39

54 Miles Clearing and Grubbing @ $400 per Mile.................................... 21,600 00

$3,766,838 39

The two columns marked "Total Excavation," and "Total Embankment," show the quantities as estimated on the Profiles. But the total quantities to be moved affected by borrowing and wasting, will be found under the heads "Clay and Gravel," "Common Earth and Sand," "Clay," &c., &c.

It will be seen on reference to the table of total quantities of excavation, that a little less than one quarter of the whole amount of earth-work is of solid and loose rock. This, however, should not be looked upon as a bad feature, especially in a country where the rains are sudden and heavy, as the cost of repairs of a road built upon a rock base, would necessarily be less than one built upon an earth base.

Superstructure.

For the superstructure I have estimated a T rail of 70 lbs. to the yard. From Paso de la Puerta to Xochiapa, there is the greatest abundance of *encina* (a species of live-oak), suitable for cross-ties. Sub-sills have not been estimated for, for the reason that the nature of the road-bed will not require them; besides, they are falling into general disuse on account of enhancing the cost of repairs.

One-mile Estimate for T *Rail.*

T rail 70 lbs. to the yard, 123·2 tons, at $40,*	$4928·00
2310 cedar, encina, or caoba cross-ties, 7 to the length of each rail of 18 feet, at 25 cts.,	577·50
660 cast-iron chairs, 20 lbs. each, at 75 cts.,	495·00
Switches, frogs, &c., per mile,	30·00
5290 lbs. rail-spikes, at 6 cts.,	317·40
Laying track, distributing timber, iron spikes, chairs, frogs, &c.	750·00
Contingencies,	40·00
Total cost of one mile of track,	$7137·90

The prices of the rails, chairs, spikes, &c., include that of freight to the Isthmus in the above estimate.

Equipment Estimate for opening the Road from the Rio Jaltepec to Ventosa.

4	Locomotives for passengers, 21 tons, at $9,500 =		$38,000
6	do. for freight, 24 tons,	10,500 =	63,000
10	Passenger cars,	2,500 =	25,000
4	Second-class do.,	1,400 =	5,600
6	Baggage, express, and mail cars,	1,400 =	8,400
100	Freight cars,	800 =	80,000
30	Platform "	650 =	19,500
25	Gravel "	425 =	10,625
10	Hand "	150 =	1,500
	Total, including freight to the Isthmus,		$251,625

* Iron is admitted on the Isthmus free of duty.

Station Buildings.

Jaltepec—temporary engine, passenger, and freight houses, machine-shop and fixtures,	$40,000
Ventosa—engine, passenger, and freight houses, machine-shop and fixtures,	90,000
Five intermediate water-stations, and wood-sheds, at $2,000,	10,000
	$140,000

With this equipment, at least 100,000 passengers and 100,000 tons of freight could cross the Isthmus in one year.

Equipment.

Estimate for opening the Road from Mina-titlan to Ventosa.

6 Locomotives for passengers, 21 tons..... at	$9,500	$57,000
8 " for freight, 24 tons...........	10,500	84,000
14 Passenger cars	2,500	35,000
6 Second-class cars	1,400	8,400
8 Baggage, express, and mail cars	1,400	11,200
120 Merchandise cars	800	96,000
40 Platform "	650	26,000
30 Earth "	425	12,750
12 Hand "	150	1,800
Total................		$332,150

The above estimate, in every item, includes the freight; but if the cars be made so as to be taken in pieces before they are shipped, and then put together on the Isthmus, the cost of their transportation may be materially reduced.

Station Buildings.

Mina-titlan—Machine-shop and fixtures, engine, passenger, and freight houses, wood-sheds, and water	$80,000
Plains of Sarabia—Engine, passenger-house, wood-sheds, and water...	20,000
Ventosa—Machine-shop and fixtures, engine, passenger, and freight houses	90,000
8 intermediate water-stations, wood-sheds, &c.... at $2000	16,000
	$206,000

Auxiliary Carriage Road.

It will be seen, on reference to Plan No. 2, that the country between the Jaltepec and Jumuapa rivers is characterized by two main dividing ridges, one running in a southerly direction from Rancho Amate to Paso de la Puerta, the other from Suchil parallel to the Jaltepec.

With regard to the construction of a carriage-road over this portion, extending from the Jaltepec to the plains of Xochapia, Mr. Avery, from whose report I have extracted at length, says:

"A good carriage-road may be constructed from the Jaltepec River to the plains of Xochiapa, at a small expense, and at no point very distant from the line of survey. In building a carriage-road, most of the difficulties encountered in the construction of a railroad are obviated, as, not being so much limited in the matter of grades and curvature, advantage may be taken of the peculiar formation of the country, which is remarkably well adapted to the construction of good roads in certain directions. For a great portion of the distance above referred to, the road can traverse the summits of elevated ridges or natural turnpikes, having a perfect drainage, and forming a hard gravelly road-bed.

Supposing the carriage-road to terminate on the Jaltepec River, the route thence to the plains of Xochiapa presents the following characteristics. From the Jaltepec to the Rancho Amate, a distance of four and a half miles, the ground is but slightly undulating, and the soil a gravelly clay. The proposed route crosses the Amate Creek twice, and also two or three smaller streams in this distance. The cost of bridging these will be light, as there is abundance of heavy timber on the ground. For a short distance back from the Jaltepec it may be necessary to throw up a light embankment, to insure the road being above overflow.

From the Rancho Amate to within one-half mile of the Jumuapa (a distance of ten and a half miles) the road will traverse the summit of an elevated ridge, avoiding the necessity of crossing any streams. For the first four miles of this distance, the road will be somewhat hilly, and will involve considerable expense in its construction; but for the balance of the way, nature seems to have shaped the ground expressly for a road; it is *even now passable for carriages, and but little labor is required to put it in excellent condition.*

The Tortugas Creek and Jumuapa River would require bridging, and also a light embankment to be thrown up across the bottom-lands bordering these streams, which at this point are about half a mile in width; or a good corduroy or plank road might be made across the ground subject to overflow. These bottoms are not marshy, and are never flowed to a depth of more than three or four feet, and then only for a short time.

Leaving the Jumuapa River, the road will follow the summit of a gravelly ridge for nearly the entire distance to the Sarabia, only crossing three small streams in this distance. This portion of the route is remarkably well adapted for the construction of a permanent road, and will require for this purpose but a very small outlay.

For crossing the Sarabia River and bottoms, nearly the same constructions will be required as at the Jumuapa; thence to the Malatengo River the road crosses but three or four creeks, and will be very cheap of construction. It will intersect this river at a point about three-fourths of a mile to the eastward of the line of survey, and where the banks of the river are above overflow; so that by simply bridging the stream, it will be entirely clear of high water. After crossing the Malatengo, the road again traverses the summit of an elevated gravel ridge for a distance of some three miles, when it commences the ascent of the Xochiapa hills. The summit of these is gained by an easy grade from the north, requiring but a moderate outlay. By keeping a considerable distance back from the river, we avoid crossing more than one or two streams on this part of the route. The descent from the summit of these hills towards the Xuchiapa Creek is more rapid; but, by taking advantage of the formation of the ground, the grade of the road need not exceed three or four degrees. After crossing the Xuchiapa, it will require little grading as far south as our surveys extended—this portion of the route traversing an open prairie, with a smooth surface and a hard gravelly soil.

For nearly the entire distance above described, the route either lies through open prairies, or has been cleared of timber for a sufficient width to admit of the passage of wheeled vehicles. The importance of this auxiliary road in facilitating the construction of the railroad will be evident."

Should the best route be found through the hills of Xochiapa, via the *Mesilla* or the Nisi Conejo Pass and the Almoloya, a bridge over this stream would not be necessary, for as the road would cross near its source, there is seldom water enough to prevent fording with carriages. Besides, it has a good, hard, gravelly bottom. From the Rancho de Calderon over the plains to the summit of Chivela Pass, no difficulties whatever will be met with.

The five bridges at the crossings of the Jumuapa, Sarabia, Malatengo, Los Perros, and Tehuantepec rivers may be built on strong timber bents. As the freshets are sudden and quickly subside, it will probably only be necessary to build the bridges across the main channels, in order to clear the highest water. They can thus be built with less spans than the railroad bridges.

From the summit of Chivela Pass to the Pacific plains, at the Rancho de la Martar, is about six miles. Upon this distance the engineers of Señor Garay have already constructed about two miles of carriage-road, which was designed as a preliminary step to the accomplishment of his project. Between the end of this and Torrente Masahua, there is about two miles more of pretty difficult road to construct, being round the west end of the limestone mountain called " Cerro Prieto."

From Torrente Masahua to the end of Cerro de la Martar, the carriage route might be made to keep to the left of what is now called Rio Verde, down to a point opposite the end of Cerrro de la Martar, and then recross this stream to the plains of the Pacific; thence on nearly a direct line to San Geronimo, Comitancillo, to Tehuantepec and Ventosa.

From the foregoing it may be inferred, that should the railroad be ultimately located on the west side of the Coatzacoalcos River, and via Chivela Pass, the auxiliary road can be run in its immediate vicinity, nearly all the way from the Jaltepec to Ventosa.

72   ENGINEERING REPORTS.

Distances by the Coatzacoalcos River from the Bar, and from Mina-titlan to Suchil and the Railroad crossing of the Jaltepec River.

	Intermediate Distances.	From Bar of Coatzacoalcos.	From Mina-titlan.	Time from Mina-titlan. 8 miles per hour.
	Miles.	Miles.	Miles.	Hours.
To Paso Nuevo	—	12	8	
" Uspanapa	5	17	3	
" Mina-titlan	3	20	—	
" Almagres	23½	43½	23½	
" La Horqueta	17	60½	40½	
" Mouth of Jaltepec	52	112½	92½	
" Suchil	3	115½	95½	12
" Railroad crossing of Jaltepec	—	121½	101½	13

Table of Distances by Auxiliary Road from Suchil, and from the crossing of the Jaltepec to Ventosa.

	Intermediate Distances.	From Crossing of Jaltepec.	Travelling Time. 4 miles per hour.	From Suchil.
	Miles.	Miles.	Hours from Suchil.	Miles.
To intersection of Picaduras	—	6·6		11·4
" Paso de la Puerta	10	16·6		21·4
" Cerro Sarabia	16·5	33·1		37·9
" El Barrio, via Xochiapa	21	54·1		58·9
" La Chivela	13	67·1		71·9
" Rancho de la Martar	7·1	74·2	20	79·0
" San Geronimo	8	82·2	22	87·0
" Comitancillo	7	89·2	23	94·0
" Tehuantepec	12	101·2	26	106·0
" Bay of Ventosa	12	113·2	30	118·0

It will thus be seen that by shoal-water navigation and the auxiliary road, the Isthmus may be crossed in *less than two days* travelling time.

ENGINEERING REPORTS.

Estimate of Cost of Auxiliary Road from Suchil, and from crossing of Jaltepec to Ventosa.

Most difficult part, over summit between Jaltepec and Jumuapa Rivers, 9½ miles............at $3000				$28,500
To El Barrio,	44½	"	800	35,600
" La Chivela,	13	"	700	9,100
" Rancho de la Martar,	7	"	3000	21,000
" San Geronimo,	8	"	600	4,800
Over plains to Ventosa...................				10,000
Total cost.........................				$109,000
Five bridges over Jumuapa, Sarabia, Malatengo, Los Perros, and Tehuantepec rivers..........			3000	15,000
				$124,000
Add five miles if Suchil be selected............			1400	7,000
Total cost of Auxiliary Road..........				$131,000

This amount is sufficient to cover all possible contingencies.

As it appears to be for the interest of the company to open the line of transit as soon as possible, the first work to be done would be the immediate improvement of the present mule-road; three or four bridges constructed, with a view to be used for wheeled vehicles hereafter—some of its steep declivities could be avoided, its crooked turns cut off, and deviations made from it in some places.

A good road for mules and litters could thus be made in from three to four months, so as to accommodate travel throughout the year. It would be necessary to use mules and horses from the Jaltepec or Suchil, whichever may be determined upon, to the foot of Chivela Pass; here a relay of carriages and wagons could be in readiness to take passengers and baggage over the plains to the Pacific.

This arrangement, which seems to be necessary at first, even if the final location of the railroad should not be made on the west side of the Coatzacoalcos River, would make 79 miles by mules, and 39 miles over the plains by carriages.

The country traversed by this portion of the common road comprehends the most beautiful and healthy part of the Isthmus, presenting the greatest variety of romantic, wild, and picturesque scenery, affording at once an agreeable and interesting journey.

To locate the railroad, and construct the necessary auxiliary road contiguous to it on the east side of the Coatzacoalcos (should the route on that side of the river prove the best), would involve so much delay in making surveys, opening *picaduras*, bridging the Coatzacoalcos, and other streams, that, in order to accommodate the immediate wants of travel, it would be unadvisable to attempt the construction of a carriage-road east of the Coatzacoalcos.

As it would be almost impossible to build a railroad through a country like this, where a wheel was never seen, except on the plains of the Pacific, without first constructing an auxiliary road contiguous to it, in order that every point of the line of railroad may be accessible for all implements, provisions, and every thing necessary to its construction, I have thought proper to embrace the foregoing estimate as an item in the cost of the railroad.

The present mule-road from Suchil can now be travelled for eight months in the year the whole distance to Ventosa, with the exception of three or four miles near the northern terminus. To put this in a condition for travel the year round, it is calculated that one-half, or $65,000, the estimated cost of the auxiliary road, will be amply sufficient.

In order to arrive at an estimate of the business which such a road would do, it is only necessary to mention, that during the three years ending Dec. 1st, 1851, upwards of 225,000[*] passengers and 45,000 tons of freight have crossed the Isthmus of Panama *alone*. This gives an average yearly transit of 75,000 passengers and 15,000 tons of freight (*not including the mails*).

Now, considering the constantly increasing travel, the great natural advantages of the Tehuantepec route, the healthiness of its climate, and the saving (over the present routes of travel) of from 1500 to 2000 miles in distance between the United States and California, we may safely assume, as a basis of calculation, 50,000 passengers and 10,000 tons of freight, or *two-thirds* of the yearly number *which have actually crossed* Panama within the last three years, for the number *which will cross* Tehuantepec.

---

[*] Vide Revenue and Income, page 121.

This gives *an average* per day for the whole year of 140 passengers and 27 tons of freight, or 400 lbs. per passenger;[*] but as steamers carry from three to six hundred passengers, and from fifty to one hundred tons of freight, it would be necessary to provide mules for the transportation of the whole with the least possible delay. Consequently it has been thought proper to calculate for 2500 mules, including those for relays, to put on the route at the commencement.

With these elements, the extreme cost of opening the communication, and the approximate income therefrom, would stand as follows:

Repair of road from Suchil to Ventosa	$65,000
Buildings for accommodation of passengers at the termini, and at regular stopping-places along the route	40,000
Station-houses and boats at Ventosa	10,000
2500 mules with saddles and *aparejo*, complete, at $50	125,000
150 carriages and wagons, harness complete, for Pacific Plains, at $200 (delivered)	30,000
2 light-draught steamers for the Coatzacoalcos River	50,000
4 barges " " "	12,000
Contingencies, 10 per cent.	35,000
Total cost of opening road	$367,000
Yearly receipts on 50,000 passengers, assuming the price at $25 each	$1,250,000
10,000 tons of freight at $100,[†] or $5 per 100 lbs.	1,000,000
Total receipts	$2,250,000
Keeping up stock, care of mules, feed, and all other expenses, 40 per cent.	900,000
Total yearly net income	$1,350,000

This supposes the company to undertake the whole matter of transportation, as seems proper they should do, in order to secure the comfort and speedy transit of passengers. If it be allowed that one-half of the transportation is effected by the inhabitants of the Isthmus, even then the estimated proceeds of the mule-

---

[*] This result is obtained by averaging all the freight amongst all the passengers; but it must be recollected that there are sometimes whole mule trains of freight with but few passengers, and at other times a great many passengers with scarcely any freight.

[†] $300 to $400 per ton has been charged on the Panama route.

road would contribute yearly a large sum towards the construction of the railroad.

We give the above result, based upon prices actually below what have been charged upon the Panama route, to enable persons to form their own ideas of what may be the probable business upon this road.

The opening of the Panama road may reduce the fare across that Isthmus to $15 or $10; but considering the time which will probably elapse before the completion of that road, the saving of sea distance by Tehuantepec, and the consequent reduction of the price of the whole passage to California, we can safely assume the price by the latter route, or until the opening of the Panama Railroad, at $25 each, and for freight at $5 per 100 lbs., or $100 per ton.

The time by light-draught steamers from Mina-titlan to Suchil, as may be seen on reference to the tables, page 72, is 12 hours (8 miles per hour), and from Suchil to Ventosa is 30 hours (at 4 miles per hour); making 42 hours, travelling time, from Mina-titlan to Ventosa.

Summary of Cost of the Railroad from Jaltepec River to Ventosa.

Opening auxiliary road necessary for the operations of building the Railroad,	$131,000·00
Clearing, grubbing, graduation, masonry and bridging, from Rio Jaltepec to base of mountains,	3,766,838·39
Do. do. from base of mountains to Ventosa,	345,819·60
Superstructure—Jaltepec to Ventosa, including six miles for stations and side-tracks,	785,882·79
	$5,029,540.78

The above shows the total cost of the road, with superstructure and every thing complete, and ready for the engines and cars.

In accordance with the assumption that at least one hundred thousand passengers, and one hundred thousand tons of freight, would cross the Isthmus yearly after the road is opened, an equipment capable of doing that amount of business has consequently been calculated for.

To this estimate must also be added the cost of light-draught steamers and barges, to run on the river between Mina-titlan and the head of shoal-water navigation. They, of course, must be capable of doing the same amount of business which has been estimated for the railroad.

The cost of light-draught steamers on the Ohio River varies from twelve to sixteen thousand dollars. The expense of refitting and taking to the Isthmus would be from five to ten thousand dollars. A light-draught boat would therefore cost, delivered at Mina-titlan, at the outside, $25,000. Barges can be bought for a sum ranging from six hundred to one thousand dollars each. Refitted and delivered on the Isthmus, their cost would reach, at most, from $2500 to $3000. And as I have estimated for three steamboats and six barges, the total cost of opening steam communication between Mina-titlan and Ventosa, by means of light-draught steamers and locomotives, would stand as follows:

Cost of road as above,	$5,029,540.78
" engine, cars, &c.,	251,625.00
" station buildings,	140,000.00
" three light-draught steamers,	75,000.00
" six barges,	18,000.00
" engineering and contingencies, 8 per cent.,	440,000.00
Total cost,	$954,165.78

This has reference to the Jaltepec terminus and a connection by shoal water. Should the road be extended to Mina-titlan, we should then have the following result:

Auxiliary road, between Mina-titlan and the Jaltepec,	$62,000.00
" " Jaltepec to Ventosa,	131,000.00
Clearing, grubbing, graduation, masonry and bridging—Mina-titlan to Jaltepec,	1,180,666.00
Do. do. Jaltepec to Ventosa,	4,112,657.99
Superstructure—from Mina-titlan to Ventosa, including eight miles of station and side tracks,	1,243,422.18
Total cost, exclusive of equipment and engineering,	$6,729,746.17
Engines, cars, &c.,	332,150.00
Station buildings,	206,000.00
Engineering and contingencies, 8 per cent.,	580,000.00
Total cost of road,	$7,847,896.17

Which completes the estimate for the *road*, from ship navigation at Mina-titlan to ship navigation at Ventosa.

Table of Comparative Cost of the Construction and Operation of some of the principal Railroads in the U. S.

Name of Road.	Length.	Total cost of Road and Equipment.	Cost per Mile.	Total Receipts for One Year.	Cost of Working for One Year.	Return for One Year.	Ratio of Expense to Receipts.
	Miles	$	$	$	$	$	
Western Railroad	156	9,900,154	63,462	1,332,068	652,357	679,711	48·9
Eastern "	58¼	3,095,394	53,139	479,158	182,266	296,892	38·0
Boston and Worcester.	66½	4,650,393	69,925	716,284	381,918	334,366	53·3
Boston and Providence.	47½	3,031,107	63,813	354,375	182,288	172,087	51·4
Boston and Lowell	27½	2,013,687	73,225	461,339	268,707	192,632	58·3
Georgia	213	3,551,975	16;766	582,015	195,783	386,232	33·6
Boston and Maine	80	3,371,832	44,648	511,628	256,535	255,093	50·1
Baltimore and Ohio	179	10,096,571	56,405	1,241,245	644,634	596,611	51·1
Syracuse and Utica	53	2,363,043	44,585	432,562	195,263	237,299	45·1
Hudson River	143	10,000,000	70,000				
Tehuantepec (estimated cost) :							
Jaltepec to Ventosa	104	5,861,170	56,000	In connection with light-draught steamers.			
Mina-titlan to Ventosa.	166	7,847,900	47,000	From ship navigation at Mina-titlan to ship navigation at Ventosa.			

Table of Comparative Cost of the Construction and Operation of some of the principal Railroads in England.

Name of Road.	Length.	Total Cost of Road and Equipment.	Cost per Mile.	Total Receipts for One Year.	Cost of Working for One Year.	Return for One Year.	Ratio of Expense to Receipts.
	Miles	£	£	£	£	£	
Great Western	205	11,655,850	56,370	1,183,326	316,734	866,592	26·8
London and Birmingham	164	6,997,065	42,520	1,291,592	385,830	905,762	30·0
Southeastern	88	4,306,478	48,937	567,728	246,924	320,804	43·4
Manchester and Leeds.	56	3,372,240	60,220	492,426	185,868	306,558	37·7
North Midland	72	3,846,133	46,474	338,984	113,252	225,732	33·4
Eastern Counties	51	2,954,755	57,956	425,562	195,948	229,614	46·0
Grand Junction	82	2,597,317	31,686	645,324	192,672	452,652	29·8
Liverpool and Manchester	38	1,798,506	47,329	399,468	131,220	268,248	32·8
Southwestern	94	2,620,724	27,879	505,688	161,110	339,578	32·8

Proposed Lines.

In any surveys which may be made hereafter, I would recommend that the country traversed by the river Almoloya should be thoroughly examined; for as good, if not a better route can be found along the valley of this stream, or via what is called *Llano de Gavilanes*. In running down the Almoloya, we begin to descend almost directly at the summit of Masahua Pass, whereas at Nisi Conejo, twelve miles further north, we are sixty-two feet higher than the first-mentioned Pass, and have consequently that much less distance to run down upon. The object in running the line through Nisi Conejo Pass was to take advantage of the plains of Xochiapa and meet the survey coming up the Malatengo from Boca del Monte. But these plains being found much higher, or rather the valley of the Malatengo so much lower than was expected, the line in consequence is rendered more difficult. Judging from the characteristics of the valley of this stream, its rugged, almost perpendicular banks, the sinuosity of the stream itself, and its depth below the general level of the ground, I am forced to believe that the route of the Almoloya must be considerably better. At all events, it is quite certain that the grades* by way of this stream will be much easier; and every thing else remaining the same, it seems that it would be better to run the line via the Almoloya if for no other reason than the improvement in the grades, even were the distance a mile or two miles longer. It is not, however, certain that the distance will be at all increased.

A survey would have been made by way of the Almoloya as well as through Chivela Pass, had not the Governor of Oaxaca sent orders to stop the work.

The results of our surveys have changed the longitude of the Coatzacoalcos, from above the mouth of the Malatengo River to the Gulf, from eight to sixteen miles west of the position represented upon previously existing maps, thus making the proposed line *east* of that river now appear the shorter; whereas before, it was supposed to be the longer route: besides, the favorable reports of Messrs. Murphy and Avery of the country on the east of the Coatzacoalcos, in the neighborhood of the Upper Uspanapa, and the probable mineral wealth of that region, would seem

---

* See maps numbers 1 and 2.

to render a survey through it advisable before the final location is made.

The amount of water-way, for which masonry and bridging have been calculated, over the most difficult part of the route which we have surveyed between the Jaltepec River and the Pacific plains, allowing for the heaviest freshets, amounts to 3804 feet in 69 miles. This includes all the spans of the culverts and bridges. Now, in considering the immense range of mountains which bound the apparent plains on the east of the Coatzacoalcos, around the summits of which collect and discharge all the great body of clouds passing over that part of the Isthmus, and the amount of water-way for which a railroad running nearly parallel with their base must necessarily be provided, I am led to the conclusion that the drainage on the east of the Coatzacoalcos must be as great, if not greater in proportion to the distance, than that on the west, from the Jaltepec to the Pacific plains; and, as the distance along the base of these mountains is some 70 miles, the aggregate amount of water-way would be in proportion much greater than on the other side of the river. Still, there may be other and sufficient reasons, such as the presence of coal, iron, silver, &c., in the mountains, which would fully justify building the road on the eastern margin.*

By crossing the Coatzacoalcos at A,† and running down the east side of the river, we avoid the heavy drainage opposite to the line AB on the west; and by recrossing again on this same line, we avoid the heavy drainage on the east side, and below the crossing, and run upon a similar character of profile.

A line should also be run down from a point near Lake Otiapa to the base of Mount Pelon, at La Barrilla, where the coast line seems to indicate that a good and capacious harbor may be eventually constructed. In the final location, the shortening of the line some twenty miles, and the advantage of saving river navigation, may be considerations of sufficient magnitude to justify a thorough survey of this line, and its terminus.

---

* It is said that in the district of Acayucam (west of the Coatzacoalcos) there are several coal-beds, which are continuations of those in the adjoining province of Oaxaca.   † See map number 1.

Mountain Passes.

There are, properly speaking, no less than six mountain passes on the Isthmus of Tehuantepec, whose summits divide the waters of the Atlantic from those of the Pacific ocean. Commencing at La Chivela, the one farthest to the west, they occur in the following order:

	Elevation above Pacific.	Authorities.
La Chivela	780 feet	Barnard.
Masahua	843 "	"
West Piedra Parada	800 "	Estimated.
East Piedra Parada	825 "	"
Tarifa (Portillo)	684 "	Moro.
Convento	750 "	Estimated.

It is possible that another passage may be found through the mountains, near the head-waters of the Rio Almoloya, following down the south side of Cerro Huacamaya to the foot of Chivela Pass.

From the summit of Masahua, at grade, there is a total fall to the plains at the foot of the mountains of 553 feet; consequently, as the summit of the Pass is 793 feet at grade above the Pacific, the plains are at this point on grade 240 feet above: to reach which we ran down on a distance of ten miles, and on an average of 55 feet to the mile.

The Pass of Chivela presents less space for the development of the line than the Pass of Masahua, but it has the advantage of a summit 63 feet lower.

Coming up from towards Juchitan, or when on the elevated part of the plains immediately south of Portillo de la Martar, an apparently low depression in the mountains is seen just east of Cerro Prieto, through a gap in the Masahua range. This gap (a little north of Rancho de la Cueva), on closer examination does not present the favorable appearance seen from the plains, and I think is quite impracticable for a railroad. If, however, the appearance from the plains were as favorable in reality, and a good line could be laid through the gap, it would then be of very little, if any importance; for, after gaining the north side of the mountain through this gap, it may be said you are *still on the Pacific plains*, and have the main and only difficulty to overcome, viz., to find a passage through the mountains north of, and parallel to, the Masahua range.

I have deemed it proper to say this much in regard to the lower portions of the Masahua mountains, because it has been thought, that once through this range, there would be no trouble in finding a passage to the Chivela plains; and to show that any gap in the Masahua has little, if any thing, to do with getting a railroad line through the mountains.

As to the low depression formed by Arroyo de Juan, immediately at the east base of Cerro Prieto, I am of the opinion, from the appearance of the formidable hills between this chain of mountains and Chivela, that there are almost insurmountable difficulties to be overcome, unless it should be thought advisable to cut a tunnel from one to two miles in length, near the source of Arroyo de Juan, through to the plains of Chivela.

The same may also be said of the openings through the mountains at the west end of Cerro Masahuita, formed by Arroyo de Molino.

The four Passes of East and West Piedra Parada, Tarifa, and Convento, can be reached with a railroad line by coming up the valley of the Tarifa River, and so on to the plains of that name. The Chivela and Tarifa plains are distinctly separated by a long dividing ridge, whose principal point is Cerro Timbon.

HYDROGRAPHIC REPORTS.

In the establishment of a great inter-oceanic communication, like that projected across the Isthmus of Tehuantepec, the hydrographic results constitute an important element of success, and as full reports were made on this subject, I cannot do better than give the details in the language of those to whom this branch of the survey was confided.

Extract from the Report of Mr. W. G. Temple, U. S. Navy, to Major J. G. Barnard, on the Survey of the Coatzacoalcos River.

Under date of December 30th, 1850, I received from you the following instructions:

"There are two principal objects in your survey of the River Coatzacoalcos: 1st. To determine the proper head of sea navigation; 2d. To ascertain its capabilities for navigation by light-draught vessels as far up as Paso Sarabia.

"As to the first point, it does not appear from the configuration of the river, that even if it is equally navigable, any point between Mina-titlan and the Island of Tacamichapa is preferable for the terminus to Mina-titlan itself, unless local circumstances, such as a peculiarly favorable site and a high ridge of land leading to it, should render it so. There is little doubt that the road will lie on the west or left side of the river, hence your exploration should be directed particularly to that. It is said that sea-vessels can ascend the Brazo Mistan as far as La Horqueta: should this be the case, the road would be materially shortened by selecting a terminus somewhere on this arm. It may be, however, that this branch, though deep, may be so narrow as to be unfit for sea-steamers, and be particularly difficult of passage for sailing vessels. Such considerations, of which you will judge, would decide the point in favor of Mina-titlan. You will, however, note all favorable sites within the limits of sea navigation. It is said that Almagres is high, and that a road could be run across the island to it. You will observe, therefore, whether the island appears to be above overflow, and whether this road, crossing the Brazo Mistan, would, from the east, approach the Brazo on favorable ground. To shorten the line materially, such a road should follow a line or lines as I have sketched on the map from Almagres. To terminate on the Mistan, it should follow the same direction on one of the three other lines sketched from Tesistepec below. You will therefore get as much knowledge of the country back from the river as you can. The difficulty, I fear, in these approaches is not high or mountainous ground, but wide margins of overflowed lands.

"You will, in your notes, give the topography of the banks within view or access. Note the geological characteristics, the growth, character, and names of timber, its value if you can ascertain it, its application to various purposes, and availability for commerce. As to your plan, within navigable limits, it should be something like the one you have to Mina-titlan,—lengths being estimated or measured, and soundings giving greatest *depth* in channel. As the river is not at low water, you cannot tell exactly: and hence may not be able to decide the limits of fifteen feet low-water depth—but you can judge of the limits of sea navigation pretty nearly.

"2d. As to the river for shoal-water navigation, you cannot judge as well now as if it were lower; but you can survey all the shoals and ascertain of what they are composed—observe whether the shoal is due merely to an expansion of the stream (in which case it might be deepened by confinement and excavation), or whether it is due to a sudden fall over a hard ledge: in this latter case the chance of improvement is not so good, particularly at extreme low water, for the ledges are natural dams, which make intermediate reaches of deep water. Perhaps the sounding-rods I had made would be useful to you to judge the character of bottom.

"If the road should connect with shoal-water navigation, I imagine it will be at Suchil, just above the Jaltepec; for the rapids or rock ledges are above that.

"You might ascend the Jaltepec, if practicable, fifteen or twenty miles, to observe the character of a railroad crossing, and the nature of the country on its banks." * * * * *

Upon your instructions, and upon sundry conversations and letters that have passed between us, have been based the operations of the hydrographic party, with such results as follow:

1st. With regard to determining the proper head of sea navigation in the Coatzacoalcos River. The survey of the bar,[*] made by Lieut. William Leigh, of the U. S. Navy, in January, 1848, shows a depth of twelve and a half feet in the shoalest part of the channel at extreme low water of spring-tides; and I find now on a thorough re-examination, that his chart still remains accurate, no changes having occurred since that time. The sketch of the river[†] from its mouth to Mina-titlan, made during

---

[*] See map number 3. [†] Plan number 4.

the war, by Lieuts. Alden, Blunt, and May, of the U. S. Navy, and which you directed me to assume as correct, shows that this depth may be carried as far as their examinations went. The present survey resumes the work where they stopped, and extends to the rapids of Suchil, on the Coatzacoalcos River, and to stake No. 47 of the railroad "*picadura*" on the left bank of the Rio Jaltepec.

This work has been done as you directed, and in the following manner:

The course of the river was determined by compass-bearings of points upon its banks, taken successively as the work progressed, and usually with the greatest ranges afforded by the bends of the river. The distances between these points were measured by Massey's patent log. By graduating the one-mile circle of this instrument to every five-hundredths, these distances were easily read to the nearest one-hundredth of a mile; and by measuring the strength of the current with an ordinary log-reel, and noting the time occupied in running from one station to another, the corrections for current could be determined and applied to the reading. But as it was always necessary to return over the same ground, the distances were measured and the elapsed times noted both ways, and the correction for current proportioned from these data: thus any error arising from an inequality of the current in the bends and reaches has been avoided. At the same time a sketch-book was taken in the boat, and an outline of the banks of the river, embracing the topography so far as it was visible or easy of access, was made as an illustration of the notes.

The line of deepest soundings, as laid down upon the chart, was run for the most part by the eye and judgment, inasmuch as the channel may easily be traced from the appearance of the banks, and from the general law in all rivers, of following the bends. It did not, therefore, seem advisable to waste time in zigzagging the whole river, but wherever there was room for a doubt as to the precise locality of the deepest channel, or whenever shoaler water was found than had been met with below, a careful and minute examination was made; and even without these causes operating, cross-sections of the river were frequently sounded to determine if the deepest water had been found.

The chart has been constructed upon a scale of $\frac{1}{40000}$,* and as a continuation of the one already referred to of the river below Mina-titlan. The soundings are expressed in feet, and give the greatest depth in channel, reduced throughout to the lowest stage of the river.

From this it appears that a greater depth than can be brought in over the bar can at all seasons be carried up to within about a mile of the junction of the Brazos Apotzongo and Mistan, a distance of more than thirty miles from the bar. At this point there is a small island, and above that an extensive mud bank, with nine feet in channel for a distance of more than a quarter of a mile. A deeper channel might easily be dredged out through this bank, and the increased depth probably made permanent by a dam built obliquely from the upper end of the island to the left bank above, so as to close entirely the smaller branch; a dam apparently very cheap, efficient, and easy of construction, were it not for the periodical overflow of the river.

In connection with the depth of water in the channel, the heights of the banks and the width of the river must be considered to determine the proper head of sea navigation. If this obstacle be removed, the limits of sea navigation, so far as regards depth of water alone, will be extended to a point near the Rancho de Mariscal on the one branch, and to the mouth of the Estero Monzapa on the other, distances of near two and four miles respectively. Above them it would be impossible to go, for the greatest depth in channel decreases gradually with every mile in both branches. A depth of only three feet occurs before reaching Almagres or Hidalgo-titlan; and opposite this in the Mistan, there is but four feet, till at length it is impossible to bring more than two feet into the main channel at La Horqueta through the Brazo *Apotzongo*, and three through the *Mistan*.

With regard to the height of the banks, there exists no point, between Mina-titlan and the nine-feet shoal already referred to,

---

* The published copy has been reduced to one-third the original.

which is not subject to an annual overflow. If, however, the limits of sea navigation be extended to the Rancho de Mariscal and the Estero Monzapa, there will be found at each of these places a height of bank sufficient to insure against overflow during the rainy season. The first, which is on the left bank of the Brazo Apotzongo, about three-quarters of a mile above the junction, and therefore on the Island of Tacamichapa, is an isolated table-land of moderate extent, and surrounded by lagoons and low land, over which it would be exceedingly difficult and expensive to bring a railroad. The second, which is at, and above the mouth of the Estero Monzapa, and on the left or western bank of the Brazo Mistan, about three miles above the junction, is a bluff bank seventeen feet above the lowest level of the river, and about five above the highest traces of overflow. It was impossible, with our means, to penetrate the jungle, with which this last is covered, and ascertain its extent back from the river; but its fall is very small, and the whole appears to be nothing more than a little hillock. If this be so, it is liable to the same objection with the first; but even if it be the abutment of a high ridge of land upon the river, it is still objectionable as the terminus for sea navigation, inasmuch as the Brazo Mistan does not average more than 250 feet in width, and is very crooked and full of snags. Its narrowness alone would render it wholly impracticable for shipping, and still more for sea-steamers, which could neither turn round nor back down past the sharp bends. * * *

In view of all these considerations, I do not hesitate to discourage all thought of improving this part of the river for sea-steamers, nor to name Mina-titlan as the proper head of ship navigation; for although there may be seasons of the year when sea-steamers would find a sufficient depth of water as far up, perhaps, as the mouth of the Jaltepec (provided their great length would admit of passing the sharp elbows in the river), yet the proper limit should be fixed at a point which could be reached, and at the same time be free from overflow, at all seasons of the year; and Mina-titlan is the highest point on either bank of the river that combines all the requisite advantages.

2d. With regard to the capabilities of the river for navigation by light-draught vessels, I am satisfied that the soundings as expressed upon the accompanying chart are reduced to the very lowest level to which the river ever attains. It follows, therefore, that it is navigable *at all seasons of the year* for any vessel drawing less than two feet as far up as my survey reaches, and although it may be possible to carry that depth much higher, yet beyond that the bed of the river is frequently broken into rapids, up which no steamer of sufficiently light draught would have power to ascend; and in many places it is so choked up with little islands as to be wholly impassable for any thing larger than a canoe. I therefore deem it utterly impossible to navigate the river beyond the Isla del Suchil in its present condition and at all seasons. In fact, the rapids at this point present an insuperable obstacle; for in addition to the great fall in the bed of the river (some two feet in fifty—I had no means of accurate measurement), the channel makes nearly a right angle with itself, both at the head and foot of the rapids, and a steamer could neither ascend nor descend without risk of serious damage. Even canoes find the greatest difficulty in avoiding the banks in their descent. Straightening the channel would but increase the grade of fall, and dredging out would but remove the rapids higher up.

As appears, too, upon the chart, several rapids will be encountered below this point; but these are "rapids" only when the river is reduced to its lowest stage; and even then they can be easily overcome by a light-draught steamer, and present no obstacle to an uninterrupted navigation of the river. A heavy rain in the upper country will cause the river to rise almost immediately, and then these rapids become merely a strong current of some three or four knots per hour.

In connection with this I would remark also, that this river is exceedingly sensitive to rains; and I have known a heavy thunderstorm of three hours' duration, crossing the head-waters from east to west, to create a rise of two feet at the mouth of the Jaltepec within twenty-four hours; which rise did not subside again for three days, and was speedily followed by another. And I am convinced that the minimum depth of water in the channel as laid down upon the accompanying chart will seldom be found at any season of the year.

The Jaltepec River affords the same depth (two feet) as far up as you directed the survey to be carried, and though narrow, and in some parts very crooked, containing several rapids, too, at extreme low water, I have no doubt it could be rendered serviceable for light-draught steamers to within three-quarters of a mile of the limits of our survey, by simply clearing it of snags. Should it be decided, however, to connect the railroad with shoal-water navigation by means of this river, it might become advisable, by reason of its inferior width, to construct steamers of a smaller size than could be used if the connection were at or near its junction with the Coatzacoalcos or at Suchil.

The strength of the current varies in the upper portion of the river from two to three miles per hour, and decreases gradually in its average towards the mouth, till at length it becomes lost in the tides. During the rainy season of course it increases at the same place with the increase of the volume of water.

The traces of overflow indicate an extreme rise of twenty-two feet at the mouth of the Jaltepec, and fourteen at La Horqueta.

The influence of the tides is perceptible as far as the junction of the Brazos Apotzongo and Mistan, and becomes lost in making the circuit of the Island of Tacamichapa. Northers, too, affect the height of the river very sensibly as far as tide-water extends; but above that, any increase in depth of water is attributable entirely to the state of the weather in the mountains.

If the final decision of the company be that the railroad shall connect with sea navigation, there will exist no physical objection to a *temporary* arrangement by which they will be enabled to throw the whole force at their command upon that portion of the work embraced between the head of shoal-water navigation and the Pacific, thus making the entire connection by steam in a much shorter time than could otherwise be done. After which the road can be extended more at leisure, if, in the mean time, it be not demonstrated that such an arrangement will satisfy all the permanent demands upon the route. For this

I would recommend the selection of some point between Suchil and the mouth of the Jaltepec as a terminus, unless other than hydrographic reasons forbid it.

The extensive reconnaissances of the country between Boca del Monte and Tesistepec by means of the tributaries of the Coatzacoalcos, which you marked out in your instructions for the hydrographic party, have not been made, owing to the character of the country upon the river banks, covered as it is by an impenetrable jungle. It was found impossible to acquire any useful information of the topography of that region by exploring the different streams, or in any other manner, except by following the roads leading from the several ferries to the towns between Mina-titlan and Acayucam. This portion had already been examined, and nothing could have been gained by the proposed reconnaissance. Subsequently, as you know, lines were run through this whole extent by the railroad parties, and all the desired information obtained. The same considerations prevented my ascertaining the limits of overflow on either side.

In compliance with your instructions, attention has been paid to the natural productions and geology of the banks of the river, and I have already forwarded to you a report upon the first by Passed Midshipman John McL. Murphy, of the U. S. Navy; and another, upon the second, by Mr. Walter W. de Lacy.

The bar of the Coatzacoalcos River has been examined to determine its nature, the practicability of deepening it, and to test Leigh's chart, according to your instructions. As I have elsewhere remarked no changes have occurred since Lieut. Leigh's survey in 1848.

My efforts to ascertain the precise character of its formation were not entirely successful, inasmuch as I failed to get a specimen of the bar itself; but I convinced myself that it is of limestone, mixed with indurated clay in some parts, and covered with a light layer of coarse, loose sand. The *Stellwagon lead* of course would bring up nothing but the sand, but the presence of the rocky foundation was satisfactorily proved by probing the bottom with a long pole, the heavy end being shod with a sharp iron pike. As well as could be judged with these means of investigation, the layer of sand was, on an average, about four inches deep at the time of our survey; and beneath that was almost everywhere a soft stone. Several loose specimens of pure limestone, and of limestone mixed with clay, were picked up on the beach, and accompany this report, as also a specimen of the sand taken from the bar. From the appearance of these stones they have evidently been long exposed to the action of the water; and, from the *feeling* of the rock on the bar, I am of opinion that they are a portion of the same ledge—perhaps detached from it in the channel by some vessel's anchor, and afterwards washed up by the tides. If this be so, it will not only be practicable to deepen the channel over the bar, but the increased depth will remain permanent; for this is the only bar (known to me) on this coast of rock formation, all the others being of shifting sand, sometimes covered with a deposit of mud, although their respective rivers have their origin and course in similar regions with the Coatzacoalcos. It would seem, therefore, that this ledge had been laid bare by the running waters, rather than that it should be the accumulation of ages of deposit. And this appears the more probable, inasmuch as all the local testimony coincides in representing the action of the freshets here to be one of removal, instead of, as at the mouth of the Tobasco River, one of deposit; the layer of sand of which mention has been made, appearing only when the river is low and the current weak.

In conclusion, I will take this occasion to say, that should the result of our labors be deemed satisfactory, it is because I have been seconded by such able and zealous assistants and men as those composing the Hydrographic Party. I am particularly indebted to Mr. Murphy for many valuable suggestions, and to all for their cordial co-operation.

The following extracts from the Report of Mr. John McLeod Murphy, U. S. Navy, contain the results of a reconnaissance of the Rio del Corte, and a survey of the Uspanapa.

LEAVING the Hacienda of Tarifa, I took the road for San Miguel Chimalapa, lying in an easterly direction, and crossed the Plains of "Las Tablas," which extend to the base of the Cerro Convento, a distance of one and a half Mexican leagues. These plains, consisting of black loam and variegated marl resting upon sandstone, are covered with long grass, and present a broad extent of excellent grazing land. They are, however, traversed in an east and west direction by the Arroyo Paso Partida, a tributary of the Chichihua. This arroyo for a greater part of the year is dry, but in the rainy months—July, August, and September—it overflows, and covers the entire plains on the south side to the depth of three and four inches: later it serves as a natural drain for the land.

Entering the Paso Partida, the small hillocks clustering round the bases of the adjoining mountains are covered with oaks and pines; and further beyond, the road lies through a magnificent forest of the latter, extending for more than a league over the entire pass, which consists of compact limestone and clay slate, mingled with fragments of diorite. The pine-trees here are similar in all respects to those of the southern portions of the United States, and vary in diameter from one and a half to three feet. Of their importance and value, either for timber or as yielding tar, resin, and turpentine, there can be little question, especially when their proximity to the proposed railroad, and the facility of transportation over a level plain is considered. East of the pass, and to the right of the Convento Grande, the road winds through a valley covered with every variety of trees and plants; among which are the mahogany (often four feet in diameter), the *ocosote* (yielding a fragrant oil), the guayacan, the guaco, the cuapinol, the tamarind, &c. Subsequently the road passes around, and over a number of moderately elevated *cerritos*, alternately covered with wood and pasture, until reaching the banks of the Rio Chicapa, where it descends to a rich valley, in which, on the north side of the river, is the village of San Miguel Chimalapa. The Chicapa, at its lowest stage, has an average depth of from two to six feet, and runs over a bed of slate and dioritic rock. Near this point it has two tributaries, viz., the Xoxocuta and the Monetza—small mountain streams; one draining the southern slope of the Albricia range and the other Convento Grande; but from the rapid descent of their beds, serving to swell the Chicapa in the rainy season from nine to fifteen feet, at which heights it continues during the months of October and November: thereby affording abundant opportunity and means for the transit of the rich timber (abounding in the immediate vicinity) to the lagoons, and thence at small expense to the shores of the Pacific. The quantity of valuable wood, especially the pine and the oak, of which there are two varieties of each, that might thus be obtained, either for the construction of wharves, docks, ships, or other building purposes, should not be lost sight of by the company. At present nothing is known of the immense value of this timber by the inhabitants, but the time is not distant when the demand will be great, and when the means of procuring it a question of no inconsiderable importance. In addition to this, the Chicapa has a number of excellent mill-sites on its margins, and where lumber sufficient for the supply of a goodly portion of the Pacific coast might be manufactured.

In accordance with instructions to note the natural products of this portion of the Isthmus, I observed growing in great abundance either at San Miguel Chimalapa, or in its immediate vicinity, the ocote, guayacan, rose-wood, capalchi, mahogany, ebony, tamarind, oak, guanacaste, cascalote, cedar, fustic, mangle, sangre draco, masahua, ratan, mesquite, guamuchi (the bark of which is useful for tannin), the vanilla, sarsaparilla, cuapinol, india-rubber, Brazil, achote, campeachy, and an infinite variety of medicinal plants and trees, distilling either gums or balsams. Among the cultivated products are maize, cotton, tobacco, pepper, ixtle, cacao, and sugar-cane.

Passing out of the valley of the Chicapa, the road lies for

more than a league through a forest of pines, over a sharp, sinuous ridge, formed of clay-slate and limestone rock, intersected by veins of quartz and felspar. Beyond this, the vegetation is more varied, and the intervening valleys rich with trees of every description, among which are the ash and the cypress.

Between La Cofradia and El Ocotal, the road is extremely difficult, and winds over a succession of steep hills and through deep gorges, in which occur granite, mingled with crystals of quartz, and the slate so common on the Isthmus. Here also the aspect of the forests is different, and the vegetation (arising from the richness of the soil, traversed by frequent small streams) more profuse and, if possible, more varied than before. On this part of the route, the india-rubber tree is very abundant. Rising to the Cerro Jacal de Ocotal is a magnificent grove of pines or *ocotes*, which extend for some distance, and give name to the place. Here is found claystone, sandstone, sand, porphyry, and jasper; and further beyond, in the neighborhood of El Chocolate, the same geological characteristics, with the addition of argillaceous stone, ferruginous clay and jasper, resting upon slate.

Along the banks of the Milagro, within a mile of Santa Maria Chimalapa, the land is lower, and covered with plantations of maize and tobacco, the stalks of the former standing, not unfrequently, fourteen feet high, and the ground yielding annually two crops. Of the richness of the soil in the river-bottoms, it is difficult to find terms which might convey an adequate idea. Yet the inhabitants are deplorably ignorant, and cultivate only the cleared portions of the land, where the maize and tobacco (for the sake of economizing room) are planted in the same field; but even under these circumstances, the exportations to other towns, as El Barrio, Petapa, &c., are very considerable; while the cotton raised here, though small in point of quantity, is not inferior to that of Louisiana or Mississippi.

At Santa Maria Chimalapa the ixtle is by far the finest on the Isthmus, and the yield very great. Much attention is also paid to the raising of oranges, which form an important part of the trade of the town. These, with a small quantity of cacao, constitute the chief products. On both sides of the Rio del

Corte, the forests are very similar to those which skirt the margins of the Chicapa, and present a reeking mass of vegetation in endless variety.

The chief object of your instructions having reference to an exploration of the Rio del Corte, I obtained a *balsa*, with proper guides, and on the morning of the 15th of April reached a point a short distance below the Chimalapilla, beyond which I did not deem it necessary to explore. Between this point and the place of setting out, called the *Paraca Nicolas*, one and a half leagues N. 33° W. from the puebla, the river is exceedingly tortuous and narrow, with frequent strong rapids, and a depth varying from two to twenty-seven feet—the bottom alternating between granite, slate, and limestone, with pebbles of quartz and jasper, and large boulders of conglomerate rock. The Rio del Pinal, at its junction with the main stream, forms an angle of 22°, and has a general direction of N. E. by N. Its entrance, however, is blocked by sharp, jagged rocks, which extend for some distance up, and its banks are formed by sharp, conical cerros, covered with a rich growth of trees, indicating, from the water-marks upon them, a rise of twenty-nine feet. At the mouth of the Pinal is a road leading to the head-waters of the Chalchijapa, by which the Indians often pass to the Coatzacoalcos. On the opposite shore is another leading to the village of Santa Maria Chimalapa, and known as the "*Picadura de contrabandistas.*" Below this are several large *milpas*, located on points doubtlessly cleared by the Spaniards in obtaining timber for the Naval Arsenal at Havana. Nearer the Paraca Nicolas is a succession of high cliffs of limestone rock, overhanging the river, and making its shores bold and deep. Prominent among these is the *Piedra Lagarta*, which, from the close similitude of one of its projecting points to a huge alligator, presents a singular feature in the natural scenery of this wild and romantic region. On the opposite shore the cliffs rise perpendicularly to a height of more than four hundred feet, and are studded with lofty pines, which, when cut, are precipitated from the summit into the river.

After much difficulty I succeeded in obtaining another balsa (with the guide who had accompanied Col. Robles, during his exploration in November, 1841), and was thus enabled to prosecute my labors. Setting out on the morning of the 17th from the Paraca Nicolas, we reached a huge rock in the river, called the Piedra Magare, thirty-three and a half miles above Mal Paso, and camped for the night. In descending to this point there are three tributaries to the Rio del Corte, viz.: the Milagro, Iscuilapa, and Coyoltepec. Before reaching the first of these, there are fourteen rapids, many of them strong and dangerous, with narrow channels filled with sharp rocks—the river in many places not exceeding thirty feet in width, and varying in depth from two to fifteen feet, with a bottom of slate overlaid by sand and pebbles. In this part of the river, which has a mean direction of S. W., the inclination of its surface to the Gulf is very perceptible, while the current has an average strength of four miles per hour. The banks are generally high and thickly wooded, with occasional low strips of ground, upon which are numerous milpas, and two small plantations of cotton and tobacco. The Milagro, at its confluence with the Rio del Corte (four and a half miles below the point of embarkation), runs east and west for a short distance, with low cultivated margins and a narrow entrance. Three miles below this, on the same (left) bank, at a sharp bend in the river, the Iscuilapa joins, running W. S. W., and in point of size is very similar to the Milagro; the main river, in the mean time, pursuing a southwesterly course, and its banks exhibiting nearly the same characteristics as above; the evidences of cultivation, however, diminishing with the increase of distance from Santa Maria Chimalapa—there being but nine milpas between the Milagro and the Iscuilapa. The current is also feebler, and the stream wider—sometimes three hundred feet. The rapids are likewise less frequent, and the depth more uniform. The Coyoltepec enters with a cascade six and a half miles lower down, and is but a small stream, branching off from the Iscuilapa some distance in the interior. Between the two last-named tributaries the Rio del Corte presents no features worthy of note except the Piedra Alta, a high perpendicular cliff of limestone rock, on the right bank. Here the passage is narrow, and the water, which has worn a complete archway along the base of the precipice, twenty feet deep.

Leaving the Magare at daylight, a series of swift rapids served to bring us to the Angostura, a deep narrow passage, formed by a sharp bend running from N. N. E. to S. W., with clumps of dark slate projecting from either shore, upon which are traces of iron. Beyond this, at a distance of three miles, is the island of Capiango, from whence to the Cerro Encinal, the banks are more like those of the lower Coatzacoalcos, and the stream itself wider and deeper, but with frequent rapids and a marked depression in its bed. At the Encinal is another large island, and on the left bank nearly opposite a mule-road leading to San Juan Guichicovi. A mile below this, at a bend in the river running east and west, is a large milpa, belonging to the Indians of San Juan. From the mouth of the Malatengo, a distance of two miles, the banks of the river are low and the current stronger, with shoaler water, and a mixed bed of slate, limestone, sandstone, claystone, jasper, porphyry, and grüneisentein, all of which (with the exception of the latter) may be said to exist in a greater or less proportion from the Milagro. At the confluence of the Malatengo the river is spread over a broad space, and forms a triangular island, with a narrow passage, over a strong rapid, under the left bank. The Malatengo comes in at an angle of N. 56° W., and its mouth is much obstructed by rocks, which give it the appearance of a feeble and shallow stream. From this the river bends sharply to the eastward for some distance, and then assumes a northerly direction to beyond the Rio Chico, a small tributary on the right bank; after which its general course is N. N. W., until reaching the bend forming the rapid of Alto Mayor, the largest and most dangerous in the river. Here the fall is sixteen feet in two hundred, and the current not less than twelve miles per hour. It is passable, however, by a very narrow and turbulent channel on the left. Getting over the rapid, the water is from fourteen to sixteen feet deep, and the river one hundred and fifty feet wide. At this point an extensive saw-mill might be erected, at small expense, to supply the lumber necessary for the construction of works at Suchil or other points on the Coatzacoalcos. The upper regions of the Rio del Corte abound in pine, oak, and cypress of the finest quality, which in two days might be floated by the current, even in the *dry* season, down to the Alto Mayor, and there sawed into lumber of every size and description, and in quantities sufficient for the supply, if need be, of the whole Gulf coast of Mexico. Of the facilities for transportation below the point in reference, it is unnecessary to speak.

Between the Alto Mayor and Mal Paso, the river is exceedingly winding, but pursues a mean course of N. 6° W., although some of the extreme bends diverge as much as 22° to the southward of east and west. The water, however, is deeper and the river broader, with frequent high barrancas of red clay on either hand; but the fall is very apparent, and the number of rapids fifteen. The current under these circumstances is swift, especially in the bends and reaches approximating in direction to the general course of the river, the geological features of which are exhibited in the form of granite, limestone, and slate, accompanied by indications of what I supposed to be anthracite coal.

Lastly, with regard to the greatest rise of water in the Rio del Corte: At a point opposite Santa Maria Chimalapa, the *average* height, during the rainy season, is between thirty-eight and forty feet, and at Mal Paso between seventeen and eighteen. These figures cannot, however, be depended upon as exhibiting the maximum point at all times, for from repeated careful examinations of the river banks at both places, there are indications which induce the belief of an overflow even beyond the points named. This opinion is further confirmed by information derived from the fishermen on the river, who state that in the month of September, 1827, a greater portion of the country bordering the upper Coatzacoalcos was entirely submerged, that the water rose upwards of sixty feet in the river near Santa Maria Chimalapa, and twenty-nine feet at Mal Paso. Subsequently, in 1835, another *cresciente* occurred, but of a more mitigated form. I have sought in vain for information by which these freshets might be referred to certain periods, and to ascertain if indeed they are periodic at all. To what extent the recurrence of similar floods may affect the line of country between the Sarabia and the Jaltepec, is a question which should not be lost sight of in the future location of the railroad, whether it be east or west of the Coatzacoalcos.

As your instructions required likewise an exploration of the Uspanapa River, I repaired to Mina-titlan, and after equipping a canoe with the necessary men and provisions, left that place on the morning of the 7th of May, accompanied by Mr. George E. Evans and Padre Romay. Establishing a base at Mina-titlan, a series of compass courses and distances were run to the mouth of the Uspanapa, in order to determine its relative position, and to connect the work with the surveys of the other parties. Entering the river, these operations were continued successively until reaching the Playa del Tigre, a point on the left bank, 45 miles from its confluence with the Coatzacoalcos, and beyond which it was impossible to go, without violating your instructions respecting our return to Mina-titlan by the 25th of May. Yet while it is to be regretted that the subsequent acts of the Mexican government, in reference to the grant of Don José de Garay (upon which all our surveys were necessarily predicated), precluded a renewal of the exploration of the Uspanapa to its head-waters, I have endeavored to add to the utility of the limited results obtained, by locating such of the elevated points as would prove valuable sites, and by designating the names and places of the most useful trees and plants, where they are particularly abundant. In addition to this, the character of the bottom has been carefully noted, in order to present at a glance such portions of the river as are susceptible of improvement; and embodied in the notes of the accompanying map are the water heights at various points, the usual rise and fall of tide, and the months of the rainy season. From these, it will be seen that as far as the reconnaissance extended, the Uspanapa is superior to the Coatzacoalcos, not only as regards the richness of its margins, but in its greater depth, and better chance of improvement.

Among the tributaries to the Uspanapa are the following, viz., Arroyos Totuapa, Chichigapa, Mexcalapa, Francia, Naranjo, that of the Urgells, and the Tecuanapa. The first of these is an insignificant stream entering on the left bank of the river, one and three-quarter miles from its mouth, and draining the western slope of a small clump of hillocks a short distance above. Nearly a mile further on is the island of Uspanapa, which is low and thickly wooded, but passable on either hand; the inner channel admitting vessels drawing seven feet, and the eastern one a draught of not less than twenty. At the upper end of this island, lying contiguous to each other on the left bank, are the ranchos of *Angelillo*, *Longinos* and *La Monteria*. Leaving these, the river bends sharply to the eastward, and subsequently to the south, until reaching the Chichigapa, a distance of ten and three-quarter miles from the mouth of the river. Up to this point the least depth in channel is sixteen feet. This arroyo joining on the left is quite large, and is said to connect near its head-waters with the river Coachapa. In fact, all the immense tract of land lying opposite Mina-titlan, and bounded by the Coatzacoalcos and Uspanapa, as far up as the junction of these last-named tributaries, is known as the "Potrero de la Isla." The Chichigapa, although narrow and tortuous, is sufficiently deep to admit of schooners ascending it for some distance. Its chief characteristic now is the abundance and excellent quality of fish in its waters. Immediately opposite the entrance to this stream, and rising somewhat abruptly from the river margin, is the Cerro Doña Maria, a circular hill of considerable magnitude, densely studded with mahogany, guapaque, cedar, zapote, and macaya, all or either of which may be shipped from the spot, as the bank is sufficiently high, and the water deep enough to admit of a vessel's loading there without difficulty. Above this, the river becomes exceedingly sinuous for a distance of five miles, with low banks, which are subject to overflow, and its least depth in channel is twelve feet, with a bottom alternating between blue clay and basaltic sand. This portion is termed the "Torno Ceiba," at the termination of which is the small Remolino (or whirlpool) of Amate, and the beginning of a broad reach extending in a northeast direction for two miles. At its upper extremity on the right shore is an out-cropping of sandstone rock, the strike of which is N. 22° E., and the dip 20° 30′ E. This is called by the Indians *La Laja*, and gives name to the bend. Within the distance of half a mile on the same margin is the Arroyo Mexcalapa, connecting with, and furnishing an outlet for, a lagoon of the same name, lying between the Tancochapa and San Antonio rivers, and *said* to be several leagues in extent, with sandy shores like the sea.

One and a half miles above the Mexcalapa is the site of a French colony, located in 1823. Notwithstanding the favorable character of this point, the abundance of valuable timber growing on it, the depth and width of the river, and the elevation of the ground above overflow, the settlement has long since been abandoned, and the ruined houses are now scarcely discernible amid the densely luxuriant foliage. Diagonally opposite is the Arroyo de Francia, which drains an extensive protrero, stretching inland to the eastern margin of the Tancochapa; and six miles further on, in a direction nearly east, is a singular island called *El Rompido*, signifying "the break." The tortuous flexures of the river at this point are very great, and the aberration from the direct line of descent has been in part restored by the water cutting through the narrow isthmus which originally separated the two curves. Thus the extreme sinuosity of the river having caused it to return in a direction contrary to its main course, the peninsula was subsequently consumed on both sides by currents flowing in opposite directions, and the island formed. This contingency has had the effect to check the course of the stream, and cause an extensive deposit of sedimentary matter in the reach above, which may be permanently cleared by confining the river within narrower limits, and preventing the water from making the circuit of the island. The bend referred to, called *Torno Guineos*, exhibits a depth of only six feet, in the shoalest part of the channel, which gradually increases to fourteen at the entrance of the Arroyo de los Urgells, twenty-nine miles from the debouche of the Uspanapa. Ascending this stream for seven and a half miles, we reached El Paso, a small point belonging to the Messrs. Urgells, who annually ship from it large quantities of cacao to Mina-titlan, whence it is carried on mules to the Paso San Juan, or finds a transit by sea through the Coatzacoalcos. The arroyo is exceedingly winding and full of snags, but of depth sufficient to admit canoes drawing three feet. From the Paso we procured horses, and visited the Hacienda of San José del Carmen, situated on the western bank of the Tancochapa, and accessible by an excellent mule-road, which lies for four miles over high and undulating prairies. This point is, without doubt, one of the most salubrious, and for agricultural purposes, one of the most advantageous on the Isthmus. While here, I made a reconnaissance of the river, in the direction of the Gulf, for thirteen miles, and found, as the least depth in the channel, nineteen feet. Subsequently, on a second visit, in company with Mr. Avery, this examination was extended for twelve miles above the Hacienda, with such results as are marked in the sketch appended to the accompanying map.

Passing some four days at the Hacienda in making reconnaissances in various directions, I returned again to the Paso and continued the survey of the Uspanapa. From the entrance of the Arroyo de los Urgells, the river bends, gradually, from E. 15° S. to S. 12° W., forming a broad reach, called the *Torno Bonito*, the shores of which are thickly wooded with valuable timber. From the left bank an extensive sandy shoal stretches to nearly half the width of the stream, and in many places is bare in the dry season. But a good and sufficiently wide channel, admitting a draught of six feet, exists under the right bank. At the distance of two and a half miles from the arroyo, on the east side of the river, is the *Rancho Maria del Carmen*, a bluff above overflow, and surrounded by a forest of india-rubber trees. This point is a most valuable site, and the land throughout its vicinity incomparably rich. Here a cross-section of soundings to the opposite shore showed a continuous depth of eight feet at all seasons. Leaving the Rancho, the river continues a southwesterly course for two miles, until reaching a high perpendicular barrancas of ferruginous clay, known as *El Tamulté*, back of which is an immense forest of guapaque, mahogany, palo-amarillo, and india-rubber. At this point there is a sudden depression or break in the bank, through which a small creek drains the waters of a neighboring lagoon. Between this point and the Rancho, the least depth of water in the channel is five feet, over a hard, white, sandy bottom. The river now pursues a southerly course for a mile, and then forming a sharp elbow, bends round to the same direction again for a mile and a half further, with low marshy banks, and a depth in channel of eleven feet, which soon after shoals to five. At the end of this turn is the Arroyo Tecuanapa coming in on the right, and draining a broad extent of paririe land, stretching to the cerro which gives name to the stream. Above this the river continues a southwesterly course for two miles, sweeping along the base of a range of hills upwards of 400 feet in height. From the summit of these I was enabled to over look the surrounding country for many miles, and to determine approximately the position of Mt. Tecuanapa. All this portion of the river bank is densely wooded with cedar, and the depth of water in channel sufficient to admit schooners. Three miles above the hills referred to, at a sharp elbow bending from S. W. to east, is a perpendicular bank of white clay and lithomarge eighty feet in height, and distinctly stratified; beneath the lead-line showed a depth of thirty-seven feet. Back from the margin are three small conical peaks, which afford excellent building sites, and between them an extensive lagoon, called *El Tortugero*, from the abundance of turtle found in its waters. This lake, which receives the drainage from the southern slope of the hills, connects with the river through a narrow and tortuous little stream. On the opposite shore is a broad and beautiful potrero, covered with a reeking growth of luxuriant grass. Between El Tortugero and the Playa del Tigre, a distance of three and a half miles, the river gradually sweeps round to S. E. by E., and carries a depth of five and a half feet in the shoalest part of its channel. The left bank is somewhat elevated, and exhibits an abundance of guapaque, which clearly indicates that the ground is not subject to overflow. Indeed, the presence of this wood may be relied on as furnishing an invariable rule for the selection of an elevated site.

Finding it impossible to prosecute the survey beyond the Playa del Tigre without violating the order to return by the 25th of May, I reluctantly abandoned the work at that point, having thus completed a survey of forty-five miles from the junction of the Coatzacoalcos River.

Subsequently, on my arrival at Mina-titlan, while waiting the concentration of the parties, I induced Mr. Avery to accompany me on a reconnaissance to San José and the Tancochapa, the results of which are already in your possession.

In a review of this survey, it is evident that vessels drawing eleven feet of water may ascend at all times to the island of El Rompido—a distance of twenty-six miles from the debouche of the river; and that five feet may be carried without difficulty to the Playa del Tigre. It is unnecessary to speak of the importance of these results, in connection with the valuable timber along the margins, or the surpassing fertility of the soil, and the number of sites for colonization throughout the whole extent of this rich and luxuriant region, which is destined to become one of the most thriving and populous portions of the Isthmus.

PACIFIC PORTS.

Extract from the Report of P. E. Trastour (on the Harbor of Ventosa), addressed to the President of the Tehuantepec Railroad Company.

THE bay of La Ventosa, situated on the southern coast of the Isthmus of Tehuantepec, at twelve miles distance, in a S. E. direction from the town of that name, is formed by the Pacific Ocean; and lies between 16° 11′ 36″ and 16° 12′ 49″ north latitude, and 95° 13′ 26″, and 95° 15′ 52″ longitude west from Greenwich.

Its western extremity is formed by the Cerro Morro, an isolated rock of oblong shape, rounded at the summit, about 150 feet high and 2600 in circumference; and a little more to the south by a pointed rock, separated from the former by an interval filled in with sand, and forming an angular projection into the sea, known under the denomination of the Point of the Morro.

On the west, the Point of the Morro is contiguous, by its base, to an uninterrupted series of rocky hills, lining the beach and covering an extent of 6000 feet. They cut perpendicularly the flank and rear of an agglomeration of moderate heights, somewhat rugged and precipitous at their summits, and forming together a thick cluster of granitoidal structure, disposed in strata, wherein feldspath and amphibole are predominant. It is the last link of that chain which, detaching itself at the northwest from the Cordillera of Oaxaca, descends by an irregular series of decreasing heights, passes to the north of Huamelula, turning it at the southeast, and terminates at the Pacific Ocean, where it separates the bay of La Ventosa from the bay of Salina Cruz.

The sandy strand of La Ventosa commences at the foot of the lateral portion of the Cerro Morro, facing the east, and describes from the south to the northeast an arc nearly two miles and a half in length; then takes an easterly and almost rectilinear direction, but drawing a little towards the south, extends on about six miles further, where it runs into the sea: after which it turns back again abruptly and inclines towards the north, though "trending" all the while in an easterly direction.

From the summit of the Cerro Morro looking towards the east, the beach loses itself in a distant horizon, and unfolds to the eye a long belt of white sand from two to three hundred feet wide, terminating inland by a vast plain, scarcely broken upon by the isolated hillocks of Huazontlan. This plain, of a slightly undulating nature, is composed of sand, clay, and vegetable earth. It is covered with trees of middling size, which grow both thinner and smaller, as one advances towards the east. But in the direction of the Cordillera which separates the Isthmus into two parts, north and south, this alluvial country is generally flat, presenting at rare intervals detached heights, easily avoided in the planning of a road of any character whatever, offering to the view fields of corn, indigo, sugar-cane, palm-trees, nopals, bananas, orange-trees, cocoanut-trees, and plants of which the vigor and variety bear witness to the great fertility of the soil.

The sandy beach of La Ventosa itself is cut by lagoons of little depth, having several outlets into the sea, and by the bed of the Tehuantepec River. At the time of the periodical overflow this current flows over a low country before reaching the Pacific Ocean, in which it then empties itself, not only by its mouth, situated 16° 12′ 40″ north latitude, and 95° 15′ 25″ west longitude, but also by means of those lagoons, its sole outlets during the dry season.

The volume of the water of the river is subject to very great variations in the course of the year. In the rainy season it reaches twelve feet depth, in years of an extraordinary character.

The rainy season usually commences in the month of June and finishes in the beginning of October. The Isthmus, in general, offers as many different climates as localities, differing from one another by their situation, the nature of their soil, the atmospheric phenomena, and the position of their mountains in respect to the cardinal points.

The immense basin of La Ventosa presents a safe and commodious harbor to vessels of all sizes. Closed at the west by the heights of the Morro, it is open at the south and east. This configuration of the bay allows vessels to have ingress and egress irrespective of the quarter from which the wind blows. Throughout its great extent, and on entering it from the sea, no shoals are to be met with; everywhere a good anchorage is to be found. The bottom is of compact sand, and a great proportion of it is mixed with clay.

The depth is almost regularly graduated: it presents at from 350 to 8000 feet distance from the shore, a progressive running from 17 to 53 feet, and averaging, for the first thousand feet, two feet increase per hundred feet, and about six inches per hundred feet for the following thousand feet.

The greatest difference that has been observed in the level of the water was six and a half feet.

Besides the variable winds, which are rather light, and the land and sea breezes of the morning and evening, two prevalent winds, the north-northeast and south-southwest winds, reign during a great portion of the year on the southern coast of the Isthmus. The first of these two atmospheric currents is not felt at sixty miles east of La Ventosa, beyond the Barra de Tonala; nor at sixty-two miles west, beyond the mountain of Chahuhé, which bounds on the west the lagoon of Tengulunda. * *

The north-northeast wind usually begins to blow about the 15th of October and ceases in the forepart of April. In the month of November it blows without interruption, and at that time it reaches its maximum. Towards the middle of December it ceases during intervals of from ten to twelve days, and then begins anew to blow one or two weeks. These alternations or interruptions and renewals are reproduced at short and unequal periods. But the length of the period of discontinuance goes on gradually increasing till the wind only blows one day, and finally ceases completely.

The Indians of Santa Maria del Mar are familiar with the indications announcing the coming of the north-northeast winds. In the evening at about sun-down, if the summits of the mountains of Guichicovi and San Miguel Chimalapa (seen from the coast), are concealed from the view by quantities of slate-colored vapor, it is indicative that the northers will blow the day following, and will last as many days as the summits of those Cordilleras continue to be covered with similar clouds. Vapor of a corresponding hue, seen at the same hour, at the horizon of the Pacific Ocean, announces that the south-southwest wind will blow on the day following.

The south-southwest wind, which in winter succeeds the north wind, during one or two days at most, is the only general wind prevailing during the months of June, July, and August. After some gales of more or less intensity, which may be compared to the violence of the north wind, and not exceeding one hour and a half or two hours' duration, the southerly wind is definitively fixed. Towards evening its intensity decreases till the next morning, when the same phenomenon is renewed. Still, this wind is subject to more interruption than the north wind, and the intervals of repose last longer. The south-southwest wind, passing over the ocean, reaches the coast of the Isthmus laden with vapors, which at certain hours of the day resolve themselves into abundant showers.

In winter and in summer, during the prevalence of the southerly and northerly winds, the current of the sea is from east to west; its greatest velocity is about one mile and a half per hour. This continual movement in the waters of the Pacific is only discernible at a distance of about 6000 feet from the shores of La Ventosa.

The bay of La Ventosa is much safer than the harbor of Vera Cruz. Violent tempests frequently render the latter inaccessible during several days, and even when the north wind blows the communication between the town and the vessels in the harbor is interrupted. During our sojourn at the Isthmus of Tehuantepec we have never had to record one tempest or hurricane on the Pacific Ocean.

In December, 1850, while we were at La Ventosa the north-northeast wind blew* with extreme violence from the 7th to the 17th of that month, and we remarked, with surprise, that the sea was not agitated.

To enable you to appreciate the condition of the sea at La Ventosa, such as it actually is, it would perhaps be well here to mention that our soundings were effected by means of an open boat, five feet beam by eighteen feet long, which we had brought from New Orleans, and which was conveyed across the Cordillera; with this boat we were able to sail out eight miles into the open sea.

We have one more practical proof to furnish which will radically destroy all the doubts that might be conceived on the subject of the practicability of Ventosa as a harbor. It comes from a seaman of too much ability for it to be refuted. Below I give an extract from a letter of Captain Mott of the steamer "Gold Hunter," which anchored at Ventosa. This is dated April 11th, 1851.

"I am much pleased with this port, Ventosa. The holding-ground is excellent, and the depth of six and seven fathoms almost all over the bay very convenient. During the four days we have been here, we have had two fresh southerly winds, and two strong northers. The former did not agitate the sea much, and the latter, though blowing very strong, has not straightened out the chains. We are still riding by the 'bight,' which is buried in the clay-bottom."

If a practical knowledge of this bay of Ventosa naturally suggests to the mind the means of rendering it available as a harbor, we must not, on the other hand, lose sight of the fact, that it *must* be the terminus of the road for powerful reasons.

---

* Off shore.

There cannot be a shadow of a doubt resting on the fact that the route of the Tehuantepec Road, going through a beautiful country, perfectly healthy, possessing mineral wealth, offering, with a great variety of sites and climates, immense agricultural resources by the superior quality of its soil, will one day attract to the Isthmus considerable immigration. Moreover, the advantageous position of the Coatzacoalcos on the Atlantic, and of Ventosa on the Pacific, two excellent ports of the shortest route between Europe and Asia, will make it the central point of the great commerce of the world. The merchandise and passengers, either in Europe, in Asia, or in the isles of the Pacific Ocean, can reach their destination by the safest and most economical route, and without those stoppages which always occasion great loss of time and money; and, though the remark may perhaps be deemed out of place, this great work is one whose influence will tend to bind together the Northern, Middle, and Southern States, and by making them all interested in one and the same enterprise, and common participators in the interest and advantages resulting therefrom, the Union will thus become more and more indissoluble.

The foregoing remarks naturally lead me into an examination of the nature of the port required by the exigencies of the moment, leaving to the future inhabitants of the city that will spring up at Ventosa, the duty of executing the work and constructions in harmony with wants at present unknown.

There are few localities where maritime works are not necessary for the protection of vessels against the sea and winds, and to facilitate the approach to the coast; and a port is not merely a basin where vessels may sojourn, sheltered from the wind and agitation of the waters, but also, according to the maritime and commercial importance of the place, a safe spot, where the operations of repairing, freighting, &c., may be executed."

Here follows a detailed description of Mr. Trastour's mode of improving the harbor, the cost of which he estimates at $300,000; also a description of Boca Barra, which he proves entirely impracticable for the purposes of a harbor.

In reference to the temperature of the Isthmus he says:

"On the Isthmus there are but two seasons, winter and summer. In winter the north wind materially diminishes the intertropical heat on the southern coast. The average temperature in October and March, at six o'clock in the morning, is 74° Fahrenheit, and at twelve, in the shade, 81°, and has never fallen lower than 78°. The average temperature is 75° between eight P. M. and two A. M., and 71° from three to five in the morning.

"The influence of the rainy season also tends to lessen the great heat of the summer. The temperature during the hottest part of the day when it rains does not exceed 81°. At eight o'clock in the morning it maintains itself at 75°, and at three o'clock in the morning it seldom falls as low as 73°. Usually the nights are of almost uniform temperature.

"In summer, when the sky is clear and the sun shines with all its brightness, the thermometer varies between 87° and 90° from eleven in the morning to four in the afternoon. At eight o'clock in the evening it falls to 79°, and at four in the morning to 75°.

"The month of November is the coldest month of the year, and those of May and June the warmest. Towards the close of April, the thermometer, at twelve, in the shade, occasionally ascends to 90°, and rarely descends to 85°. The forepart of the night on such occasions maintained itself at 79°, and in the second part the temperature descended to 74°.

"In November the thermometer never falls below 70° from nine to five o'clock in the day; at eight in the evening it has never stood at less than 59°, nor less than 55° from four to six in the morning."

Mr. Trastour, having been engaged upwards of a year on the Isthmus, has collected much valuable information, which could not be prepared in time for this report. He is now employed in drawing up a large map of his survey of the southern division, embracing sixty miles of the Pacific coast.

As Mr. Trastour has made full and complete surveys of the harbors on the Pacific, I have only deemed it important to make the following extracts from Mr. Temple's Report, as to embody the whole would have been but a repetition of Mr. Trastour's results. Mr. Temple says:

"I have carefully examined the charts of Mr. Trastour, and have not the slightest hesitation in expressing my confidence in his accuracy. I should therefore have been merely repeating the work which Mr. Trastour has just completed with so much industry. In all points where I have obtained results in determining the latitude, the variation of the compass, the rise and fall of the tide, and the time of high water at the full and change of the moon, and in sketching in the topography of the adjacent country, our conclusions coincide."

Again, he says in another place: "From all the foregoing considerations, I am of opinion that La Ventosa is not only the best, but *the* point for a harbor on the Pacific coast of the Isthmus. It is a far safer and better port than either Valparaiso in Chili, or Monterey in California; ports in constant use the year throughout. I speak from personal observation, as well as from an examination of the several charts, and their similarity of outline has suggested the comparison; for, although the indentation of the coast is possibly a little deeper at each of these places than at La Ventosa, yet they are both open to the northward, and as the general 'trend' of the coast is nearly north and south, the prevailing gales blow directly *along* shore, and *into* these harbors, creating a heavy swell, and often forcing vessels to 'slip and go to sea' for safety: whereas, at La Ventosa the 'trend' of the coast is east and west, so that the 'Northers' blow directly off shore, and create no swell whatever. The danger being from the *sudden* strain brought upon a cable by the surging of a vessel in a sea-way, and not from the steady strain caused by the wind, it follows that northers may be disregarded in an estimate of the safety of this anchorage, as was satisfactorily shown in the case of the Gold Hunter. But northers, although frequent during the winter, and seldom occurring at other seasons, are the only gales that blow in this region. The southerly winds, characteristic of the summer and autumn, are said to be nothing more than thunder squalls of short duration, and incapable of raising a sea. Even the fresh and steady sea-breezes that prevailed during the latter portion of our stay at La Ventosa, were unaccompanied by any increase of swell.

"I find in Mr. Trastour's chart of La Ventosa a moderate and almost uniform grade of bottom, beginning with three fathoms at about 100 yards from the beach, and deepening to seven and eight fathoms at a distance of 1000 yards. He also shows a good anchorage there, which he represents as a muddy bottom, nearly in the shape of an ellipse, of which the transverse axis is about twenty-seven hundred feet (extending from within 400 feet of the point of the Morro, in nearly an E. N. E. direction), and with a conjugate axis equal to 1800 feet. The sufficiency of this holding-ground was well tested under our own observation by the steamer Gold Hunter. She anchored upon it with a southerly wind, and subsequently swung to a norther, which, although of considerable force and duration, she rode out without '*tautening*' her chain.

"A temporary arrangement (or until the artificial works are made) for the transmission of passengers, baggage, mails, and articles of freight may be made at once, without subjecting them to any risk or discomfort in the landing or embarkation. This would be effected by the establishment of a station-house at La Ventosa, near the foot of the Morro, provided with large surf-boats, similar to those used by the U. S. Army at Vera Cruz—each with a crew of seven men."

GENERAL SUMMARY.

IN a brief review of the results just given, it seems proper, before speaking of the probable revenue and income arising from an opening of the Tehuantepec route, to refer in general terms to some of the more important points determined by the surveying parties. Of the question of *practicability* (hitherto so often mooted) little need be said. In the Engineering Reports, it has been shown that the surveys connect ship navigation on both sides of the Isthmus; and it is evident, even from a glance at the topographical features of the country, that no difficulties exist in the way of constructing a railroad over those divisions which lie on either side of the dividing ridge. It remains, then, only to speak of the practicability of the middle district, in which is comprised the route through the mountains, separating the two oceans. On every part of this, on the line of location, detailed estimates have been made of the earth to be moved, and the masonry and bridging to be constructed, all of which have been given in Tables marked Divisions II., III., and IV., and indicate the extremely favorable nature of the work. Yet the quantities of graduation and masonry laid down, for this as well as other portions, will be found, on the final location, considerably in excess, for the reason that the line surveyed is by no means over the best route. That other and better ones than this exist, there is little doubt, and but for the edict of the Mexican authorities, would have been examined. As our operations were therefore confined to a single line, it would be somewhat anomalous if, in view of the difficulties which necessarily assail engineering operations in a country so entirely new as the Isthmus was to us, we had hit the most favorable ground in the offset of the work. The estimates have nevertheless been drawn up in the same manner as if no other or better line existed. It is consequently but reasonable to infer that a great reduction, in cost and quantities, will be made on the ultimate location of the road.

The surveys over the Atlantic and Pacific plains bear more the character of *reconnaissances* than absolute surveys, and although compass and level lines were run over these portions to determine beyond question their entire practicability, detailed estimates and minute instrumental observations were not so necessary as on the middle division, where all the doubts and difficulties were centered. In this connection, moreover, it is well to bear in mind, that the New Orleans Company, in sending the expedition to the Isthmus, desired not so much to *locate* a line as to demonstrate the question of practicability within a reasonable cost, and the existence of efficient harbors at each termini of the road.

With reference to the *expense of construction*, as already given, it is only necessary to say, that the items embraced in the table are put down at prices nearly double those for the same character of work in the United States. But even were the Tehuantepec road to exceed three or four times the estimated cost, the certain income derivable from its opening would more than justify the outlay.

In estimating for the *equipment*, a basis has been made upon a certain number of passengers, who have actually passed over the different routes to and from California for the last three years, and upon a certain yearly average of tons known to double Cape Horn, which it is but reasonable to suppose would take the Tehuantepec route, when established, in preference to any other. I am free to acknowledge, however, that the estimate of equipment is extremely low, and that great additions will necessarily be made from time to time as trade increases. Yet while I have endeavored to limit the number of engines and cars so as to fall on the safe side, it is difficult, indeed, to calculate with any degree of certainty on the amount of business the road will command, when an uninterrupted communication between the two oceans shall have been effected.

The next point which claims attention is the amplitude and security of the *harbors*, and the capacity of the *rivers* for ship and shoal-water navigation. First, then, with regard to the Coatzacoalcos. The fact of there being no delta at the mouth of the river, and the constancy of the depth upon the bar, which has remained unchanged, according to the history of the country for nearly three centuries, proves that it has attained its "*regimen*," and indicates that any improvement by deepening the channel may be relied on as permanent. Of the precise character of the formation of this bar, many opinions are entertained; and although its position and circumstances seem hardly to justify the conclusion that it is rock, Mr. Temple has so stated, and I have consequently consulted Mons. Maillefert (a gentleman whose experience in marine blasting entitles his views to credit) with reference to the possibility of deepening the channel to 18 feet, which, for a width of 300 feet, he estimates at $135,000. If Mr. Temple's impressions are correct, this item of cost, in connection with the importance of a permanent depth of 18 feet on the bar, can hardly be considered as one of magnitude. The following extracts from a letter written by Capt. R. W. Foster, of the steamer "Alabama," who crossed the bar several times, and subsequently sounded it, furnish some interesting details.

"Sailing vessels bound for the Coatzacoalcos ought to make the land to the eastward. This precaution is necessary on account of the prevailing trade-winds which cause a strong westerly current, also in case of a norther, to have the advantage of sea-room. The entrance to the river may be known by the Vigia or tower, situated upon the western side, likewise from the sand cliffs extending from that point to the westward.

"The best mark for crossing the bar is to bring the Tower to bear S. $\frac{3}{4}$ W. by compass. Having passed the bar, haul up to the eastward of south, and steer in midway between the two points that form the entrance to the river. The wind, after crossing the bar, often falls to calm; for this reason it is necessary to have the anchor ready to let go, as the current on the ebb, even in the dry season, sets out strong.

"The extent of the bar east and west is about 220 fathoms, and the breadth by actual measurement 108 feet. The bottom, composed of sand and clay, is hard, on which account it is not liable to shift. At high water, on the full and change, the depth is about 13 feet, and falls as low as 11 feet. The general depth, however, is 12 feet, from which, in sailing, it deepens gradually to five and six fathoms. Except in heavy northers, there is a regular land and sea breeze: the latter sets in between the hours of 9 A. M. and noon.

April, 1851. R. W. FOSTER.

"N. B. The bar, being composed of sand and clay, as already stated, and only 108 feet in width, could easily be deepened for vessels of the largest draught to enter."

In view of all the testimony, it is presumed that no one will now question the practicability or security of this harbor. Second, with regard to the capacity of the river itself: From Mr. Temple's report, the head of ship navigation is placed at thirty miles from the mouth, and ten above Mina-titlan. In other words, any depth not exceeding twelve and a half feet, which is the maximum draught admissible over the bar at the lowest tides, may be carried to within a short distance of the junction of the Brazos Apotzongo and Mistan. By deepening the bar to admit vessels drawing eighteen feet this depth may be brought, without difficulty, to Mina-titlan; thus forming a secure harbor for nearly thirty miles, along which the track may be laid to any desirable extent. Lastly, the results of Mr. Temple's survey show that light-draught steamers of two feet may ascend at all seasons to beyond the confluence of the Jaltepec—a distance of ninety-five miles by the windings of the river from Minatitlan.

Not less gratifying are the results of the survey of the Uspanapa, from which it is evident that vessels drawing eleven feet may ascend it for twenty-six miles from its junction with the Coatzacoalcos, and that those requiring five feet will experience no obstacle as far up as the Playa del Tigre, forty-five miles from the mouth of the river.

Passing to the southern side of the Isthmus, we come to a consideration of Ventosa, which can now be used in its present condition in the same manner as Panama, by employing lighters, but under circumstances far more advantageous, from the fact that vessels of the largest class may lie within a few hundred feet of the shore. Whereas at Panama the approach to the beach is extremely shallow, and vessels seldom lie nearer than three miles of the town.

Already a number of plans for the permanent improvement of Ventosa have been suggested. Mr. Temple recommends a breakwater, extending from the extreme outer point of the Cerro Morro, in a direction about east 2000 feet, and with an angle at the centre of 150°. Mr. Trastour, on the other hand, proposes the construction of a timber breakwater, or port, about one and a half miles to the east of Cerro Morro, on the opposite side of the mouth of the river. A third plan is to carry a breakwater out from near the middle or inner point of Cerro Morro, in an easterly direction, on a curved line—at first about 1500 feet—so as not only to serve as a protection to the entrance of an inner basin to be formed by dredging out the Laguna del Morro and the western mouth of the Tehuantepec River, but to form likewise an outer harbor. An important preliminary step to this plan would be to throw a dam across the Tehuantepec River, and confine it exclusively to its eastern channel. This would prevent the accumulation of deposit and sedimentary matter now fast filling up the indenture in the coast. An approximate estimate of this method gives, in round numbers, $490,000

GENERAL SUMMARY. 117

as the total cost.* But whatever mode of improvement the company may think proper to adopt, it is enough for present purposes to know that Ventosa may now be used without artificial works, as previously stated.

Capt. Mott, of the "Gold Hunter," to whose letter reference has already been made, says of Ventosa:

STEAMER GOLD HUNTER,
Port Ventosa, April 11, 1851.

MY DEAR SIR:—I beg to return you many thanks for the tracing of this port which you so kindly sent me, and which I received on my return from the Boca Barra. I must confess I was much disappointed with that place. Instead of twenty-three feet on the bar, as marked on Moro's chart, I found but eight; and on the inner bar, where eight and a half feet are marked, but one and a half at high water, and quite dry at low. I am convinced that no use whatever can be made of the Boca Barra as a port for any class of vessels, for in addition to the heavy breakers constantly raging on the bar, in which my boat, a fine large sea-boat, was capsized, and the crew narrowly escaped being devoured by sharks, this part of the lake is crossed in all directins with shoals and sand-pits, rendering it unnavigable for the smallest vessels.

I am much pleased with this Port Ventosa. The holding ground is excellent, and the depth of six and seven fathoms almost all over the bay very convenient. I see nothing wanting but a breakwater carried out some 500 or 600 yards from the outer point of the Moro Rock, to protect the landing from the surf, to make it an excellent port. During the four days we have been here we have had two of fresh southerly winds, and two of strong northers. The former did not agitate the sea much, and the latter, though blowing very strong, has not straightened out the chains. We are still riding by the bight which is buried in the clay bottom.

T T MOTT.

P. E. TRASTOUR, Esq., Tehuantepec.

But under any circumstances Ventosa can be improved at an expense comparatively insignificant, and in such a manner as to enable ships to receive and discharge their cargoes directly from the shore.

In closing the operations of the survey, I cannot omit mentioning, in terms of commendation, the indefatigable zeal and un-

---

* An idea of this plan for improvement has been traced on Mr. Trastour's map of La Ventosa.

tiring industry of the assistant and sub-assistant engineers while engaged on field duties.

To assistants W. B. Williams, W. L. Miller, C. C. Smith, J. B. F. Davidge, D. J. Johns, J. M. Mercer; sub-assistants H. H. Burnett, O. W. Follin, J. H. Bradley, J. Laffont, Geo. R. Ferguson, W. A. Coburn, R. E. K. Whiting, L. M. Davidson, the company are, in a great measure, indebted for the results contained in the engineering part of this report.

REVENUE AND INCOME.

EVEN a cursory glance at the results of the survey of the Isthmus of Tehuantepec, will satisfy the most skeptical that the project of constructing a railroad or transit route to connect the two oceans, is not only eminently feasible, but practicable, at an outlay much smaller than the magnitude of the enterprise might suggest. This point being placed beyond doubt or conjecture, the question naturally follows, What would be the income from the Tehuantepec Railroad, and from what sources would that income be derived? This is a most important inquiry: for unless there was a probability of its paying a dividend commensurate with the cost of construction, repairs, and keeping it in travelling order, no capitalist would be disposed to invest his means in the enterprise. That such a probability exists, nay, that the income to be derived from the undertaking would certainly be such as to amply warrant the necessary subscription of stock (separate and apart from considerations of a national and patriotic character), there is hardly room for a doubt. The sources from whence this income would be gathered are twofold, viz., the *through* and the *way* traffic; which latter, though apparently insignificant, would be found more important than might be imagined.

If we look at the map of the American continent, it will be seen that the Isthmus of Tehuantepec is the most favorable point at which an inter-oceanic communication can be established, whether we consider it in reference to the United States alone, or to the American, European, and Asiatic countries. From Europe or the United States to the Pacific it is the *shortest* route of any, either now in operation, or that is at present contemplated. This is clearly exhibited by the following table, showing the respective distances from England, New York, and New Orleans, to the port of San Francisco, in California, by the routes of Panama, Nicaragua, and *Tehuantepec*, compared with the voyages from the same places round Cape Horn, and showing the distances each would respectively save by traversing the American Isthmus.

Voyage to San Francisco, in California.	Round Cape Horn.	*Via* Panama.	*Via* Nicaragua.	*Via* Tehuantepec.
	Nau. Miles.	Nau. Miles.	Nau. Miles.	Nau. Miles.
From England (departure from the Lizard)	13,624	7502	7041	6671
From New York	14,194	4992	4531	3804
From New Orleans	14,314	4505	3767	2704
		Distance saved *via* Panama.	Distance saved *via* Nicaragua.	Distance saved *via* Tehuantepec.
		Nau. Miles.	Nau. Miles.	Nau. Miles.
Saved by England		6122	6583	6953
" by New York		9202	9663	10,390
" by New Orleans		9809	10,547	11,610

These figures cannot be disputed: they are, indeed, of that class which are not "figures of speech." It is therefore plain that the superiority of Tehuantepec over all other routes is immeasurably great; and (considering the identity of conditions and the limited distance between Panama and Nicaragua) we may, in a discussion of relative advantages, regard them as one and the same point. The geographical position of the Tehuantepec Isthmus would at once secure to it the whole of the vast trade and emigration which have sprung up between the Atlantic portion of the American Republic and the new State of California on the Pacific—a trade which, when we consider the short time that has elapsed since our acquisition of that territory, and the still shorter time that has intervened since the discovery of the gold mines within its bosom, is unequalled in the history of commercial intercourse. This trade and emigration will increase from year to year, as long as the gold deposits are unexhausted. The Hon. *George M. Dallas*, in a recent communication, says:

"I cannot resist the impression that this junction of the two oceans of the Isthmus of Tehuantepec would Americanize this vast and augmenting portion of the commerce of the world. It would give to the people of the United States the overwhelming advantage of an abridgment, by fully one-half, of geographical distances. Against the merchants of Europe it would give ours two voyages to one. There is scarcely a region in the limitless South Sea, with which a trade would be lucrative, that could not be reached by them in half the time that would be consumed by English, French, Spanish, Dutch, or Swedish navigators. 'If,' says Mr. Scarlett, 'this scheme were realized, it has been calculated that the navigation from Philadelphia to Nootka Sound and the mouth of the Columbia River, which by Cape Horn is now five thousand leagues, would be reduced to three thousand only.' In fact, the reduction would be greater. But, at this rate, what would the reduction necessarily be as regards the navigation, in that direction, from New Orleans, Mobile, St. Augustine, Savannah, and our entire southern sea-board? The interchanges of commodities between our great and teeming valley of the West, and the rich and rising region of the Pacific, would be accomplished almost at the mouth of the Mississippi."

The following table exhibits (as nearly as can be ascertained from the most authentic data) the number of vessels and passengers, tons of freight, value of gold, and average weight of mail between California and the Atlantic States for four years, ending Dec. 24, 1851.

Route.	No. of Vessels.	No. of Passengers.	Tons of Freight.	Gold.	Average weight of Mail per steamer.
Panama	1183	227,001	46,584	$138,620,400	(17,000 lbs.hvst.) 9000
Nicaragua	71	14,521	425		
Overland		171,420			
Total	1254	412,942	47,009	$138,620,400	

To this number of passengers may be added 11,021 who have gone by sea around Cape Horn, making a total of 423,963 persons—of whom only 8100 belong to the year 1848. In order, however, to arrive at a yearly average, we may safely leave out that year, and divide the total number of passengers by 3 (representing respectively 1849, '50, and '51), which gives 141,320 as the lowest annual estimate of emigration between the Atlantic States and California. The receipts arising from this source alone would amount to a large sum, and justify the commencement of the Tehuantepec road at the earliest day. Nor is it unreasonable to conclude that even the existing trade and emigration would seek a route so advantageous in point of time and distance as this is proven to be. But there is a reason more cogent than all this, which will go far to secure to the Tehuantepec Isthmus the California travel. We allude to *climate*. In forming an estimate of this, personal *experience* is, beyond question, the best criterion. During a residence of eight months, exposed to every danger and privation, camping night after night in the open air, not a solitary case of malignant fever or dysentery occurred among the (more than fifty) members of the surveying expedition, who returned in health at the close of their labors, delighted with the salubrity of the atmosphere, the purity of the water, and the magnificence of the scenery of the Isthmus. In judging of climate, however, *medical* men are perhaps most competent to give an opinion; and the intelligent reader is referred to the report of Dr. Kovaleski, appended to the article on "Climate," for an exposition of the sanitary condition of Tehuantepec.*

Having now shown the great advantages of the Tehuantepec route in point of time, distance, and climate, the next consideration is the harbors on its coast, and their facilities for the reception, shelter, and safety of ships; for without these requisites the projected communication would be an idle dream. Fortunately, the results of the survey show this is not the case; and the relative merits of the points selected are so clearly set forth in the reports of Mr. Trastour on Ventosa, and of Mr. Temple on the Coatzacoalcos, that a repetition of their numerous advantages here would be superfluous. In connection, however, with the gratifying results obtained by the Hydrographic Engineers, the *practicability* of the Isthmus ports has been fully demonstrated, as will be seen by the letter of Captain Mott, of the steamer "Gold Hunter," and of Captain Foster, of the "Alabama," which will be found in another part of this work. Without

---

* See "CLIMATE," page 173.

drawing any invidious distinctions, little is therefore hazarded in the assertion that both Ventosa and the Coatzacoalcos are superior in *all* respects to the ports of Panama and Nicaragua—a superiority which will be greatly enhanced on the completion of the projected improvements—especially when we consider the loss of time, and damages to cargo unavoidably resulting from distant lighterage in Panama, and the terrific violence of the *papagayos* along the Nicaraguan coast.*

One of the readiest sources of revenue to the Tehuantepec Railroad, would be the products of the immense whaling fleet in the Pacific. In a communication to the Hon. J. A. Rockwell, made during the second session of the 30th Congress, this subject is so thoroughly discussed by *Lieut. Maury* that we quote him at some length. It is proper to state, however, that this estimate of returns had reference only to the income of the Panama project. As its application was admitted with regard to that route, it is presumed that no one will question its extension to Tehuantepec, where, from all that has been shown, the argument applies with a force which is precisely equivalent to the superiority of its advantages over Panama. Lieut. Maury says:

"According to the *Whaleman's Shipping List*, of Jan. 9, 1849, published at New Bedford, there were at that time out upon the high seas a whaling fleet of 613 vessels, carrying, in round numbers, 200,000 tons. We subjoin a comparative statement, drawn from the same authority, as to the quantity of bone and oil (sperm and right) imported for the last nine years:

---

* In the recent work of Mr. Squier on *Nicaragua*, we find the following:—"There is one grand objection to this port (San Juan del Sur), as *also to all others* which are found on the coast of the Pacific parallel to Lake Nicaragua, viz., the character of the prevailing winds. These are called *papagayos*, literally *parrots*, probably from the crooked bill of that bird, which illustrates their revolving direction. They render approach to this portion of the coast *extremely difficult.* They prevail from Punta Desolada on the north, to Cape Velas on the south, a distance of not far from two hundred miles, and are supposed to be caused by the northeast trades, which, as I have said, sweep entirely across the continent and Lake Nicaragua, and encounter other atmospheric currents on the Pacific. These trades are strongly felt, blowing off the shore for a distance of fifteen or twenty miles, beyond which the conflicting or revolving winds, or papagayos, commence."—*Vide Sir Edward Belcher's Voyage round the World*, vol. i., p. 185.

REVENUE AND INCOME.

	Bbls. Sperm.	Bbls. Whale.	Lbs. Bone.
Imports for 1848	107,976	208,856	2,008,000
" " 1847	120,755	313,150	2,341,680
" " 1846	95,217	207,493	2,276,939
" " 1845	157,917	272,730	3,167,142
" " 1844	139,594	262,047	2,532,445
" " 1843	166,985	206,727	2,000,000
" " 1842	165,637	161,041	1,600,000
" " 1841	159,204	297,348	2,000,000
" " 1840	157,791	207,908	2,000,000
	1,271,171	2,047,300	20,926,206
Average for nine years	141,242	235,456	2,324,578

The present value of sperm oil is $1.40 per gallon, but usually about $1.00, equal to $32.00 per barrel. The value of whale oil $10.54 per barrel; and of bone 33 cents per pound—equal to $4,519,744 for the average of sperm, $2,472,288 for whale, and $367,110 for bone: Total, $7,356,142, annually fished up out of the sea. This is a sum far greater than that which is annually gathered for commerce out of all our magnificent forests.

We are not able to state the precise number of vessels employed in the Pacific, or how much of this seven millions and a third should be credited to that ocean, though in 1846 there were 292 vessels fishing on the northwest coast alone; and they took, while there, 253,000 barrels of oil. We may safely assume that two-thirds of the whole number of vessels engaged are employed in the Pacific; and that three-fourths of the oil taken come thence, for the vessels of the Pacific are larger than those in the Atlantic fishery.

This would give for the Pacific, in round numbers, 400 vessels, yielding annually five millions and a half of money.

The cost of outfit and vessels for this fleet is about $28,000 per vessel; the average length of a voyage (mean of right and sperm whales) is three years; of which one-third is lost in going and returning from the whaling grounds, lying in port to re-cooper, refresh, &c., leaving but two years of actual fishing, or eight months in twelve.

The rate of insurance upon vessels and outfits is three per cent. per annum, and the legal interest upon money invested in ships and outfits, which make no return until the end of the voyage, is six per cent. The loss by leakage is five per cent. during the voyage.

If this oil, then, instead of remaining on board the vessel from one to two years (for that which is taken the first year remains on board two years, and that which is taken the second, one year), as dead capital, could be sent home across the Isthmus at reasonable tolls, the gains would be great, for there would be a saving of both time and substance; the leakage would amount to but one per cent. instead of five; half the time, at least, that is now employed in consequence of having to desert the whales to cooper the oil, refit, and refresh, would be saved; the whaling year might be made to consist of ten instead of eight months, with, of course, a proportional increase of profits on the original outlay for additional two months of fishing; the vessels employed in the business, instead of being large ships, capable of holding 2800 barrels—the proceeds of three years—would be small ships, capable of holding only one year's gathering; and the cost of smaller vessels, say one-third the size of those now employed, instead of running up to $28,000 each for vessel and outfit, would, by a liberal estimate, be brought down within half that sum.

Estimating the charge per ton for storage, freight, and handling, at the enormous rate of $20.00, or $2.00 per barrel across the Isthmus (this is 20 cents per ton per mile over railroad), and the freight thence to the United States to be $1.00 per barrel, or $10.00 per ton, the following comparative statement is obtained, in illustration of the importance to this interest alone of such a communication:

Cost, Outfits, and Expenses of Vessels on a Three Years' Whaling Voyage in the Pacific Ocean.

Cost of 400 vessels of 2800 barrels, at $28,000	$11,200,000
Six per cent. interest on same for one year	672,000
Three per cent. insurance on same for one year	336,000
Ten per cent. wear and tear on cost and outfits	1,120,000
Two year's interest on $1,833,333, being one-third of the value of oil taken during three years, of which one-third is kept on board ship, dead capital for two years	220,000
One year's interest on oil taken second year	110,000
Leakage, being four per cent. on $5,500,000	220,000
Annual average disbursement per ship, $2000	800,000
Original outlay and expenses of one year's whaling in Pacific	$14,678,000

Credits and Receipts.

Value of vessels and outfits after one year's wear and tear	$10,080,000	
Value of cargoes returned	5,500,000	15,580,000
Gross profits		$902,000

Per contra: Supposing a communication across the Isthmus, and the whaling business to be revolutionized by the substitution of vessels of one-third the present size, and half the cost, and by sending the oil home once a year:

Cost of 400 vessels of 933 tons, at $14,000	$5,600,000
Six per cent. interest on same for one year	336,000
Three per cent. insurance on same for one year	168,000
Ten per cent. wear and tear on same for one year	560,000
Annual disbursement per ship, $1000	400,000
Loss by leakage, one per cent. on $6,875,000	68,750
Freight, &c., railroad, of 48,240 tons, at $20.00 per ton	970,800
Freight thence home, at $10.00 per ton	485,400
Original outlay and expenses of whaling one year, and sending proceeds home by railroad	$8,588,950

Credits and Receipts.

Value of vessels and outfits, deducting one year's wear and tear	$5,040,000	
Value of bone and oil collected by fishing ten months instead of eight months	6,875,000	11,915,000
Gross profits via railroad		$3,326,050
Gross profits around Cape Horn		902,000
Margin in favor of the railroad, on account of the whaling business		$2,424,050

Two millions and a half is a large margin; but there is room for a larger margin. Whether the national wealth would be increased to the full extent of it or not, it is evident from the exhibit that the communication, in reference to this one interest alone, is of sufficient national importance and magnitude to command the most attentive consideration. The prospect of gain is, to say the least, inviting."

It is unnecessary to pursue the source of revenue derivable from the Pacific whale fishery any further. Its existence is indisputable, and it only remains to construct the railroad for the certain security of a greater portion of this ~~work~~ *business*

The opportunities for whalers to refit and replenish at Ventosa are too apparent to require comment.

The next point of income would be the transportation of Western produce and domestic fabrics to the shores of the Pacific. According to the most reliable information we have concerning California, that new State, in consequence, principally, of the absence of rain in the summer months, never can be, to any extent, an agricultural region. Enough of garden vegetables, and perhaps of esculents, may be produced in the valleys for the use of the population, although this even is to be doubted, but for cereal food of all kinds it must unquestionably depend upon the Atlantic States. Doubtless, large quantities could be raised in Oregon, but agriculture in that territory will not, in all probability, become a leading occupation as long as the gold of California offers such prospects as it does for the speedy accumulation of wealth. As it is, a great many farmers in Oregon have forsaken the plough and the sickle, in the hope of amassing money more speedily in the mines of California than by tilling their fields at home.

Within the past two years an enormous sum of money has been expended in the purchase of flour, produced from wheat grown in Chili and other South American Republics, and a proportionate sum paid in duty to the United States government. This duty, combined with the saving that could be effected in sending flour from the Atlantic States, *via* the Isthmus of Tehuantepec, would be virtually a prohibitory tariff against the admission of flour from those countries; and while the demand would stimulate agriculture in the United States, the transportation across the Isthmus of what would be required for consumption in California, would add largely to the receipts of the railroad. Again, so long as California preserves her identity as a *mining* State, and her people their present character, she cannot, in the nature of things, become for many years a *manufacturing* region. It is plain, therefore, that her dependence in this respect must be upon her Atlantic sisters, and the measure of the demand will be equivalent to the golden inducements which she offers for rapid and speedy settlement.

Some idea of the dependence placed by the people of California on the crops of South America may be gleaned from the following extract from the *Alta California* of Dec. 15, 1851:

"It is now *twenty-eight days* since we have had an arrival from the American Atlantic ports. This causes more firmness in many articles. The arrivals of flour have also been very small, including a certain number of *pounds* (we forget how many), as reported in one of the papers from Oregon.

The attention of wheat-growers in Chili has been much interfered with by recent disturbances there, and should they continue to this month, which is the period of saving their grain, the results will be unfavorable as to *expected supplies*. The news from Valparaiso has had sufficient effect to cause parties who offered to sell on Saturday, to put their prices up considerably."

These facts, in combination with those expressed in the recent report of the Secretary of the Treasury (showing a balance of trade against us for the year ending June last of $38,000,000), clearly indicate the necessity on the part of the United States government for the adoption of some measures which shall end to create other markets for export than those we now have. Already we see the anomalous picture of two sections of our country suffering from this cause—the one from the want of *demand*, and the other from the want of *supply*. The remedy of the evil consists simply in the *security* of *some* route that shall guarantee cheap and rapid transit. It is unnecessary, after all that has been advanced, to designate which is *shortest, healthiest*, and *best*.

Another consideration, of perhaps more importance than any of the preceding, is the fact that the construction of the Tehuantepec Railroad, in view of what has been stated, will create a revolution in the carrying and passenger trade between the Asiatic and the European worlds. This will be hastened by forming a line of steamships to connect San Francisco with Macao or some other port in China. During the last session of Congress a project of this kind was favorably reported upon by the Committee on Naval Affairs, to whom it was referred. On this subject the Committee say:

"The acquisition of California presents facilities for trade and intercourse with China which ought not to be neglected. It is believed that steamers can regularly make the voyage from the Bay of San Francisco to China in twenty days; and by the *circuitous route over the Isthmus now necessarily used*,* communication is maintained between the western coast and our Atlantic cities in little more than thirty days. Thus the establishment of a line of steamers on the Pacific would place New York within less than sixty days of Macao. The trade with China in sailing vessels, which go around the Cape, now labors under a great disadvantage in the length of time required for the voyage. It may be assumed that an average of ten months is required to make the return; and the voyage from Europe to China and back, may be considered as occupying an average of full twelve months. With the facilities now existing, and with the addition of the Pacific line proposed by the memorialists, the communication between Liverpool and China would be reduced to sixty days, and the return of an adventure from London to China might be received by the way of the United States in less than five months, less than half the time now required.

"The commerce of India has always enriched the nation enjoying it. The exports of China have so much value in proportion to their bulk, that they can well afford to bear the cost of steam transportation. With all the advantages which will be possessed by a line of six steamers of enormous capacity for freight, wearing the flag of the United States, commanded by officers of the Navy, making their trips with regularity, and much more speedily than on other routes, it is certain that the rich stream of Eastern commerce would flow

---

* The Committee refer to Panama.

into the United States; that new markets would be opened among the dense population of the East for our varied productions; and that a great increase of public revenue would result from increased importations; and if goods imported be not entered, but warehoused, vast advantage would follow to our commercial and shipping interests. Shippers of goods to be warehoused and sent to a more favorable market, would necessarily draw on their consignees, and the additional great commercial advantage of exchange would thus be secured to our merchants.

"The competitors for the China trade are the British and American merchants. The commerce of the United States with China has been steadily increasing, and it can scarcely be doubted that the contemplated facility of communication by steam will give to our enterprising countrymen advantages which cannot be countervailed by those of any European nation.

"*One of the greatest and most important effects of the concentration of this commerce at some point in the Bay of San Francisco (where must necessarily be located the depot on the Pacific), and the extension of our intercourse with the Asiatic nations, would be to hasten the adoption of some practicable plan for connecting the two oceans by a railroad across the continent; thus binding together two widely separated members of our confederacy, not only by the moral influence of the same constitution and laws, but by another link in that vast system of improvement by which the common welfare is to be so greatly promoted, and by which alone the remote State of California and the coterminous possessions of the United States can be brought into those easy and intimate relations, and that constant intercourse which ought to subsist between all parts of the same government.*"

This picture is far from highly colored. All the advantages which are foreshadowed in the Report of the Committee would assuredly flow, not from the establishment of a line of steamships alone, but principally from the opening of a railroad to connect the Atlantic with the Pacific oceans. Such a communication would of itself effect the revolution we speak of; for whether a line of steamships be built or not, the whole of the commerce between England and France with China, and between the United States and China, should in the nature of things pass over this route in preference to any other. Hitherto England has had the advantage over us in the Pacific and Indian trades. Lieut. Maury, in his letter to the Hon. Mr. Rockwell, says:

"Owing to the course of winds, the direction of currents, and other physical circumstances, British merchants are ten days' sail and upwards nearer than we are to all the markets of the world, except those of the Caribbean Sea and Gulf of Mexico. They are next door to all the markets of Europe; to Brazil, to Cape Horn, the Cape of Good Hope; and, consequently, to all the ports beyond them, they are practically some ten or fifteen days' sail nearer than we are. A vessel from the United States bound to the Southern Hemisphere first sails nearly an east course until she arrives in the vicinity of the Azores and Canary Islands; she then puts her head south for the first time. Now, while the American vessel is sailing this route, the English vessel that sailed on the same day for the same market has passed those islands and is far on her way. For the reason that the Cape de Verde Islands are some ten or fifteen days nearer to England than to America, England is that much nearer to the Southern Hemisphere; for vessels generally, whether from the United States or from England, are in the habit of passing by these islands on their way thither.

"Therefore, the Englishman meets the American in all the markets of the world, except those of the Gulf and Caribbean Sea, with the advantage of ten days and upwards.

"Notwithstanding this disadvantage, the United States, in their commercial race with England, have for the last fifty years been gradually gaining. They have been coming up all the time, and at last the contest has become so close that England is hardly a throat-latch ahead. Cut through this Isthmus, 'Uncle Sam' will then turn the corner, and England will be distanced. Instead, then, of meeting us in India, China, and even on our own Pacific coast, with the advantage of some ten days' sail or more, the scales will be turned, and we shall have the advantage of some twenty or thirty days, thus making a difference in our favor of thirty or forty days under canvas."

But the proof does not rest on Lieut. Maury alone. The following extract from (an eminent English engineer of the present day) Allan Macdonnell's project of a railroad from Lake Superior to the Pacific, will be read with interest:

"Without directing attention to the trade carried on throughout the Pacific, by France, by Holland, and other nations of the European continents, as also by the United States, let us look only to England.

IMPORTS *into Great Britain from the following Ports:*

From Bengal, Madras, and Bombay, as taken from *Hunt's Merchants' Magazine* for March, 1843, including all to continental Europe, and North and South America, annually	£12,000,000
Less for the amount to France and America	2,489,340
	£9,510,660
From Sumatra and Java	215,216
The Philippine Islands	346,692
New South Wales and Van Dieman's Land	1,118,088
Mauritius	806,593
Chili (estimated)	1,500,000
Peru "	1,000,000
	£14,497,249
From China, total amount of various productions	5,000,000
	£19,497,249

"To which must be added the *exports* from Great Britain which are sent in exchange for the above productions. The imports and exports of the Dutch East Indies and the French East Indies should also be considered, as also the exports and imports of the United States."

The same writer, while arguing the necessity of overcoming by *art* the *natural* advantages which are within the reach of the United States for constructing such a communication as is here proposed, and while urging the feasibility of building a railroad through the British American Possessions to the Pacific, says in reference to the Isthmus route:

"Through her geographical position the United States can more readily avail herself of the benefits to be derived from this course than any other nation. Her fleets would steam in one unbroken line through the Gulf of Mexico; her naval power would overawe our settlements upon the northwest coasts; and her influence extend itself throughout all our Indian possessions. The Marquesas Islands, in case the project be carried into effect, lying directly in the route of the navigation to India, would at a step advance into one of the most important maritime ports in the world, whilst the Society Islands, also in the possession of France, would enhance immensely in their value; more than all, returning back, the vessels of all Europe would ere long procure their tropical productions from the newly awakened islands in the Pacific Ocean: in just the degree that their value would increase, the West India possessions would depreciate. * * * The power and advantages of Saint Helena, Mauritius, Capetown, and the Falkland Islands, commanding the passage round Cape Horn, would be transferred to New Orleans and other cities of the United States bordering upon the Gulf of Mexico."

In the construction of the Tehuantepec railroad these conclusions are irresistible. "National predilection cannot prevent freights from taking the course which is speediest and cheapest. The whole of the East India carrying trade must therefore speedily fall into our hands." The proof will be found by comparing the routes from England to China, via Panama, Suez, and Tehuantepec.

Liverpool to Canton via Panama .... 15,624 miles = 50 days.
    "   "   via Suez*............   = 54 "
    "   "   via Tehuantepec...... 13,425   " = 40 "

---

* Length of passage from Southampton to the undermentioned ports, including all stoppages:

To Gibraltar.........	7 days.		To Ceylon	42 days.
To Malta	11 "		To Madras........	45 "
To Alexandria.......	16 "		To Calcutta	48 "
To Constantinople....	16 "		To Hong Kong	54 "
To Bombay	35 "			

In our estimate of the time upon these routes, the speed of ocean steamers has been calculated at the rate of thirteen miles an hour. The average has been deduced from passages of the Atlantic steamers to New York, from September 21, 1850, to January 1, 1851.

The time upon railroads has been computed at twenty miles per hour—a rate assumed from the general operations of railroads in the United States. No deductions have been made for stoppages. We have thought the difference of twelve days sufficient to cover all stoppages and loss of time as to the Suez route, whilst the time lost by stoppage upon the Panama and Tehuantepec routes would be about equal; these routes across the Pacific being identical from a point off Tehuantepec.

The ocean distances on the route from Liverpool via Panama has been taken from the report of the Hon. Mr. Rockwell, in his able report to Congress, from which we have before quoted.

A writer in *De Bow's Review* thus disposes of the question of distance, as compared with Tehuantepec:

"The advantage offered by the Tehuantepec route, to compensate for its increased length, is the saving of sea distances from each direction to its termini on the Gulf and Pacific, being 1200 miles north of Panama. This saving in sea distance is estimated at 1700 miles, in making the trip from New Orleans to San Francisco; the distances being stated at 5000 miles from New Orleans to San Francisco, by way of Panama, and as being only 3300 by way of Tehuantepec; and being from New York to San Francisco, by way of Panama, 5858 miles, and by way of Tehuantepec only 4744 miles—being a saving, by Tehuantepec, of 1100 miles. This immense difference in the sea distances, other things being equal, would seem to be conclusive in favor of the Tehuantepec route."

It is unnecessary to add any thing to this. The position is defined, and the immense saving in point of time and distance by way of Tehuantepec cannot be gainsaid. The same writer, after alluding to the project of constructing a railroad across the peninsula of Florida, says:

"It is a magnificent idea to dwell upon, that, by the construction of 270 miles of railroad, New York and San Francisco are brought within 4300 miles of each other, and New Orleans within 3000 miles; thus cutting off nearly 10,000 miles of the voyage round Cape Horn. And it will not be deemed an extravagant supposition, that, when constructed, 20 days will suffice to reach San Francisco from New York, and 16 days from New Orleans."

Since this was written telegraph lines have been established between the northern cities and New Orleans, as far north, indeed, as Montreal. It follows, therefore, that by the way of Tehuantepec, San Francisco, and New York, Montreal and St. Louis will be brought within sixteen days of each other. This certainly is progressing with the spirit of the age. It is unnecessary to allude to the importance which this rapid communication would exercise on the commerce of the country, or on the revenues of the company. They can be perceived at a glance, and need not be pointed out. But what can be said of the tremendous revolution that is destined to take place in the course of commerce between Europe and the East, when the best connection between the two oceans is established? "Doubling the stormy cape" will then be unknown, and "voyages" *around* the world will be changed to "trips" *across*. The American continent will then become the *entrepôt* for the commerce of the universe, and the United States the "mistress of the seas."

The Tehuantepec route is, of all the routes proposed from the Atlantic to the Pacific Ocean, the true American route. It is the route which is entirely commanded by our possessions on the Gulf of Mexico, and not domineered over by any British possession whatever. In case of a war with Great Britain, our vessels, bound to Chagres, would be obliged to sail almost within gun-shot of the British forts at Jamaica, while any number of men and provisions could at any moment be sent down from New Orleans to the mouth of the Coatzacoalcos. The Mississippi River being the great artery of the West, and the Mississippi Valley destined to be the great reservoir of the population, enterprise, and nationality of the United States, we are at all times better prepared to defend, occupy, and *keep* the Isthmus of Tehuantepec than any other position on this side of our continent south of New Orleans.

In connection with the establishment of a steam marine in the Pacific, to which reference has already been made, it may be well to mention, incidentally, another important source of revenue to the Tehuantepec railroad. To the present time no *coal* mines of importance have been opened or worked on any part of the Pacific coast contiguous to San Francisco, so as to be available for the supply of steamers. It therefore follows, as a matter of course, that until these rumored coal deposits are mined and proven adequate to the demand, supplies of this article must be drawn from the Atlantic side. But the question arises, How is it to be sent? The answer will be found by an examination of the facilities for shipping coal down the Mississippi to New Orleans, and thence by sea 960 miles to the Coatzacoalcos River—from whence it can be transported to the shores of the Pacific by railroad on the day of its arrival from the United States. At a glance this item of coal may appear insignificant. Suppose, however, that on the completion of the Tehuantepec railroad, there should be 50 steamers in the Pacific, which burn an average of 30 tons per diem. Now allowing these steamers to consume each 4000 tons in a year, this fleet would require, at the least calculation, 200,000 tons of coal, which may be shipped from Pittsburg to the Pacific, via the Mississippi and Tehuantepec, in less than three weeks.

Another source of revenue would be the tolls received from the United States government for the speedy transportation of supplies for the naval and military service in the Pacific and the China and India seas—for it is not to be supposed that the government would not avail itself of the saving which could be effected by transporting its supplies across the Isthmus of Tehuantepec, in preference to sending them around the southern capes—a voyage which often destroys provisions necessary for the use of the naval service, such as bread, flour, pork, beef, &c. This subject engaged the attention of the United States government during the war with Mexico. It will be recollected that when a treaty of peace was proposed with that republic, the security of a right of way across the Isthmus of Tehuantepec, for the purpose of forming a communication between the two oceans, was almost made a *sine qua non*. Indeed, so much impressed was the administration of Mr. Polk at that day, with the importance of securing this route to the United States, that Mr. Trist, who was sent to Mexico with the view of negotiating a treaty, was authorized by Mr. Buchanan, then Secretary of State, in the following words:

"Instead of $15,000,000 stipulated to be paid by the fifth article, for the extension of our boundary over New Mexico and Upper and Lower California, you may increase the amount to any sum, not exceeding $30,000,000, payable by instalments of $3,000,000 per annum, provided the right of passage and transit across *the Isthmus of Tehuantepec*, secured to the United States by the eighth article of the *projét*, shall form a part of the treaty."

This offer (sufficient to build *two such railroads as the Tehuantepec* company propose), it must be remembered, was made *before* the acquisition of California, or the discovery of its gold. How much greater is the value of the right of way *now*, when we consider the immense concession of lands embraced in the grant, and the magnificent empire which has so suddenly sprung into existence amid the wilds of the Pacific coast!

In the opening of the Tehuantepec route the United States government would realize the most incalculable advantages. Within a single week an army of 50,000 men might be landed on the shores of the Pacific, with all their munitions and appointments, without exposing them in the slightest degree to the incursions of a West Indian fleet. Our naval force in the Pacific and Indian seas would be permanent establishments there, drawing their supplies from the United States in one-tenth of the time now occupied for their transportation, while our immense whaling fleet, already referred to, would become the nursery of the noblest seamen in the universe. The world of the West would be born again; and the commerce, wealth, and power of our country increased, diffused, and strengthened in such a manner as to distance all competition and to make rivalry a preposterous idea.

Thus far no especial reference has been made to the *American* trade with foreign countries on the west coast of America. In the recent report of the Hon. Secretary of Treasury, we find the following statement, which, while it exhibits the extent and value of that trade, indirectly indicates the influence which California has already exercised over our commercial destinies:

American and Foreign Vessels which cleared from Ports of the United States during the Year ending June 30, 1851.

	American.	Tons.	Foreign.	Tons.
Dutch E. Indies	11	4,070	8	3,320
British do.	62	29,389	5	2,138
China	33	11,830	10	3,106
Asia generally	15	6,213		
Pacific Ocean*	76	24,430	3	349
Indian Ocean	26	6,780		
Sandwich Islands*	108	31,623	66	11,970
	331	114,335	92	20,883

American and Foreign Vessels which entered the United States from the same Places during the Year ending June 30, 1850.

	American.	Tons.	Foreign.	Tons.
Dutch E. Indies	8	3,689		
British do.	51	23,537		
China	41	21,969	23	7,445
Asia generally	3	945		
Pacific Ocean	90	30,502		
Indian Ocean	15	3,679		
Sandwich Islands	39	9,267	24	4,195
	247	93,588	47	11,640

This tabular statement exhibits the extent and value of our foreign commerce in the Pacific, and the urgent necessity for the establishment of *some* inter-oceanic communication, which (in combination with the advantages arising from superiority of ships and vessels) shall enable America to distance England forever in the world-wide race for dominion of the seas.

In the prospective ship canal through Nicaragua the attention of our merchants has necessarily been diverted from the Tehuantepec route, notwithstanding the saving in distance to be accomplished by it. But, unfortunately, the hopes which were foreshadowed in the projected union of the two oceans are fastly waning; and the feasibility of a scheme so universally beneficent, and so inviting as Nicaragua promised to be, is becoming, on a closer inspection, a widely mooted question. In the excellent publication of Mr. Squier, late Chargé to the Republics of Central America, we find the following statement:

---

* Principally whale ships.

"The proposed canal must then be of larger dimensions than that of Scotland or Holland. Admitting, for the sake of instituting comparisons, that a canal 30 feet deep, 50 feet wide at the bottom, and 150 at the top, would fully answer to these conditions, we have the following comparative results, in respect to the amount of excavation :

Caledonian Canal	183,902,400	cubic feet.
Holland do.	422,400,000	" "
Proposed do. on Baily's line	4,927,577,800	" "

That is to say, apart from any other portions of the proposed line, *the single section from Lake Nicaragua to the Pacific*, would require more than *ten* times the amount of excavation performed in constructing the Holland Canal, and *fifty* times that of the Caledonian Canal, which, from the nature of the ground overcome, locks, &c., affords the best standard of calculation. At the same ratio of expense, *this section alone* would cost $250,000,000!

"An open cut canal, therefore, from Lake Nicaragua to the Pacific, to be supplied with water from the lake, on *any line hitherto surveyed is impracticable*,— if on no other ground, certainly on that of cost. It has been proposed to avoid or obviate this objection by the construction of a tunnel, for a part of the distance, where the height of land is greatest. But any canal designed for the passage of large ships which requires the construction of a tunnel of any considerable length, is *prima facie* impracticable. In the particular instance before us, if the open cuttings were carried upon either side of the summit until they became 90 feet deep, yet there would still remain 5888 yards, or upwards of three miles of tunnelling, to be accomplished. But neither Mr. Baily nor the most daring of those who have made this suggestion, have ventured to propose a tunnel of this length. They have suggested a tunnel commencing at an elevation of 122 feet above the lake, which would reduce its length to a trifle over a mile, but increase the vertical lockage from 128 to 372 feet. The fatal objection to this plan, however, is a lack of water to supply the upper levels, and to lock down vessels both to the lake and the ocean. Mr. Baily suggests the collection of the waters of the little streams and rivulets, by rising on this narrow isthmus, and the '*sinking of Artesian wells*,' to furnish the requisite supply! I have no hesitation in saying, after passing over these heights, that the whole amount of water which it would be possible to collect from these sources, would not supply the simple *leakage*, to say nothing of the *evaporation* of a canal of the kind required.

"These *few* stubborn facts, unless some more favorable line shall be discovered, must settle the question so far as regards a canal across the narrow isthmus intervening directly between Lake Nicaragua and the ocean. For although here appears to be the natural and most obvious route for the work, yet its practicability must be tested by the same standards which regulate the construction of all works of improvement and public utility."

In view of these obvious difficulties, to which might be added the lesser ones of distance, inefficiency of ports, and unhealthiness of climate, it seems a useless occupation of time to consider the comparison of Nicaragua with Tehuantepec longer. Existing circumstances warrant the belief that even the holders of the canal grant are doubtful of the practicability of their project; and the increase of clipper ships within the last year, both in England and the United States, conclusively shows that confidence in the ultimate construction of the canal is being withdrawn. But without arrogantly asserting that the union of the two oceans is absolutely impossible (for who can use that term with certainty now?), it seems but reasonable to assert, that the Nicaragua Canal is wholly impracticable in the nineteenth century. But the stern demands of commerce are only more clearly heard above the expiring throes of failing projects; and man by the whiles of *art*, is diligently seeking to overcome the barriers of *nature*. If it be admitted that the Tehuantepec isthmus is the most available point—in respect of time, distance, climate, cheapness, and practicability, at which an inter-oceanic communication can be made—it follows necessarily that the railroad to be constructed must secure a large proportion of the commerce of the world.

The additional gold discoveries in California, particularly in Mariposa county, show that the precious metal exists in that new State not only in "dust," as it is termed, in the valleys; not only intermingled in large quantities with the native quartz rock, but likewise in soft calcareous slate, to such an extent as to produce a village, yea, a town in its vicinity, as it were in a single day! These discoveries will exercise a potent influence in increasing the volume of emigration to that wonderful region. California is daily taking a deeper root in the public mind: already the voice of her people is heard in the Capitol, startling even the most visionary with the boldness, truth, and magnificence of her inevitable destiny. Every day brings us intelligence of the strides of the young giant; and every steamship that leaves us is filled to its utmost capacity with energetic and adventurous emigrants, each of whom leaves behind him a family or relations and friends with whom he will correspond respecting the prospects of his new home in the West. If such correspondence should be of a character to induce others to emigrate, as no doubt it will be, it is not difficult to imagine the increase of travel from year to year. Indeed, there seems but little doubt that the population of California will soon number half a million of souls, and that an empire will eventually be founded on the shores of the Pacific, which, in wealth, resources, and power, will rival even New York itself. The toilsome journey of a *month*, which now serves the emigrant and the returning adventurer in the youth of his Western home, will then no longer answer the conditions of maturer years; and with a characteristic spirit, he will seek a transit which shall keep pace with the rapid flow of his thoughts. Can it be doubted what route he will take?

We have thus briefly touched on the probable *through* revenue and income of the Tehuantepec railroad, the sources of which may be recapitulated thus:

1. The California travel.
2. The return of oil and bone from the Pacific whaling fleet.
3. The transportation of breadstuffs and domestic fabrics to California and adjacent points.
4. The freight on naval and military supplies.
5. The consumption of coal by Pacific steamers.
6. The American and foreign trade with the East Indies and China.

It is unnecessary to go into more minute details concerning this single source of revenue. Indeed, it would be impossible to make even an estimate susceptible of expression in the simple representative language of dollars and cents. All we can do is to state the premises as accurately and as briefly as possible, and leave the world to draw their own conclusions. The simple questions involved in the inquiry are: Is the route feasible? Is it shorter? Is it healthier? Have you safe and sufficient anchorage? These, we hope, are satisfactorily answered.

The case does not, however, rest here. No allusion has yet been made to the income derivable from the way or incidental trade of the projected railroad, which, as we have previously intimated, would be much greater than might be supposed.

In order to get at an approximate estimate of what this inland traffic would be, it is necessary to refer to the extent of territory embraced within the Mexican grant to the company; and secondly, to the indigenous products of the soil of the Isthmus and the neighboring States, and the demand for them at home and abroad. The grant of land of which mention is made is in *fee simple*, and embraces an extent of fifty-six Mexican leagues in length by twenty in width; that is, 1120 square leagues, each containing 4340 acres; thus making a total amount of nearly *five millions* of acres of tillable land, an area greater than that of the State of Massachusetts. This, with the right of making settlements within fifty leagues on either hand of the communication (also comprised in the grant of Don José de Garay), presents an opportunity for establishing one of the noblest colonies that ever existed.

Among the produce of the country, there are salt-pits extremely abundant, which might be turned to profitable account without any other outlay than the bare expenses of conveyance. California receives at present her supply from the United States by way of Cape Horn. Salt might be supplied to the countries in the neighborhood of the line of communication, such as Chiapas and Guatimala, as well as the Havana and New Orleans, where the price generally averages eight or ten dollars per ton.

The other *natural* products of the Isthmus, such as wax, honey, silk, india-rubber, cocoa, pepper, sarsaparilla, corn, rice, sugar, tobacco, cotton, indigo, hemp, vanilla, gums and resins, furs, tortoise-shell, coral and pearls, are abundant in the greatest degree. But among all these productions, the timber of its immense forests deserves particular mention. Its abundance is such, that the only limit which can be assigned to the supply it may yield, is the demand for centuries to come. From the fir, the oak, the cedar, and every description of building timber, to the dye and fine woods, their profusion is absolutely incredible. None of the countries which at present supply these species of woods could compete with the Isthmus, where they are found on the very banks of the river, which facilitate their carriage.

Lastly, the country itself can supply thousands of workmen at the moderate wages of from 37½ to 50 cents per day.

The consumption of dyestuffs, mahogany and other fine woods, such as the Isthmus can supply, amounts for London and Liverpool alone to upwards of sixty thousand tons ! the value of which, at the present market prices, exceeds $1,500,000, clear of all charges ; and when the demand for every other country is taken into account, it is but reasonable to put down under this head the sum of $2,500,000. In the port of Liverpool, during the year 1849, the imports of mahogany only, exceeded 29,012 tons. As the grant of land is made to the company in fee simple, these sources of income are of course the property of the company, and add to the value of the stock in a material degree. These resources have, however, lain dormant for ages, and would continue so if no communication between the Atlantic and Pacific oceans was made through the Tehuantepec isthmus. But no sooner would the projected railroad be constructed and in operation, than the busy hum of industry and commerce would drive the wild beasts of the forests into the distance, and a demand be created for the products of the soil, which have so long grown, and withered, and decayed, and grown again, as if in mockery of the boasted progress of man. It has been said that he who makes two blades of grass grow where but one grew before, is a public benefactor. What shall we say of those who will open to the commerce of the world a tract of land which abounds, in the greatest degree, with the commodities essential to this civilized age—not only to the wants, but to the luxuries of man—and which, indeed, possesses riches that the nations of the old world have hitherto pursued at a distance of eighteen or twenty thousand miles ?

Some idea of these products may be gleaned from the following table, showing the approximate value of what might be annually obtained by the existing population on the Isthmus even now :*

---

* It is proper to remark that the figures representing the values of most of the articles above are taken from official documents, obtained on the Isthmus during the survey. The value assigned to hides, india-rubber, valuable woods, fruits, tar, and wax, are estimated.

Indigo	$20,000	Ixtle (hemp)	$45,000
Fruits	40,000	Coffee	7,000
Hides and leather	50,000	Corn	100,000
India-rubber	350,000	Vanilla	10,000
Salt	200,000	Sarsaparilla	5,000
Cacao	75,000	Gums, resins, &c	5,000
Tobacco	50,000	Wax	5,000
Pepper	50,000	Tallow	14,000
Rice	6,000	Tar, pitch, and turpentine	10,000
Sugar	150,000	Lime	8,000
Valuable woods, dyes, &c	500,000		
			$1,700,000

The Tehuantepec Company may use the products of this field of wealth either directly, by exporting them to markets where there is a constant demand, or indirectly, by selling the land, and letting privileges to other parties. In either case the profits would go into the coffers of the company.

It will be readily perceived that there is no way of arriving at any thing like an accurate estimate of the returns that would be derived from this source. It will be seen, however, that great as the prospect is for a large income from the *through* or foreign traffic, the products of the company's territory would be immense. In this connection, it may not be inappropriate to mention incidentally, that no sooner would this railroad be opened and the Isthmus established as a point of great trade and commerce, than all the contiguous territory of the Mexican Republic extending as far as Vera Cruz, and even the capital itself, would be favorably affected by it, the results of which must be profitable to the company. In the decree of the Mexican government, granting the privilege to Don José de Garay, this point, as far as that republic is concerned, is alluded to. The decree says: " Feeling, besides, that in order to encourage the spirit of speculation, it is necessary to make concessions, by which alone enterprise has been fostered; and that by this enterprise in particular, the nation will obtain revenues on which it cannot reckon at present, derivable from foreign trade, and immediately reap the advantages which must result from commercial intercourse, *when its soil shall become the emporium of commerce, and consequently teem with wealth and abundance,* when its various products shall become articles of exportation, &c." This decree, issued in March, 1842, was signed by General

Santa Anna, who, it is well known by the people of the United States, is one of the shrewdest and most sagacious statesmen whom the Mexican Republic has ever produced. We have said that what would conduce to the interest of the owners of the grant would also conduce to that of Mexico herself, by connecting railroads, which, from the necessities of the case, and in order to supply the wants of commerce, would be constructed. The topography of the contiguous portions of the Mexican Republic exhibits such favorable features that at a comparatively small outlay, roads can be built which will bring into the lap of the Isthmus the mineral resources and dyes of Oaxaca, the indigo of Guatimala and Chiapas, the sugar and cotton of Vera Cruz, and the tobacco, coffee, and chocolate of Tobasco. But apart from this, the sources of income, derivable from the introduction of "such articles as are intended for consumption in the interior," together with "the one-fourth part of the net produce of the dues that are paid for the right of transit," would be to Mexico an abundant, sure, and never-failing support. Instead, then, of languishing as now, under the burden of her foreign debt, with blockaded ports and ruined trade, her treasury would be replenished, and her people stimulated to enterprises of the most magnificent character. The world would then behold two of the most powerful nations on its surface allied by a common interest, and bound hand in hand in the fellowship of republicanism, controlling, extending, and protecting the commerce of every land and sea. Bonds of union would thus be forged which no political contingency could destroy; and 'the star of empire, which, in its westward course, has so long lingered on the brow of the Cordillera, would rise again, under the developing power of free institutions, and pass to its culminating point in the Oriental world.'

We cannot, in a work like this (which is intended more as a manual of reference to the advantages that are placed at the disposal of the projectors of the Tehuantepec railroad, than an enumeration of their importance as far as present and prospective value is concerned), dilate on the profits which would, in a comparatively short time, accrue from the single source of *way* trade alone. Sufficient has been said to show beyond cavil or question, that the revenue arising from the incidental traffic would of itself justify the construction of the road.

Thus far we have considered only the circumstances of existing trade and travel, without attempting to draw from them the irresistible conclusions which they suggest. Let us look for a moment on the consequences to England's Pacific possessions, from the establishment of the communication of which we speak. Hitherto her people have been adverse to emigration, and the comparatively few who have reluctantly sought new homes, are of the middle class, as merchants and shopkeepers. But in her nervous efforts to render herself independent of America, her colonial policy has undergone a recent change. By reference to the British tables of emigration, it will be seen, that during the years 1848, 1849, and 1850, no less than 72,032 persons, chiefly farmers and agriculturists, have passed around the southern capes to the Australian colonies and New Zealand. Within a year, however, a new Ophir has sprung up in these Pacific possessions which bids fair to rival California; and thousands upon thousands are now daily seeking the new land of gold. A change has thus come over the emigrant's dream, and in lieu of calculating on what his prospects are to be in his colonial home, his eyes are turned towards the *West* as the *natural* path which leads him soonest to the scene of his future labors. He realizes (though perhaps for the first time in his life) that *time* and *money* are equivalent terms. A glance at the map shows him that a line drawn from England, through the narrowest portion of the Mexican territory, passes also through the Indian colonies; and he sees that the course of the emigrant ship is long, circuitous, and uncertain; but he embarks under the necessities of his case, wondering and sorry that no inter-oceanic communication exists. Can it be questioned for a moment, if he alone were consulted, in what path his footsteps would be bent?

The same arguments may be applied to the French, Dutch, and Portuguese settlements in the Pacific, setting time and distance aside, were it only to avoid the dangerous effects of the *monsoons* in the China and Indian seas.

Some of the advantages to our own government and that of Mexico have been referred to; but who can speak with accuracy of all the glorious consequences, or even enumerate the changes which the opening of the Tehuantepec route is destined to bring? Indeed, the mind becomes lost in the magnificent mazes of the labyrinth, and our speculations of futurity are but the shadows of what is to come.

But there may be still some skeptic to whose lips will rise the involuntary question, "Will it pay?" Let him ask the California emigrant how much he would save in time, distance, and money. Let him inquire the price of breadstuffs and fabrics on the coast of the Pacific, and figure up what has already been expended in their purchase. Let him consult the whaleman on the length of his voyage and the meagerness of his returns. Let him calculate the difference of insurance, interest, and outlay between *six months* and *forty days* on a voyage to the Indias. Let him look at the expenses of our naval fleet, and see how much it costs to send stores around the southern capes to the Pacific. Let him glance at the prices current of California, and compare the cost with the consumption of coal. Let him investigate the demand at home and abroad for valuable woods, tropical fruits and luxuries. Let him ask the Australian emigrant which route he prefers, the Cape of Good Hope or the Isthmus. Let him examine the map, and figure out the difference between going *around* and *across* the world. Let him consider well the influences of climate, and reconcile if he can, the discrepancies between the number who have sailed to and from California via Panama and Nicaragua, and those who have reached their destination. Perhaps his question then, will be satisfactorily answered.

PART II.

STATISTICS.

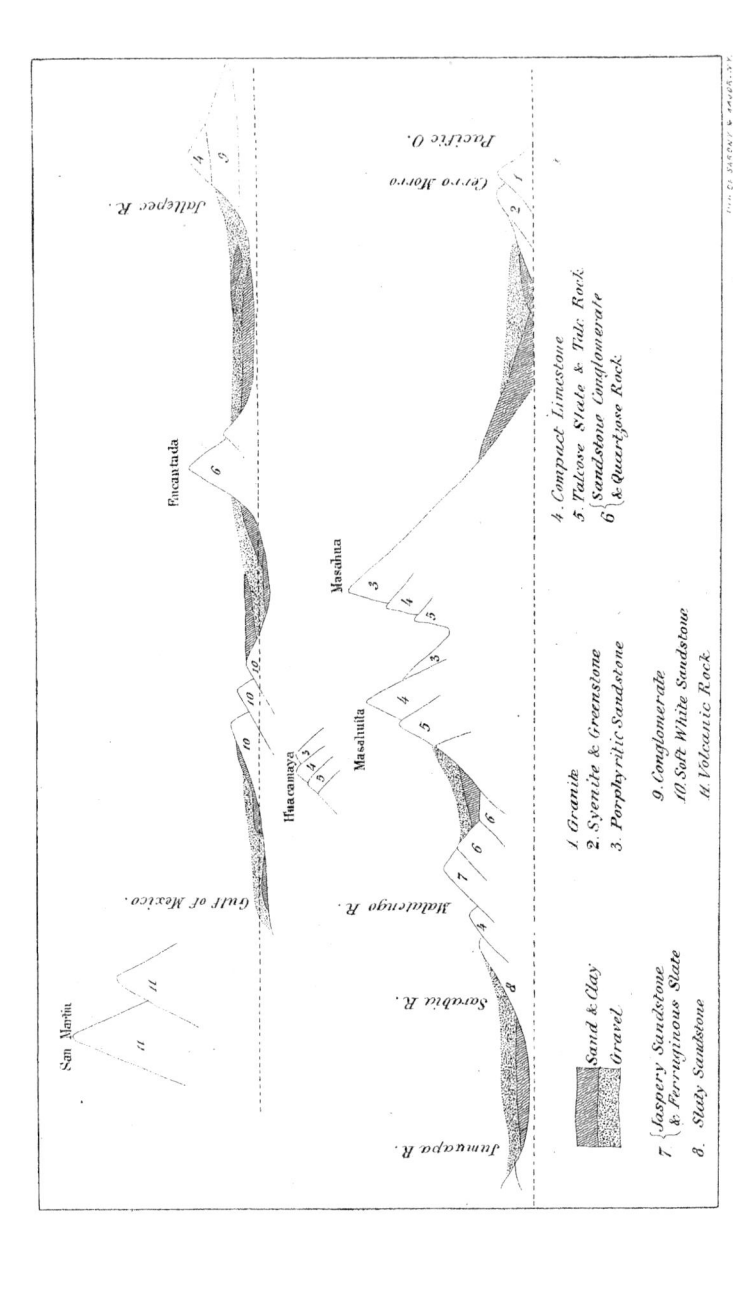

GEOLOGY AND MINERALOGY.

The geological structure of the Isthmus is less clearly marked than that of the adjoining more elevated districts of Mexico. A country having a horizontality of 135 miles from sea to sea, with an average elevation of not more than 600 feet, cannot present over its surface many exposed situations where the dip, strike, and nature of the rocky basis could be ascertained; much of the gentle slope of the northern plains being covered over with clay, sand, and gravel, and so densely wooded, that no appearance of the rock formation is discernible. The same may be said of the plains on the southern shore. On the middle more elevated regions the conformation is more evident; and what is deficient upon the sides of the hills, owing to the superficial deposits of gravel and sand, has been in great part exposed by the sections made naturally, on the large scale in the mountain passes.

The tertiary clays, gravels, and beds of detritus which cover up so much of the Isthmus along the line of survey, extend on the north side almost to the summit-level, and the base of the hills which lie east and west of it. These deposits being found pretty uniformly spread, even to the depth of thirty feet in some places, as at a point north of the summit-level, and between it and the river Almoloya, are evidences of the slow and tranquil elevation of this portion of the Isthmus above the sea, and of its comparatively quiescent condition since a very distant epoch.

Granite and granitiform rocks do not occupy much extent of surface upon the Isthmus, and perhaps were not the chief upheaving agents which elevated this district. Porphyritic, dioritic, and greenstone rocks appear in the majority of cases to accompany the most vertical of the stratified rocks, and to have been, by their intrusion and appearance upon the surface, the elevating rock. This crystalline rock (granite), however, does appear in a few places: it is first met with at the Pacific shore, where it constitutes the Cerro Morro, San Diego, Huilotepec, and extending north to the city of Tehuantepec, where it appears in the hills of Dani Guivedchi and Dani-lieza. These small hills, which are not above 500 feet above the plain, or 550 feet above the sea, are the eastern spur of a small granite range (the Cerro Verde), which passes in a westerly direction through Oaxaca towards the Rio Verde. In stretching west they become more elevated.

The scattered hills which lie along the shore between this range and the lagoons, such as Malamamlaif, and a few of lesser note, are the most depressed points of this chain. Granite forms some of the higher summits in the mountain districts north and northeast of Cerro Atravesado. It is also met with to a small extent in the low ground leading from the Portilla de Tarifa to La Venta de Chicapa, along the Arroyo del Tolistoco. This rock is not met with in place in any other part of the Isthmus; drift and pebbles of it are found in the channel of the Coatzacoalcos River, carried down from the Sierra by the mountain torrents, showing its existence in that range.

With one exception, all the islands of the upper lagoon, and the hills which lie between it and the lower lagoon, are of greenstone, sienitic greenstone, with other metamorphic rocks, such as porphyry and hypersthene. The greenstone there appears to have cut through the granitiform rocks and their contents, and the constituents of both seem to have become fused together.

The island of Mitiac-xocuan in the upper lagoon, the Cerro de Buena Vista, and the range of hills between the Espantaperros and the Niltepec rivers north of the lagoons, as well as the scattered hills east of this range, are of porphyry, with a basis of jasper and claystone. These metamorphic rocks, produced by the action of the greenstone protrusions, appear to underlie the whole of the Pacific plains north of a line drawn from Tehuantepec to Xocuapa, and extending to the Venta de Chicapa. The northern and southern slopes of the eastern Cerro Prieto, and the flanks of the Cerro de la Cienega are made of a silicious slate, or greywacke, as it has been termed in Mr. Moro's report. None of these altered rocks are on the line of survey. These hills stand prominently up out of the sandy plain in which the river and city of Tehuantepec lie. The character of the granite is more hornblendic than felspathic or micaceous, and in some positions it is a distinct sienitic rock. Along the shore, granite is not confined to the situation of a massive rock, but is found as an intruded mass, or as intersecting veins in greenstone. This may be seen in Natartiac and a few other islands in the upper lagoon. It may be that this appearance is due to the greenstone rock, which, cutting its way through a granitic or sienitic rock, ruptured off fragments, and carried them onward with the cooling mass, depositing them at a higher point as the intruding mass cooled. The axis of most of the hills near the Pacific and upon the islands lies in a direction east and west, with the gentle slopes in a southerly direction. With the exception of these granitiform rocks, the plains on the Pacific side are undisturbed by any elevated range. This large tract of country is covered over in most places by an alluvial sand. Along the course of the rivers this covering passes into a clay bottom, more or less rich, depending on the source whence the river derived its mud and detritus, the overflow of which contributes so much to enrich the land. The depth of this clay is in many cases thirty feet, mixed in layers with gravel.

The hilly ranges which obstruct the Isthmus are a few chains of low mountains that appear to be the terminating points of the sierras which lie on either side. They are the Cerros de la Hucamaya, Prieto, Masahua, Masahuita, Espinosa, and the Piedra Parada.

The Hucamaya range is a continuation of the Sierra; and the Prieto, Masahuita, and Espinosa are southeasterly prolongations of the chain. The Masahua are a parallel range to these last. Between these two runs the Torrentera de Masahua. No erupted rocks are conspicuous in these ranges; they are chiefly made up of early secondary rocks (silurian), which are very metamorphic in their physical character. The southern flank of the Masahua is a sandstone or grit, partly calcareous and ferruginous.

Higher up in the same slopes, compact limestone is met with; and this rock constitutes the highest points of all the hills upon this range, as also in the chains above enumerated which lie north. Talcose slate with talc rock constitutes the basis rock of these mountains, and is that upon which the limestone reposes. The dip of these slates and limestones varies, but averages about 45°, in a direction southwest—the bluff edges of the hills face the northeast. It is on this side that the talc rocks are easily seen underlying the limestone, nowhere more apparent than when passing along the Torrentera and looking south upon the northern sides of the Masahua, where abrupt cliffs and nearly vertical walls of rock, from 200 to 300 feet high, are occasionally met with.

The elevating force which raised these hills seems to have been exerted with more energy upon the Masahuita than upon the Masahua range, as the former is the more elevated; geologically speaking, they are repetitions of each other and of the Hucamaya, their formation (reckoning from above downward) consisting of:

1. Sandstone, grit and metamorphic.
2. Limestone, gray and dark-colored.
3. Talc, in rock and shale.

Their analogous form and conformation are given in the section, and are well marked in the view of Masahua. The lower portions of the talc slate are intermixed with greenstone and hypersthene rock; and in some places it becomes magnesian, and verges into a steatitic rock. Veins of milk-quartz cut through the sandstone, especially upon the flanks of Masahuita and Espinosa.

South of these hills, and before the Pacific plains are reached from the north, there lie several scattered hills about 200 feet high, having round rugged summits, with a gradual slope to the south. The limestone of these ranges is a very compact, light-colored stone, dense, and so altered as to become nearly a crystalline marble; it effervesces strongly with acids, burns well, and is well adapted for building purposes, for stone or mortar.

This limestone bed presents a semicircular form, commencing from the Coatzacoalcos, east of Santa Maria Chimalapa, sweeping south to San Miguel, west to the rancho del Zapotal, and thence northwest, crossing the Almoloyo and Malatengo rivers. In this latter situation it is of a less metamorphic character than near Tarifa, or on the southern flanks of the Masahua hills: where the Malatengo crosses, it is of a dark-blue color and unaltered. It is intersected by thin thready seams of calc spar; is apparently a mud limestone, not fossilliferous, and of the silurian series. It is a valuable building material.

North of La Chivela, and extending from the Rio de Chicapa in a northwest direction to the hill of Guie-xila, silurian sandstones and slates, quartz and talcose rocks, form the surface rock, intersected with layers of white quartz. These constitute almost the chief rock of the summit-level. La Chivela is placed upon quartzose sandstone, which has a slight slope to the northeast.

The crescentic margin of the limestone described previously is overlaid by a sandstone rock which slopes northerly and easterly, upon the surface of which the rivers roll; from Guichicovi, and for several miles to the east, as far as the Coatzacoalcos this sandstone becomes more ferruginous, and passes into jasper and claystone. Porphyritic alterations of the rocks here are extensive. On the banks of this river, south of where it receives the Malatengo, primary limestone crops out, as also in the stream.

The above sandstone is of a purple color, slaty and semi-crystalline. It is a durable stone, and inclined to split into flags. It forms the surface rock of the northerly course of the Malatengo, and the country thence crossing the Sarabia and Jumuapa. Along the line of survey it has a gentle dip to the northeast of a few degrees. Between the Sarabia and Jumuapa rivers the ground is elevated by porphyritic and greenstone rocks; the sandstone, however, suffers little displacement. South of the Jaltepec River, along the line of survey, the compact limestone again crops out from under the sandstone, and is accompanied by thin veins of black quartz or hornstone. The upper bed of this sandstone is a conglomerate, and occupies a considerable surface extent between the Jaltepec and Jumuapa, south of the limestone. Its direction is described further on.

Commencing at a point where the Rio Pachine joins the Malatengo, and thence in a southeasterly direction, are a range of porphyritic hills with metamorphic sandstones, claystone, and jasper, extending as far as the Arroyo de los Otates, where it falls into the Chihihua; these have the same dip, and look with their bluff faces in the usual northerly direction. In the passes between these hills run the rivers which follow the general slope of the sandstone. In that portion of the range west of the Malatengo river, and near San Juan Guichicovi, iron ore abounds. Between these hills and the Malatengo River, after it has taken its easterly course, the compact limestone, described previously, crops out upon the surface in several places along the line of survey.

Between the Malatengo and the Sarabia, and between the latter and the Jaltepec, the surface is less disturbed: granular quartz, or quartz-breccia, sandstone, and porphyritic greenstone and sandstone are the underlying rocks. None of these upheavals reach the height of the hills more to the south. While the direction of the elevating force was the same, its intensity was less. The real inequality of the surface is diminished by the accumulation of quartzose gravel and gravelly clay, which here occupy the whole surface of the level ground. Five miles south of the Jaltepec the compact limestone appears as the surface rock. Here it overlays coarse conglomerate, consisting of hornstone united by a calcareous cement. The limestone forms the crest of an elevated ridge dividing the waters of the Jaltepec and Jumuapa. It has a porous structure, but is rather hard. It is covered by a mass of weathered fragments, which, when removed, show the rock to have a dip of a very small angle to the north. The strata are nearly horizontal.

North of the Naranjo River about seven miles, a range of hills 800 feet high, chiefly composed of sandstone conglomerate with a calcareous cement, approaches the river Coatzacoalcos from the west. The dip is southward, with a more easterly strike than the other formations. Above Suchil this conglomerate is met with, the strata dipping at almost every angle. On the eastern side of the Island of Tacamichapa the compact limestone crops out on the river's edge and forms bold cliffs: here it forms the bed of the stream, and rises up east of the river into hills a few hundred feet high, and having a dip southwest of about 20°. These are repeated at the Indian village of Almagres, where the strata project into the river a little below the town. The limestone is here light, porous, and decomposed by the weather.

About fifteen miles north of the sandstone conglomerate, and west of the Coatzacoalcos, a fine-grained sandstone, whitish and very light, appears over ground. It is porous, and too soft to be used for any architectural purposes, but may possibly serve in the arts as a polishing material. This rock, on which Tesistepec is placed, covers an area of eight or ten miles square. The sloping plains have here an elevation of 200 feet above the Gulf: in their descent they suffer little deviation, as the land is but little elevated into hills on the western side of the river. At the Peñas Blancas and the Cerrito de Cuapinoloya, the white sandstone strata are almost horizontal.

The Sierras, in which the Coatzacoalcos and its eastern tributaries take their rise, were not accurately explored. Atravesado, which is 5016 feet high, has its summit of porphyry: the hills more northward reach 7680 feet, and are sienitic. Clay and talcose slates form the larger portion of the whole, while the flanks and lesser hills are made up of sandstone, porphyry, quartz, and greenstone. The compact limestone skirts the whole range. Micaceous granite occupies a few hills, and serpentine is met with in some places. Besides these, amygdaloid rocks, hornstone, obsidian, jasper, and petroleum, are met with in the bed of the rivers which have their sources in these hills.

Augitic rocks form no unimportant portion of these hills. The basaltic sand which is washed down by the streams, occasionally contains gold particles. Such was the case with that from the hacienda of San José, in a brook emptying into the Tanchochapa. Near San José are the remains of sinkings for wells, which, it is believed, have been used by the natives in former times for washing these auriferous sands. It is well known that the basaltic sand at Trinity Bluff, California, is very rich in gold; but it has been separated with great difficulty by washing, owing to the density of the sand. Skilful chemical treatment has, however, made it yield up its auriferous portion; and the basaltic sand of San José might be treated with advantage in the same manner. That gold does exist on the Isthmus is a matter of history, which is corroborated by its geological structure. Quartz, talcose slate, and alluvial sands, are here in great abundance, which elsewhere are the auriferous beds; and a rigid search through the neighboring Sierra would no doubt display the actual position of the gold. The following extracts show how abundant and easily obtained it was at one period upon the Isthmus.

Antonio de Herrera, in his "*Descripcion de las Indias Occidentales*," speaking of Tehuantepec, says: "En todo este Obispado no hay in que no lleve oro." And in another place, referring to the Estates of Marquesanas: "Cogese en el mucha seda trigo, y maiz: tiene la lengua Zapoteca: ha havido en el buenas minas de oro."

Bernal Diaz, in recording the account of the expeditions of Gonzalo de Umbria and the gold which he brought, says: "Neither did Diego de Ordas, who had been sent to the river Coatzacoalcos, return with empty hands."

Again, in reference to the march of Sandoval: "Twenty of the caziques and principal personages soon made their appearance, bringing with them a present of gold-dust in ten small tubes, besides various pretty ornaments."

At another place, in the same connection: "We arrived in the province, and began diligently to explore the mines, accompanied by a great number of Indians, who washed the gold-dust for us in a kind of trough, from the sand of three different rivers. In this way we obtained four tubes full of gold-dust, each about the thickness of the middle finger. Sandoval was highly delighted when we brought him these, and concluded that the country must contain rich gold mines."

The expedition of Alvarado to Tehuantepec, in 1522, seems to have been attended with far greater success. Bernal Diaz, speaking of this expedition, says: "Among the more powerful tribes who submitted on this occasion, was that of the Tecuantepec (Tzapotecs), whose ambassadors brought with them a present in gold; stating, at the same time, that they were at war with their neighbors, the Tutepecs, who had commenced hostilities with them because they had submitted to the Spanish crown. This tribe inhabited the coast on the South Sea, they added, and possessed great quantities of gold, both in the raw material and in ornaments." Again: "The cazique (of the Tutepecs) soon after arrived with a valuable present in gold, which he repeated almost every day, and provided the troops with abundance of provisions. When Alvarado found what a quantity of gold the inhabitants possessed, he ordered them to make him a pair of stirrups of the finest gold, and gave them a couple of his own for a pattern; and indeed those they made turned out very good. Notwithstanding all the gold which Alvarado received from this cazique, he ordered him to be imprisoned a few days after his arrival. Many credible persons have asserted that Alvarado's only motive for ill-using this cazique was, to extort more gold from him. One thing, however, is certain, that he gave Alvarado gold to the value of 30,000 pesos, and that he died in prison from excessive grief."

The same writer, in describing the expedition of Alvarado to this province in the following year, says: "From this place he marched to the large township of Tecuantepec, which is inhabited by a tribe of the Tzapotecs, where he met with the kindest reception, and was even presented with some gold-dust."

Clavigero, in his history of Mexico, speaking of the abundance of the precious metals in this country, says: "The Mexicans found gold in the countries of the Cohuixcas, the Mixtecas, *Zapotecos*, and in several others. They gathered this precious metal chiefly in grains amongst the sands of the rivers, and the above-mentioned people paid a certain quantity in tribute to the crown of Spain."

The riches of a country in precious metals does not depend so much upon the fact of its rock strata bearing the marks of upheaval, as upon the character of the rocks which have been the immediate cause of the alteration of the horizontality of the beds. The auriferous localities of California are in the alluvial sands and clays, whether they be silicious, aluminous, or basaltic; in granite and primary quartz, and lastly in talcose slate. Although the Sierras of Mexico are a more easterly range, yet their geological constitution is similar to that of California; and it is also on the eastern sides of the range that these metals have been plentifully obtained. Sufficient historical evidence of the presence of gold upon the Isthmus, or in its immediate proximity, has been produced; and there is little doubt if the sands of the Coatzacoalcos, Uspanapa, and other rivers on the east side were examined, the presence of gold would be detected.

The Andes of South America are the great storehouses of silver for the world. The richness of the mines is almost inconceivable; but their great elevation above the sea makes the climate so cold and the labor of mining so great, as not to be a profitable speculation, except in a few cases.

In Mexico the ores are equally rich, but at a comparatively low elevation, so that where the ore is found in quantity, it is always advantageous to work it. Its position is various. The silver mines of Comarga occur in sienite. In Guanaxuato, the richest mine in Mexico, the ore occurs in talcose slate. At Real del Cardonal-Xacala, in Limo del Toro, it is found in transition limestone. The average richness is four ounces in each quintal of 102 pounds.

The general position of silver ores is in veins which traverse the primary and older of the secondary stratified rocks; but especially the former, as well as in the unstratified rocks, the granites, and porphyries which accompany the above. In the limestone the silver is generally associated with lead ore, which is then termed argentiferous galena. The proportion of silver found in English lead mines is twelve ounces to the ton of 2240 pounds; but it is profitable to separate it when it is as low as eight ounces, or one grain in half a pound of lead ore. Silver is occasionally found in Northern Mexico, mixed with iron ore and ochre chiefly, as chloride of silver, or horn silver. The same system of rocks which are metalliferous in the other districts of Mexico exist upon the Isthmus; and the limestone contains galena which is argentiferous. An exploration of the metamorphic rocks might lead to the discovery of some valuable veins.

Iron ore has been found in quantity in three places apart from each other. One locality is in the hills north of San Juan Guichicovi. The second is among the shale which crop out near

Moloacan, east of the Uspanapa River, and a few miles south of Ishuatlan. Lamellar specular iron-ore has been found in the neighborhood of Tarifa. The ores in the first two localities are red hæmatite, both earthy and compact. There are, besides, in many places, deposits of ochre and umber, arising from the decomposition of the ferruginous shales. Almost all the porphyries, shales, and sandstones are impregnated with oxide of iron, which gives the red and blue tints to the sands and stiff clays carried down by the rivers. To the east of the Coatzacoalcos, in the vicinity of Ishuatlan and Moloacan, the clay iron-stone is magnetic to a marked degree. Magnetic oxide of iron occurs at San José.

The hills of San Martin, on the Gulf towards the west, are of a volcanic character, and contain cinnabar ore in abundance. From this mineral (the sulphuret of mercury) almost all the quicksilver of commerce is made. Its location here is a future source of riches to the Isthmus.

The district on the northern slope east of the Coatzacoalcos has a geology somewhat different from, and of a more recent character than that on the west. Between that river and the Coachapa the land is level, and subject to inundation over a large extent. The low hills, which here and there vary the surface, are the limestone strata, upheaved similarly to that on the Isla de Tacamichapa. Limestone constitutes a range of hills between the latter river and the Uspanapa. North of this river, between it and Ishuatlan, is a range of hills chiefly of shale, with red hæmatite. About six miles easterly of this is situated a salt and sulphur spring. In this vicinity there exists also a petroleum spring, arising from the decomposition of the vegetable matter existing in these shales. The quantity which pours out is very considerable, and, from its purity, would be a valuable article to collect. It hardens very readily into asphalte, small detrital pieces of which are picked up in the Uspanapa, and about the west base of the Cerro Acalapa. Near Moloacan lignite is met with, and corundum at San José.

Obsidian, pitchstone, and volcanic glass are met with constantly in beds of streams and in alluvium, washed from the Sierra on either side. These have not been seen in place over the line examined; but of these and other erupted or basaltic minerals there is a great abundance. Immediately south and west of San José, and following up the course of the rivers, the ground is composed of fine alluvial clay, which reaches to the foot of the mountains. This clay is auriferous, and has been previously alluded to.

Notwithstanding the chain of successive low hills which alters the horizontality of the northern plains, that alteration does not affect the general gradual slope of the land into the Gulf. The strike of these hills being generally N. W. and S. E., the southern extremity is more elevated than the northern, and the long back, or more gentle slope of the hills, is towards the Gulf. Again: the more remote from the Sierra, the less elevated the upheavals constituting the hills; and from the configuration of the Gulf coast, no hill-range exists at the mouth of the Coatzacoalcos under water. The above considerations, as well as actual observation of the river, would lead to the presumption that the bar of the river is not a rocky obstruction, but an accumulation of sand and detritus from the river.

Although muriate of soda does not exist in beds over the Isthmus, yet its great abundance on the surface justifies our notice of it under the geological description. Solar evaporation of the lagoons on the Pacific shore every year furnishes a large amount of a coarsely crystallized granular salt, which forms a crust on the margins of the lagoons to the depth of two or three inches. The same occurrence is common on the Gulf shore. The purification of the salt is simple and inexpensive, and when carried out on a large scale is profitable to the manufacturer. The country is admirably adapted to the manufacture of salt by art: nothing more being necessary along the coast and lagoons than to convey the water in a stream, and allow it to trickle over shrubs and branches of trees laid horizontally, when, from the excessive heat of the sun, most of the water would evaporate, and the salt crystallize on the twigs. By re-crystallization, the finer salt is obtained. Nature has pointed out this Isthmus as a locality where this manufacture might be carried on as a staple article of trade.

The low average elevation of the mainland of the Isthmus

above the sea-level, and the horizontality of most of the beds, show that the elevating force was small compared with that of Mexico north, or of Guatimala south. The soundings at the mouth of the Coatzacoalcos are the same now as they were when examined by direction of Cortes in 1520; so that, for three hundred and thirty-two years, there has been no elevation of the land here. Every thing on the Isthmus bears the mark of stability, and the absence of any active volcanic force. This is a point of great importance where the stability and permanence of large buildings are concerned; and in this respect, this portion of Mexico is less liable to motions of the ground than Guatimala or Nicaragua; in which latter place several alterations of level have taken place lately. Previous absence of upheaval and eruption through a long period of time is *a priori* evidence of the nonexistence of the upheaving cause; and this is the actual condition of the Isthmus of Tehuantepec.

CLIMATE.

UNDER the term climate are comprised the results of the influences of geographical position, of prevailing winds, elevation of country, and the disposition of the mountains and seas of any particular latitude. These result in producing a certain mean temperature, a certain annual fall of rain, and the stimulant effects of light and electricity; so that when the climate of any latitude is spoken of, all the circumstances enumerated above are supposed to be taken notice of.

A slight review of these circumstances as affecting the Isthmus is given here; at the same time it may be stated, that the data upon which this portion of the report is based has been necessarily limited, the time of those engaged in the survey not allowing of occupation in experiments devoted to this object. The facts stated here, however, have been derived from observation, and the inferences drawn are trustworthy.

As a regular mountain-chain the Andes may be said to descend suddenly at Panama, and are merely continued northward to join the Rocky Mountains by a mass of elevated ground, with an irregular mixture of mountains and table-land. This table-land occupies the greater part of Mexico or Anahuac. It commences at the Isthmus of Tehuantepec, and passes northwest to latitude 42°, an extent of 1600 miles. This land is narrow at its southern limit, and widens northward to the latitude of the city of Mexico, where it is 300 miles across its greatest breadth, and where also its elevation is greatest; from this point northward the plateau again descends. Southward this elevated plain borders on the table-land of Guatimala, which is much more elevated above the ocean level, except in certain passes between the two oceans. These highlands terminate in parallel ridges of mountains, called the Cerro Peladro, which run from east to west along the 94th meridian, filling one-half the Isthmus, and uniting the table-land of Guatimala with that of Mexico.

The range of mountains, the Cordilleras de la Huacamaya, Prieto, Masahuita, and others, whose extreme eastern limit is 18° west of Washington, has a convexity towards Tehuantepec, and approaches within 20 or 25 miles of the Pacific shore. The range which lies eastward of this is further from the Pacific Ocean, and runs in a southeasterly direction. The result of these two chains of mountains is to form the Isthmus valley, with a slope four times as extensive towards the Gulf of Mexico as towards the Pacific. In this valley, which has a northeast direction, the river Coatzacoalcos, fed by other rivers, runs its contorted course. The rivers which have their sources in the chains on both sides of the Isthmus, empty themselves into this common stream. On the southern side of these mountains, the proximity of the ocean, which sweeps inland with a crescentic margin, following the depression of the land, limits the river courses, and hence no large stream, fed by lesser ones, exists; but each river rolls down the sandy plains, and empties itself into the lakes by its own channel, seven of which by this configuration of the ground, necessarily converge at their embouchure within a space of thirty miles. An eighth, the Tehuantepec River, empties itself into the ocean at the Bay of Ventosa.

The land slopes to either shore from the Cordillera de Prieto, having an average summit-level of 800 feet; the descent occupying 28 miles to the Pacific, and about 110 miles to the Gulf of Mexico: this latter fall is through most of its extent very slight, the chief declivity being from the Almoloyo River to the Jaltepec, the level of which is 75 feet above the sea-level: this last fall is accomplished in 75 miles, being scarcely one foot per mile descent from that river to the Mexican gulf.

The result of this conformation is to give to the Isthmus the full benefit of the coast winds and rains from the north, which play over three-fourths of the breadth of land, and are only retarded from passing across its whole extent by the mountain land.

Physical geographers place this country in the zone of the northeast winds; and these northerly winds prevail on the Isthmus from the middle of December to the end of March, and generally blow with considerable strength. They are cool and damp winds, and are commonly accompanied with more or less rain on the mountains. At Chivela, which fronts the main pass through the mountains, there is a strong breeze throughout the entire year, and almost the whole time from the north. These winds come from the Gulf, and travel along with the warm stream, which, coming westward through the Caribbean Sea, turns northward round the Antilles, and passes into the Atlantic Ocean. The accompanying winds reaching the shore of the Gulf at the Isthmus, being saturated with watery vapor to the greatest extent they can hold in solution, and meeting with the sloping plains of Vera Cruz, and which, at all times of the year, are cooler than the ocean, are necessarily cooled in their westward course across the table-lands: they immediately deposit the greater portion of the watery vapor which they had held suspended; and when they have reached the summit-level and the mountain-chains, the increased cold condenses almost all residual moisture which had escaped deposition below. Whatever little (if any) that may have escaped deposition is not poured out as rain on the Pacific slope, for two reasons: first, on account of the aspect of the land, which, looking southerly, is warmed by the sun to a greater extent than the northern slope, and compels these northerly winds, already cooled, to expand, and rise higher in the atmosphere; and, secondly, the breeze which blows off the Pacific shore being warm, and meeting the northers coming through the passes and over the hill-tops, warms them suddenly, converts the mists into invisible vapor, and presents to the eye of the spectator the appearance of the rain-clouds suddenly vanishing into thin air when they pass southward over the hills. The cool wind of the north has a tendency at all times to occupy the lower stratum of air, owing to its density; and hence it is that it escapes southward along the mountain-passes, through which it blows with considerable violence when the northers prevail, sweeping down through the narrow gorges in the mountains leading from the elevated table-lands to the Pacific plain, with irresistible force; especially when, from meeting with the wind off the Pacific, an eddying current is produced.

On the shores of the Pacific these northers are also strong, and carry with them clouds of dust and fine sand from the plains. As they blow off shore, the sea is but little disturbed by their influence, and vessels would doubtless lay in perfect security during the hardest gales. There is thus a free circulation of air across the whole Isthmus, sweeping through the valley of Chicapa, and carrying the cool air of the north across to the Pacific shore.

The prevalent winds which blow upon the Isthmus come from a northerly point for the reason stated—i. e., the influence of the Gulf Stream : they are augmented in force and frequency by the course of the sun over these latitudes. The solar rays, playing upon the heated waters and land, warm the contiguous air, which immediately rises upwards into the higher regions, and is replaced by a current of cool air, which comes down from the north to fill the vacuum. These winds, blowing from the north so long as the sun is travelling over these latitudes, are termed *northers*, and are always loaded with watery vapor, being saturated by the evaporation of the sea.

The following figures show the number and direction of the winds, observed by the officers of the survey and by those of the United States Navy, on the northern side of the Isthmus. Thus in 104 observations made daily, there were

Winds from N.		19 days		*or*	
"	" N. E. & N. N. E.	36 "		Northerly winds	69
"	" N. W.	14 "		Southerly	31
"	" S.	12 "			
"	" S. E.	13 "		Easterly	49
"	" S. W.	6 "		Westerly	24
"	" W.	4 "			
		104			

The prevalence of northerly winds is here well shown, and their effects upon the temperature and productions of the Isthmus are well marked.

Between the tropics the rains follow the sun, and when he is north of the equator, the rains prevail in the northern tropic.

Thus the rainy season commences on the Gulf coast about the first of July and ends about the first of November. On that portion of the Isthmus included between the Jaltepec and Sarabia rivers, the rainy season commences about the first of June and ends in December; and at El Barrio it commences about the first of July and ends in October.

The rainy season, as above limited, includes only those months in which the rains prevail to a considerable extent; but there is usually a month, both preceding and following the rainy season as above defined, which is more or less showery, but these showers generally occur in the night. In some parts of the more elevated mountain districts, the rains prevail to some extent throughout nearly the whole year. This is particularly true of the northern slope of the Cordilleras, where the warm, humid air blowing from off the Gulf and across the Atlantic plains, first meets the cooler atmosphere of the mountains.

The atmosphere of the northern portion of the Isthmus, extending as far southerly as Boco del Monte, is damp; but to the south of this point, its humidity becomes sensibly less, and at El Barrio and Chivela it is quite dry, and still more dry over the Pacific plains, where it scarcely ever rains.

The sandy plains of the Pacific shore belong to one of the rainless districts of the American continent, which here embraces the plateau of Guatimala and the table-land of Mexico. The proximity of the Gulf causes the rains on the northern side for the reasons before stated. The annual amount of the fall of rain on the Isthmus is considerable, especially in the central district from the Jaltepec to the Cordillera de la Hucamaya. At Guichicovi, and San Maria Chimalapa, it rains abundantly, and very often at San Miguel. At these times the table-land of Tarifa is covered with a thin mist, which disappears upon reaching the Portillo, or pass to the Pacific plains.

These rains are not, however, of sufficient consequence to prevent out-door work for the whole of any one day. The annual fall of rain at Vera Cruz is 66 inches, just one-half the amount which falls in St. Domingo or Jamaica, and even less than that on the northern shores of the Gulf, as at New Orleans or in Florida. It is also considerably less than falls at the Isthmus of

THERMAL CURVES OF DIFFERENT SEASONS.

N° 1 1848
The dotted line for 1851

N° 2 1847

N° 3 1850

Panama. The temperature of this Isthmus is probably more favorable to human life as compared with similar latitudes elsewhere.

The mean equatorial temperature of the air in Asia is 82°.94
" " " " in Africa, 85°.10
" " " " in America, 80°.96

So that this continent is cooler under the equator than any other, owing to the abundance of sea surrounding it, and the more elevated character of the land. Similar causes lead to the depression of temperature on the Isthmus below what it is upon mainland of a like latitude. The curves of temperature appended are drawn from tables filled by the officers of the survey while on duty, and also from extracts out of the log-books of United States vessels at the mouth of the Coatzacoalcos River and at Mina-titlan. It must be remarked that these are the temperatures of the northern side of the Isthmus, while those on the southern side are somewhat higher.

In Table I. is given the temperatures obtained by the U. S. Bomb-vessel Stromboli, lying at Coatzacoalcos River in 1847.

Table II. contains the temperatures obtained by the U. S. schooner Bonita in the same river in 1848. The same table contains also a lesser curve for a short period in May, 1851, obtained by the officers of this survey while at Mina-titlan.

Table III. gives the temperatures at Mina-titlan and Coatzacoalcos in 1850–51, observed during the survey.

From an inspection of these curves, it appears that the highest temperature obtained was on May 24th, 1847, and May 21st, 1848, when it reached 98°: the lowest, the 31st December, 1850, when it reached 62°.

The mean temperature of a portion of May,....1847,......90°
" " " early part of June,.....1847,......88°
" " " greater part of April,...1848,......83°
" " " whole of May,.........1848,......88°
" " " 1st half of June,......1848,......85°
" " " part of Dec. & Jan'y...1850–51,...74°

These curves were drawn from observations taken at different periods of the day; thus, in

Tables I. and II., observations daily at meridian.

Table III., observations made twice and three times daily: chiefly at 10 A. M. and 4 P. M.

These curves in Tables I. and II., therefore, indicate the highest range of temperature on the northern coast, inasmuch as they are drawn from meridian observations, which give a higher average than those taken at 10 A. M. and 4 P. M. daily would yield; and also because they are from the sea-level, which is always warmer than the upland.

The thermal curve of December, 1850, and January, 1851, shows the influence which the fall of rain has upon temperature, by producing a mean depression of about 12°. This low temperature prevails through the succeeding months, the warmth gradually augmenting till it attains the mean temperature of 83° in April.

The temperature of the sloping plains of the north is several degrees below that given on the tables, and is considerably less between the Jaltepec and Malatengo rivers, and somewhat less still between the latter river and the summit-level.

The Jaltepec, where it crosses the line of survey, lies on a level of 75 ft.
" Malatengo,..300 ft.
" Summit-level,...800 ft.

As the temperature diminishes on elevated land at the rate of one degree Fahrenheit for every 334 feet of elevation, it follows that the mean temperatures of the Malatengo river-level and the summit-level would be always one and two degrees less respectively, throughout the year, than those given in the tables accompanying. But even this estimate is too high, for as other circumstances than elevation determine the mean temperature of any place, so in this instance the insular character and northern slope of the Gulf plains diminish the temperatures several degrees below that of the sea-level: this is clearly indicated by the character of the vegetation, the abundance of dicotyledonous trees, the appearance of the tree fern, of *pinus abies*, and other Alpine plants, which point out a modified and insular temperature. The profusion of the Myrtle and Laurel families of plants is proof that the temperature is not tropical but subtropical. The proximity of the Sierra Madre, whose summits are always enveloped in clouds, tends to lower the temperature of the upland district very remarkably.

On the Pacific plains, and about Tehuantepec, the thermometer ranges as high as 92°; but this temperature is softened down by the breezes which blow off shore and from the mountains. Señor Moro states, that when the thermometer on the plains ranges about 85° Fahr., it is not more than 56° at Chivela or Tarifa.

The altitude of the table-lands of Guatimala and Mexico has a more powerful effect in determining the climate of the Isthmus, than what the mere latitude, or its own elevation, could lead to believe. This table-land has an average elevation of from 6500 to 8200 feet above the sea, which would give a mean temperature of 20° throughout the year, less than that of the seaboard : thus, if the temperature of the coast be 85°, that of the table-land would be 65°, which is a truly temperate climate, although within tropical latitudes. This is proved by the growth of oak, cypress, pine, and fern trees, which are inhabitants of a temperate clime; and most of the cerealia of northern latitudes grow in luxuriance. The average height of the table-land of Guatimala gives a mean temperature of 60° through the year, and the lands are called *Tierras frias*. Now, it must be recollected that the Isthmus of Tehuantepec, though in itself possessing only an elevation calculated to lessen the temperature at the sea-board by a few degrees, is subject to the influences of the land in its neighborhood, and its own warmth is very much reduced by the cool air descending from the high table-lands and from the Sierra Madre, spreading over the lowland by its density, cooling the surface of the ground, and mixing with the warm air of the Pass.

The climate of the northern division of the Isthmus is damp, but as it is not so warm as that of the south, it is not of necessity unhealthy.

During the prevalence of northers on the more elevated sections to the east, as the Chimalapas, for example, the atmosphere is damp and heavy, with a chilly mist like that experienced on the northern coast of Ireland. But otherwise the climate is healthy, and rheumatism and catarrhs are the only diseases of note; sometimes fever and ague in October. There, the rainy season commences in June (latter part), and extends through July, August, September, and October. The average age of the oldest inhabitants is sixty years.

On the northeastern division of the Isthmus, bordering the Gulf, where the rainy season begins in the middle of June and terminates in November, the district appears to be unusually healthy, and it is not uncommon to meet with natives seventy and eighty years of age residing there.

The less healthy portion is, without doubt, the Coatzacoalcos River, along the mouth and delta of which, fever, ague, and remittent fever of a bilious type are prevalent during July, August, and September. The people who inhabit this region are miserably poor, and the insects numerous and annoying. There is no doubt that in alluvial plains, which are generally level and well watered, the slow current of the streams and the luxuriant vegetation give rise, by the decay of vegetable matter, to the development of miasmata and gaseous matters, which produce fevers of an intermittent and typhoid character. Mankind are not necessarily victims to these diseases, unless by absence of precaution, or a lowered state of health, the constitution becomes impaired, so that it is unable to resist the miasma. Cleanliness of skin, temperance in eating and drinking, and clothing to defend against alternations of temperature, are sure preventives against the influences of a moist climate and a damp soil—influences which are equally hurtful, whether in New England or on the plains of Mexico.

There is no reason to doubt that when the northern slope becomes more inhabited, and the forest cleared somewhat, so that the sun's rays may reach and dry the ground, much of its present injurious effect on the constitution will disappear: the demand for forest timber and the cutting down of trees for medicinal and commercial purposes will also remove the humidity and drain the soil remarkably. The use of flannel next the skin should never be omitted by inhabitants of the whole northern slope, and a small fire should be kept in the rooms during the rainy season when the thermometer sinks low.

The practice of sleeping out of doors should be avoided, likewise that of placing the bed upon or near the ground. These precautions are not absolutely necessary on the southern plains, which are so remarkably dry. It would be well, however, to observe the precautions concerning sleeping in any district.

In warm climates there is always a tendency to overaction in the functions of the liver, spleen, and skin. Temperance, especially in the use of alcoholic liquors, is a great safeguard against diseases of the first two named viscera. Drunkenness is inevitable death, and frequently within the tropics brings a speedy one; and it is the more incumbent on laborers to observe temperance, as they consume a large amount of solid food daily to support their strength, and the exertion produces the desire to drink; and fruits, juices, &c., the food of the natives, should be preferred. More vegetable and farinaceous diet should be consumed, and less animal food than is usual in northern latitudes; and the constant use of the cold-water bath whenever attainable, appropriate clothing, comfortable houses placed upon well-drained spots; these, with the avoidance of stimulating food and drink, will enable the colonist to resist the influences of climate and soil equally well as the native.

On the south side of the Isthmus the inhabitants are more cleanly than upon the northern, and bathe frequently, the streams being more shallow, and consequently free from *alligators,* which abound in a considerable degree in the rivers and streams on the northern slope.

At Tehuantepec (as has been said) the rains are of trifling character, and confined to the months of July, August, and September, and the prevailing diseases are those of the bowels. The average age of the oldest inhabitants is about 60.

The central division of the Isthmus is perhaps the healthiest— a circumstance due to its elevation and better drainage.

In October and November of 1850, the cholera broke out on the Isthmus and raged with considerable violence in the south and in the central division; but it did not reach the Atlantic plains at all.

Yellow fever has never been known to occur on the Isthmus. Since the establishment of the Mexican Republic the official returns of the population seem to indicate a sensible decrease—which is at variance with facts. The cause is, that the Indians find it to their advantage to make the returns as small as possible, as by so doing, many rid themselves of taxes and a thankless service in the army of the republic.

The northern division of the Isthmus—that is to say, from the Pacific slope to the Mexican gulf—has, nevertheless, suffered in times past from the small-pox. In the year 1828, in two small villages near the sea-coast, east of the Coatzacoalcos River, no less than 126 persons died out of a population of 800; nor were the ravages of the disease arrested until broad *picaduras* (roads) were cut through the surrounding forests to admit a free circulation of air. This had the desired effect, and the small-pox disappeared entirely. A similar instance occurred at Huimangillo, near the confines of Tobasco, where a malignant fever was entirely checked by felling the neighboring forests.

The conviction in the minds of those engaged in drawing up this report, and one founded on a residence upon the spot, is, that the climate of the Isthmus is a mild and healthy one, favorable to longevity, and free from many diseases incidental to more temperate latitudes. The health of those engaged on the survey was unusually good during their entire stay; and although frequently by accidents wetted to the skin and remaining in wet clothes the whole day, and this occurring on successive days, with limited food at long intervals, yet none suffered in consequence—a strong proof that their health was due to the favorable climate.

Compared with other places selected for forming a junction between the two oceans, this Isthmus has peculiar advantages. With less alluvial land at the sea-level, it is more healthy than San Juan de Nicaragua, and from its more northern latitude its mean annual temperature is less than that of Nicaragua or of Panama. The latter place has, indeed, a temperature and climate truly torrid, and partaking more of the character of a continent than of an island, which latter is the peculiarity of the position of this portion of Mexico.

Extract from the Report of Dr. Kovaleski (surgeon to the party under the direction of P. E. Trastour) on the climate of the Isthmus of Tehuantepec.

I HAVE the honor to present you the following report on the sanitary condition of the Isthmus of Tehuantepec; made from personal observations during a sojourn of one year in the country, under circumstances most favorable to test its salubrity. I shall state facts as they occurred, from the time of our arrival to the date of our return, adding all such reliable information as could be obtained from inquiries among the inhabitants, and such as came under my own personal observation.

We arrived at Mina-titlan on the 18th of July, 1850, and left it the 30th of the same month. This village, containing about 400 resident inhabitants, is situated on the left side of the river Coatzacoalcos, about twenty miles from its mouth, by which the river discharges its waters into the Gulf of Mexico. The country along the river approaching Mina-titlan, and for many miles beyond it, is an extensive plain, covered with thick forests and intersected by numerous tributaries. All these rivers are subject to great annual overflows, by which extensive tracts of the wooded lands on their banks become temporarily inundated. Mina-titlan itself is built on the first link of a group of elevations, which, as they recede westward and from the river, become more and more prominent, and join a platform of the country beautifully undulated by valleys, small hills, and slopes, in the direction of Jaltipan and other villages chiefly inhabited by Indians of the Aztec race, who cultivate portions of the neighboring soil. The right shore of the river opposite Mina-titlan is flat, and so continues to the heights of Hidalgo-titlan. Both north and south of Mina-titlan, a small stream furnishes the inhabitants with good drinking-water. On the south side the stream loses itself in a marsh, which, during the high waters, is overflowed to the foot of the small hill on which the village is built. On the north side there is a narrow valley extending along the bayou, which is also covered by water during the rainy season; but a little further, the land rises again in small hills, which, running westwardly, join the more elevated platform of the back country and the plain called Tacoteno, which is considerably higher than the village.

I took particular care to inquire among the inhabitants, what were the diseases from which they mostly suffered, and how strangers settling among them were affected, and I ascertained beyond doubt, that not only Mina-titlan, but the whole plain of the Coatzacoalcos River, wherever inhabited, was a remarkably healthy country. Not a single case of yellow fever has ever occurred in Mina-titlan, or any other part of the Coatzacoalcos plain, although in the years from 1829 to 1832, when the French emigrants attempted to form a colony on the Isthmus, the number of unacclimated strangers was considerable in the country, and they were exposed to every kind of privation and suffering. Neither did I learn of any dangerous form of fever existing. I heard of cases of the intermittent fever, which must have been of a very mild type, as it was usually cured by the natives themselves with remedies indigenous to the country, such as the bark of the Palo-mulató, a tree growing abundantly in the Isthmus. During the time of our stay at Mina-titlan, I met with but one case of old-standing derangement of the bowels, which terminated in extreme emaciation, debility, and death; the cause of this disease I traced to the habit of the sufferer of eating clay for many years back, a habit which in all places ultimately produces the same effects, namely, marasmus and death. This practice unfortunately prevails to a considerable extent among the Indians of the Isthmus: the eatable clay has even become an article of commerce, and is exchanged for the produce of the country; it causes the death of many children and increases mortality among the adults.

I met at Mina-titlan with several individuals who formed a part of the French colony, and who had resided there for twenty-two years; they all assured me that they enjoyed uninterrupted health. The appearance of the natives proves the country to be healthy, and our small party had no reason to complain of sickness during its stay.

On the 30th of July our party left Mina-titlan in two canoes, and an open boat, which we intended to carry over the Isthmus. The rains had already set in, and were unusually abundant this year. After fourteen days of exposure, fatigue, and privations, we landed at the Paso de la Puerta. Messengers having been immediately dispatched to Guichicovi for provisions and means of transportation, we for the first time since our departure from Mina-titlan had an opportunity of changing our garments and drying our wet clothes. We remained in this spot for fifteen days, the swollen condition of the Sarabia River, and the consequent difficulty of crossing the mules, occasioning the delay. During this time we were living on spoiled rice, worm-eaten beans, and without salt and bread. We fortunately found in the neighborhood a large field of plantains; they were unripe, but, such as they were, served us as our principal article of food, which we seasoned plentifully with red pepper, also found growing near at hand. Under these unfavorable circumstances my anxiety for the health of the party became extreme. One after another soon began to suffer from fever; and while administering appropriate remedies, I watched the progress of each case with gloomy expectations of typhoid fever, or even of uncontrollable dysentery before me; yet, to my utmost delight, a thorough sweating would put an end to all the febrile symptoms in the course of a few days, and my patients would only complain of not having enough to eat in order to recover their strength. The fever proved to be nothing more than the consequence of exposure, fatigue, and want of healthy diet during our ascent of the rivers, to which the bites of musquitoes and other insects contributed not a little.

At the Paso de la Puerta the river plains terminate. Between it and Mina-titlan there is but one inhabited place, called Hidalgo-titlan, or Pueblo de los Almagres. It is situated on the right side of the Coatzacoalcos, about twenty miles above Mina-titlan, on elevated land, and contains about four hundred resident inhabitants, chiefly of the Aztec race, who are, with few exceptions, robust and healthy. Here we also found some of the French colonists, who assured me, that as far as their health was concerned, they had no reason whatever to complain. Their cheerful countenances and robust forms fully attested the truth of their assertions.

At the Paso de la Puerta begins another region of the Isthmus, namely, that of hills and mountains. Its topographical and geological characters are entirely different from those of the plain of Coatzacoalcos River: while the latter is formed of alluvial soil, this has rock for its basis, which is covered with a variety of soil more or less deep, and of variable fertility in different places. The wave-like hills and dales, covered by rich pasture, extend along the foot of lofty mountains. They are interspersed by clusters of luxuriant trees, growing along the various tributary streams of the Coatzacoalcos, affording refreshing shelter to the large herds of cattle that range through this region. Here may be seen spots the most romantic and picturesque that the admirer of the beauties of nature can enjoy, while quietly reposing after the labors and toils of the active business of life. Here and there ranchos are to be met with, scattered among the valleys; and even among the mountains are several Indian villages, such as San Juan Guichicovi, which contains upwards of five thousand inhabitants, who cultivate the soil. This village is surrounded on all sides by the Cordillera of the same name. It is inhabited only by Indians, called Mijes, has an excellent climate, and would afford a delightful and healthy residence for our valetudinarians. Our journey from hence across the Cordillera to the plains of Tehuantepec, was a constant change of most interesting scenery, which we enjoyed greatly, notwithstanding the rain and very bad roads. This entire region for its salubrity cannot be surpassed by any country whatever. The small villages of Petapa, El Barrio, and Santo Domingo, also built on the elevated table-land, enjoy a well-merited reputation for uncommon healthiness, not only among the inhabitants of the Isthmus; but many Mexicans, as I learned later at Tehuantepec, come there, even from Oaxaca and several other states of Mexico, to recruit their health. The mean temperature of this region is much lower than that of the rest of the Isthmus. The light and variable winds that blow during the dry season refresh the air, which is always dry; and, besides, there are no musquitoes to mar the quiet of the evening, or disturb sleep during the night. The clear mountain springs furnish excellent water. There is an abundance and great variety of fruits, and the inhabitants, chiefly Zapotecos, are peaceably and quietly disposed.

The last portion of the Isthmus to be described is that of the plain of Tehuantepec, which stretches from the southern side of the Cordillera to the coast of the Pacific Ocean. The moment you descend the mountains, you perceive that you are in an entirely different region. The sturdy oak, and the thick dark-green foliage of the trees in the hilly regions, are replaced here by large varieties of bluish-leaved mimosa, of cactus, and other vegetation peculiar to a tropical climate. The soil is generally light and sandy, the rivers but few, rather small streams when compared with those of the northern part of the Isthmus. On this plain there are several large villages, inhabited by Zapoteco Indians. The city of Tehuantepec, the head of the department of that name, contains from twelve to fourteen thousand inhabitants. Although the mean temperature of this valley is higher than that of the plain of Coatzacoalcos, it enjoys a degree of salubrity not inferior to that of the region of the mountains. The season of the rains is shorter here than on the north side; and the heat of the sun during the dry season is mitigated by the north wind and the variable breezes in the wet season. I never heard of a single case of sun-stroke either among the natives or strangers. The air is pure and dry, and it never feels as oppressive as it often does in the summer-time at New Orleans. The natives complain chiefly of indigestion and some other derangements of the bowels, which are generally the consequences of all kinds of excesses; besides, these diseases are more prevalent in tropical climates than in temperate and cold ones. In some parts of the plain, as near the upper and lower lakes, in the neighborhood of San Francisco and Boca-Barra, the intermittent fevers prevail, particularly after the rainy season is over; but the yellow fever is unknown in this region, nor did I hear of any other epidemical pernicious fever. During our stay at Tehuantepec, while preparing for departure, I met with but few cases of sickness, and these were not of a character peculiar to the country, but such as would occur accidentally in all places. I saw and treated but one single case of dysentery, caused by imprudence in diet, which being for some time entirely neglected, presented at last really alarming symptoms. I was told that similar cases of dysentery generally proved fatal; all the friends, and even the father of my patient, one of the oldest and most intelligent inhabitants of Tehuantepec, the only apothecary that resides there, considered the case as hopeless, yet she finally recovered. The disease had nothing of a pernicious character in itself, was purely accidental, and I am satisfied that similar cases, properly attended to, would generally yield readily to correct treatment. Among upwards of forty Americans who arrived from California, and who partook freely of the fruits during a stay of nearly three weeks, not one got sick, and they all, as well as our party, crossed the Isthmus, and in the hot season, in the enjoyment of perfect health. It is true, that during the month of November and a part of December, the city of Tehuantepec and some villages of this valley suffered considerably from cholera; but this fact does not establish proof of the insalubrity of these places. It is an admitted fact, that cholera rages in all places, seasons, and climates indiscriminately. I am only surprised that it committed no greater ravages among a population who, through ignorance of proper treatment, generally allowed the disease to take its own course. Here the cholera was but of short duration, and having once ceased, did not appear again.

While at Huilotepec, some of our party were attacked by this disease, which also continued at our encampment at the Bay of Ventosa. We lost one of our party, victim to this dreadful epidemic, and even he perhaps would have been saved if he had not committed excess in drinking, unknown to me, twenty-four hours previous to his death.

The native population of the plains of Tehuantepec, particularly the Indians, are a race remarkably handsome, well built, and healthy. They all profess Christianity, live in houses, cultivate the soil, and are capable of further progress in civilization. They are friendly and hospitable towards strangers, and of a mild and yielding disposition, unless provoked by oppression and injustice, in which cases only they become really savage in their revenge.

To recapitulate in a few words, the facts above stated, it will be seen that the Isthmus of Tehuantepec naturally divides itself into three regions, each different from the other in topography, geological formation, and salubrity.

The plain of Coatzacoalcos River, flat and low, with an extremely fertile alluvial soil, covered with thick forests, intersected by many rivers, here and there subject to inundation, although the least healthy, yet enjoys a high degree of salubrity, and no fears need be entertained, as proved by the experience of the French emigrants, for those who may in future settle permanently in this region, and much less so for those who may cross it as travellers.

The region of hills and mountains is as healthy as the most salubrious portions of Europe; full of romantic scenery, it is even now highly attractive, and will, in progress of time, when inhabited by an enterprising and laborious population, become one of the most beautiful spots on the earth.

Last comes the plain of Tehuantepec, nearly as healthy as the hilly region, although warmer, presenting all the characteristics of a healthy tropical climate.

All these three regions together form a broad surface of country from the Gulf of Mexico to the coast of the Pacific, of a great variety of resources and of remarkable healthiness, a feature peculiar to the Isthmus, as the lands on both of its sides are very unhealthy; such as Vera Cruz and Tabasco on the Gulf, Acapulco, Huatulco, and the coast of Guatimala on the Pacific shore. This peculiar and exclusive salubrity of the Isthmus is, in my opinion, chiefly due to its configuration, which forms as it were a gate, walled on both sides by heavy masses of mountains, through which pass currents of air, that render the country they traverse so permanently salubrious. That the winds prevail only within the limits of the Isthmus, and not within a few miles on either side of it, I am informed from most reliable sources.

VEGETABLE PRODUCTIONS.

To present a full and comprehensive view of the botanical productions of the Isthmus, embracing as it does a variety of tropical and inter-tropical plants so valuable and numerous as to be unequalled within the same extent of territory, would exceed the usual limits of a work which is designed more as a record of mathematical results than a treatise on the natural resources of a country. Nor could the labor necessary for the proper classification here, of all the species be held justifiable under existing circumstances, especially when we consider the fact that the investigations of the commission were otherwise directed to subjects less secondary, and that on the Isthmus the names of plants vary with the numerous idioms of different sections. Care, nevertheless, has been taken to prepare a list of some of the most valuable species, from which some idea of the botanical riches of the country may be gleaned.*

In a mountainous country like Mexico, having so great a diversity of elevation, temperature, and soil, the variety of indigenous products must be immense, and most of the plants cultivated in other parts of the globe find in that country situations adapted to their nature. It unites in itself the vegetation of North and South America, though it resembles that of the latter more especially.

The distribution of plants on the Isthmus differs from that of Mexico in general, insomuch that the vegetation of the loftier table-lands is less distinctly marked. On the margins of the Gulf and the ocean are found the usual plants of inter-tropical shores, and upon the middle of the Isthmus, those families which vegetate favorably at elevations below 5000 feet within

---

* Vide Botanical Tables, p. 197.

VEGETABLE PRODUCTIONS. 181

the tropics; this occurring not because the elevation is sufficient to warrant the growth, but that the lower level of the Isthmus is cooled much below the average temperature of its latitude by the constant northeast winds, by the great humidity of the northern slope, and by the proximity of the lofty table-lands and mountain summits which cool the land in their vicinity. The different families of plants are, for these reasons, more scattered with apparent indiscrimination, and the mountain regions, with few exceptions, are clothed with species found in the alluvial basins; nor is it an uncommon thing to see the pines which stud the loftiest and coldest summits decorated with the fimbriated *orchidea*, or trellised with the *scitameneæ* of the plains.

The mean annual temperature of the Gulf shore of the Isthmus is 81°, as is that of the Pacific coast; and the *isotheral* line, or the curve of mean summer temperature of 8° of Humboldt, passes over the Isthmus. When this is extended into Africa it passes through the countries lying south of the Mediterranean, Algiers, Tunis, Barca, and Egypt, along lat. 30° N. In Asia it passes through Central Persia, Thibet, and China, and thence into the Chinese sea, north of the island of Formosa.

The curve of mean winter temperature, or *isochimenal* line of 70°, passes through the northern parts of Oaxaca and Tobasco, and the southern part of Vera Cruz, in lat. 18°; passes southward into Africa, through Sahara and Southern Nubia, thence along Arabia Felix through Hindostan in lat. 15° and at Tonquin, passes into the ocean about lat. 17°, indicating that the summer heat is that of latitude 12 degrees more northerly in Africa and Western Asia, and the winter heat that of its own latitudes even on large continents. In other words, it has a cooler summer and more moderate winter than similar latitudes, and it is this extreme equality of climate which gives to these lands the beauty and profusion of vegetation with which they are clothed.

The curve of mean annual temperature, or the *isothermal* line, of 75° passes through the Isthmus, through Southern Egypt and Arabia in latitude 25°, and Persia in latitude 28°, showing the mean temperature to be that of 12° more north in Central Asia. It is on the outside of the limits of the equatorial zone, and its productions are those of a tropical zone, which is an advantage this Isthmus possesses over any point hitherto selected further south, lying in the equatorial zone. Each isothermal zone has its peculiar zone of vegetation. These (25 in number) have been classified by Professor Schow.

The Isthmus is placed under the 15th region, or that of the cactus and pepper families, because these are the predominating ones found growing there. The mean temperature of this botanical region varies from 68° to 84° F., and includes among others the cultivated species: *Zea M. sorghum, jatropha, dioscorea, convolvulus, arracacha, marauta, musa, mangofera, amoma, psidium, cocos, carica, persica, bromelia, Anacardium, tamarindus, citrus, passiflora, theobroma, vanilla, coffea, saccharum, lycopersicum, capsicum, cajanus, arachis, opuntia, nicotiana,* and *gossypium.*

From the northern shore to the base of the Sierra on the south, the vegetation is that found arising from the alternating influences of heat and moisture. In the rainy season, the rivers which drain the Atlantic plains overflow their banks for a considerable distance, and disseminate over a vast extent of country a variety of soluble saline matter, with such animal and vegetable substances as are suspended in the water during that period. These borders, therefore, constantly increasing in richness, are densely studded with plants which exhibit a large and spongy cellular tissue; those which possess broadly expanded, soft leaves, furnished with a great number of cortical pores, or those whose growth is rapid, and which by depositing little oily or resinous matter are less liable to the deteriorating influences of constant humidity. Among these may be classed the cascalote, castarica, encina (live-oak), guanacaste, guayabo, huacillo, javicue, jobo, macaya, mangle, palo-baria, roble, sangre-draco, and the *crescentia cujete*, or Indian cup-tree.

On all the rivers are seen huge specimens of these most valuable trees of the equinoctial regions, mingled with a hundred varieties of *palmœ*, gracefully towering above plants of the most dense and impenetrable foliage, whose masses of verdure sweep the current at every sinuosity, and either thwart the efforts of the stream or deflect its course. Under these circumstances the view which is presented to the eye is often of the most enchanting nature. Numerically considered, the varieties of the palm are very great; but the diversity of its useful purposes is not less so. We find, for instance, one kind yielding substitutes for bread and yeast, another sugar and wine, a third oil and vinegar; a fourth milk and wax; a fifth resin and fruit; a sixth medicines and utensils; a seventh weapons and cordage; an eighth paper and clothing; and a ninth habitations and furniture.

Remote from the river margins, the limit of the periodic overflow is more particularly marked by the presence of plants which are of a fine and cellular tissue, and by trees of greater value, as the *swietenia mahogani*, the *cedrela odorata*, one or two varieties of the oak, "guapaque" (*ostrya mexicana*), the *lignum-vitæ*, "chico-zapote," "quiebra-hacha," and the "acacia;" the growth of all which, though more protracted than the vegetation of the bottom lands, is nevertheless favored by the peculiar adaptation of the soil and the predominance of silica. In a pecuniary point of view the value of these products is immeasurable, especially that which would result from the felling of mahogany and cedar alone. These trees, which often reach a diameter of five and six feet, are so abundant on the Atlantic slope that the Indians select only the trunks, which are oftentimes cut several feet above the ground to avoid the curl and twist of the grain. Notwithstanding the occasional shipments of wood from the Isthmus, there are still many trees the value of which has yet to be determined. These are generally timbers of great *specific gravity*, a circumstance which, considering the inefficient means of transportation, has hitherto prevented their introduction to market. Indeed, the abundance of these and other building timber of equivalent value, is such that the only limit which can be assigned to the supply they may yield is the demand for centuries to come.

Not less important in value, perhaps, is the *siphonia elastica*, or india-rubber tree, which is found in astonishing numbers throughout the forests that skirt the tributary streams. Its value, however, is so little appreciated there, that the gum is only gathered for foot-balls, or for some few medicinal purposes. The process of extracting the gum is accomplished by *tapping*, not *belting*, the tree. Two incisions are made through the bark, one

VEGETABLE PRODUCTIONS.

above the other, from the lower one of which flows a copious stream of milk-like juice, which, when collected in proper recipients, is speedily indurated by adding the juice of a vine, called by the Zapotecos *bejuco de joamole*, and always found coexistent with the india-rubber tree. By means of this process the *white* gum is produced. When the milk is simply left to congeal in the rays of the sun, the gum becomes dark. The fluid known as *caoutchoucine*, the specific gravity of which while in its liquid state is less than that of any other liquid known to chemists, but the vapor of which is so heavy that it may be poured from one vessel to another like water, is prepared from the juice of this tree in the laboratory, and is one of the best solvents for the rubber yet known. Taking half the number of trees found within an area of one-fourth of a square mile, on the Uspanapa River, as the basis of an estimate, and allowing none to grow on the Pacific plains, there would be found not less than 2,000,000 of india-rubber trees within the limits of the Isthmus, some of which yield four and five pounds of gum in a year. If from this prodigious number of trees, we suppose *one-half* only to be available, and that a single pound per tree per annum be the average yield, we should then have 1,000,000 of pounds, which, at the present value of forty cents, would realize the sum of $400,000 for this article alone.

Among the spontaneous products is the *bromelia pita*, or ixtle of the Isthmus, which differs in some respects from the *agave americana* of Europe, the *pulque de maguey* of Mexico, and the *agave sisalana* of Campeachy. Of this prolific plant there are numerous varieties, all yielding fibres which vary in quality from the coarsest hemp to the finest flax. Nor is the value of the plant diminished by its indifference to soil, climate, and season. The simplicity of its cultivation and the facility of extracting and preparing its products, render it of universal use. From it is fabricated thread and cordage, mats, bagging, and clothing, and the hammocks in which the natives are born, repose, and die. The fibres of the pita are sometimes employed in the manufacture of paper, its juice is used as a caustic for wounds, and its thorns serve the Indians for needles and pins. The point generally selected for its cultivation is a thick forest, from which the small undergrowth is removed by cutting and burning. The roots of the old plants are then set out, at a distance of five or six feet apart, and at the end of a year the leaves are cut and "rasped." When the pita is young its fibres are fine and white, but as it increases in age they become longer and coarser. In this manner it is easy to select the quality of fibre required. In a wild state the thorns are very numerous, but by cultivation they are diminished both in size and number, and in many instances there are none at all. Even with the imperfect instruments used in cleaning the leaves, four and five pounds of fibres per day is only a fair average for the labor of a man. At San Miguel Chimalapa and San Juan Guichicovi the cultivation of the ixtle is quite extensive. In 1831, according to the statements of Señor Iglesias, the ixtle plantations in the northern division numbered 1221.

Of the maize, frijoles, sugar, cacao, tobacco, coffee, and cotton raised on the Isthmus, it is difficult to speak in terms which might convey an adequate idea of the adaptation of the soil and climate to their cultivation, or the perfection to which they are susceptible of being brought.

This is the native country of maize, and upon the wet land, *milpas* (those subject to periodic overflow), the yield is two crops annually, each of which averages sixty bushels to the acre, and without other labor than the mere planting. Indeed, it is no uncommon sight to see the reaper and the sower in the same field. The lands usually selected, north of the Jaltepec, for milpas, are those which abound most in the palm, as being more easily cleared,—an operation which is performed by "girdling" the trees and burning the undergrowth. The planting is chiefly confided to the women and children, whose only implement is a pointed stick, with which a hole is made in the ground for the grains, which are then covered with the foot. On the margin of the Uspanapa, at some of the elevated points, *three* crops, each yielding *seventy* bushels to the acre, have been raised in a favorable year. In the central division of the Isthmus the bottom lands and borders of the streams are exclusively appropriated for its cultivation. To the east, in the valleys of the Rio del Corte and Chicapa, maize is grown in the same field with the tobacco, and on the south the broad plains of the Pacific, otherwise dry and heated, are dotted with frequent milpas, which relieve and refresh the eye. The cultivation there, however, is rendered somewhat more laborious by the necessity for irrigation, which is done by ditches from the neighboring streams. The ground is sometimes broken with a rude plough, and the maize hoed, in the absence of more perfect implements, with the bones of cattle.

The fecundity of the Mexican variety of maize is astonishing. Fertile lands usually afford a return of three or four hundred fold; even when the soil is sterile, the produce varies from sixty to eighty.

The general estimate for the Isthmus may be considered as one hundred and fifty fold. Of all the gramina cultivated by man, none is so unequal in its produce as this, varying so much according to season; and it is owing to this fact that famine so frequently arises. A proper rotation, and less dependence for food upon any one plant, obviate this unforeseen occurrence. Owing to its excessive yield, it is capable of becoming an article of great export.

The sugar-cane, though cultivated to a limited extent, except on one or two plantations (where there are mills for extracting the juice), is nevertheless of astonishing magnitude and richness; the stalks not unfrequently exhibiting *twenty-eight* joints, with a diameter ranging from two to three inches. It is even found growing wild in the valleys and *potreros*, and of a quality and luxuriance (according to Tadeo Ortiz) superior to that of the Antilles.

In the hands of an efficient planter, and with other care than the mere bounty of nature, it is not difficult to conceive the perfection and value to which the sugar-cane of the Isthmus might be brought, especially when we consider the adaptation of the soil and climate to its cultivation, the facilities of transporting it across the plains to the ports of the Pacific, and the close proximity of the markets of California. At Santa Cruz is an extensive mill, under the supervision of Don Antonio Mass, whose manufacture of sugar during the last year exceeded 160,000 lbs. There are also one or two horse-power presses near Guichicovi, which yield a considerable quantity of juice annually.

On the northern division, there are several mills and distilleries between Mina-titlan and Acayucam; but, like those of Guichicovi, their products are of an indifferent quality, notwithstanding the exceeding richness of the cane, and the abundant sources of water-power.

The cane may be cultivated generally up to the altitude of five thousand feet, and in some favorable exposures, even to six thousand five hundred feet Vera Cruz is a large export market for this article of produce.

Although the distribution of the plants of the Isthmus, as has been said, may be considered general, the *theobroma cacao* forms somewhat of an exception, and is not found south of the dividing ridge between the two oceans.

In the central sections at San Miguel Chimalapa, and at El Barrio, and Boca del Monte, some attention is paid to its cultivation; but the bulk of that grown on the Isthmus is north of the Jaltepec River, and on the lands east of the Coatzacoalcos, near the confines of Tobasco. Of this valuable spontaneous product, there are two varieties, one of which grows wild, and is little esteemed. The other, called "petaste," produced in considerable quantities near Huimangillo, has a delightful aromatic flavor, and is greatly preferred. This latter is grown from the seed, which is always sown under the shade of the *madre*, that the poisonous influence of the tree may prevent the destruction of the young plant by birds and insects. At the expiration of the fourth year from the original planting, the madre is cut down, and the cacao-tree left to take care of itself. In the fifth year it attains its full growth, and yields abundantly. The quality is said to be superior to that of Guayaquil or Maracaibo, and the prolific return which characterizes its cultivation is sure evidence of its importance and value. The lands east of the Coatzacoalcos seem particularly adapted to its growth.

The plantations of tobacco (the *nicotiana tabacum* of Linnæus) are both numerous and considerable, especially in the northern and central divisions of the Isthmus. That raised in the Chimalapas and on the uplands generally, is known by the name of "tabaco del monte." This variety is powerfully narcotic, coarse, and grows to a large size, the leaves averaging *thirty-*

three inches in length, and *fifteen* in breadth. Another kind, cultivated on the plains, and called "corral," is smaller, and of a flavor and quality which is said to be superior to the best *vuelta de abaja* of Cuba. On the plantations, near Jaltipan, the quantity raised is very considerable, and the natives understand very well the method of its production. With regard to the pecuniary results arising from an extensive culture of the tobacco of the Isthmus, it is only necessary to say that the soil is admirably adapted, and it can be grown equally well in all parts.

The land east of the Coatzacoalcos, and that which skirts the Mexican gulf, is characterized by the abundance of allspice (*myrtus pimenta*) disseminated over its surface. According to the calculations of Señor Ortiz, this fruit might be gathered annually to an amount of $50,000. Its cultivation is entirely neglected. Near Ventosa, on the Pacific plains, the cassia-tree (*C. fistula* of Linnæus) is somewhat plentiful, but the only use made of it is for occasional purposes of construction.

The banks of the Coatzacoalcos exhibit, in a wild state, the greatest abundance of *coffee*, and with few exceptions no pains are taken to cultivate it, although the quality is admitted to be very superior. This neglect may be readily accounted for in the universal preference which exists among the natives for chocolate. The only coffee plantation worthy of note is one on the island of Tacamichapa, opposite the village of Almagres.

The amount of *rice* cultivated on the Isthmus, compared with the quantity the land is susceptible of yielding, is exceedingly insignificant. At San Juan Guichicovi some attention is paid to the raising of a species of mountain rice; and in the potreros between the Coatzacoalcos and Tonala rivers the plantations are of considerable value. Tadeo Ortiz, referring to this portion of the Isthmus, says, "that which most particularly characterizes this privileged region, is the singular fact, that one single sowing of rice will yield successively two large crops without the slightest additional labor." Like the theobroma, it is not adapted for the Pacific plains.

The *cotton* plantations of the Isthmus are so trifling as scarcely to deserve the name, but the fitness of the soil and climate to

VEGETABLE PRODUCTIONS.

produce it are beyond question. There are two varieties, one of which, raised in the neighborhood of Mina-titlan, is not inferior in texture, whiteness, or length of staple, to the finest uplands of the Southern United States. With the single exception of Acayucam, there are no gins in the country, and as the seed is therefore separated by hand (a work which is tedious and protracted), the cultivation of cotton in other parts is necessarily small. At Santa Maria Chimalapa some attention is paid to its culture, and although the lands are incomparably rich, the yield does not exceed half a dozen bales per annum. The Pacific plains present many fine sites for its production, and it is not difficult to foresee the advantages which would result from an extensive cultivation of this staple. The other variety referred to, called *coyote*, is less white—often tinged with yellow, and in many respects very inferior. What would seem to favor the cultivation of cotton, is the sheltered condition of the table-lands and savannas, and the entire absence of the *army worm*, which so seriously damages the cotton crops of the Southern States. It is entirely unknown to the natives.

The enumeration of all the vegetable dyes found on the Isthmus, with all that might be said of the numerous varieties, would constitute matter for a well-filled volume on botany, rather than the general details of a statistical report. Many, nevertheless, deserve an especial notice either from the brilliant colors which they yield, or the pecuniary considerations involved in their growth and production. Among these may be classed the indigo trees, which are indigenous to Mexico. There are two varieties of *indigofera:* one grows in the wildest profusion throughout the southern portions, called "*añil cimarron*" (the *indigofera citisoyedes* of Lindley), and that of Guatimala (the *indigofera tinctoria* of Linnæus), which is extensively cultivated.

The method of extracting the dye is, however, very primitive, and in the few instances which were witnessed by us, mostly confided to the women, who put the branches of the plant into a large vat containing hot or lukewarm water, and after having stirred them for a sufficient time with a stick, the water (when sufficiently impregnated with the dye) is passed into pots or cups, where it is left until the solid part of the dye is deposited.

The water is then passed off and the residuum exposed to the sun or to the action of fire until it becomes hard. The great number of abandoned vats visible in various localities would seem to indicate a serious decrease in the indigo trade of the Isthmus.

The abundance of the "achote" (*bixa orellana*) which grows in all parts is not less worthy of attention. The process observed by the Indians in extracting the dye is exceedingly laborious. They simply rub the seed with their hands, which are previously dipped in oil. By this means the viscous substance that surrounds the seed and contains the coloring matter is removed. When this reaches the consistency of paste it is scraped from the hands and made into thin cakes, which are dried in the sun. This plant, from the luxuriance with which it grows, might furnish Arnotto in such quantities as to make it a profitable article of export. At Santa Maria Chimalapa some attention is paid to its cultivation, and it forms an important item in the productive industry of the place.

The growth of the *cæsalpinia crista* (Brazil-wood) and *hæmatoxylum campechianum* (logwood) is so great in every part of the Isthmus, that notwithstanding the well-known value of their dyes, they deserve an especial enumeration. In addition, there is also the Palo-moro (the *morus tinctoria* of Linnæus), called sometimes the "moral" and the "palo-amarillo," which yields a valuable yellow accessory coloring material, known to dyers as "old fustic." The dye is produced by grinding the wood and boiling the fibres in water over a slow fire. When an incision is made through the bark a cream-colored fluid exudes, to which certain medicinal virtues are ascribed by the Indians. With its usefulness as a dye, the wood combines great beauty and durability as a timber.

The variety of other dyewoods, especially those yielding tannin and material suitable for the manufacture of ink, is almost incredible; among these may be classed the "cascalote," the "uale," and the "guisachi," which are found in great abundance dispersed over various localities. The "ebano-verde" (*chloroxylum*) of the Pacific plains is somewhat remarkable as furnishing a brilliant green dye; and a valuable brown coloring matter is extracted from a variety of the vanilla growing throughout all the forests. Among the trees useful for the purposes of tanning, is the "guayabo" (*psidium pyriferum*), the "mangle-blanco" (*avicennia nitida*), the "guamuchi," and a vine called the "bejuco-amarillo."

In a commercial point of view, the vegetable gums and balsams are items of important consideration. In the central and southern districts, the abundance of the *myrosperum peruiferum*, yielding the balsam of Peru, and a bark which serves in treatment as a substitute for quinine, is astonishing. Not less worthy of note is the *styrax officinale* of Linnæus, the product of which is known as the liquid-amber gum. On the Atlantic plains the "palo-baria" supplies a valuable substitute for glue, and the numerous varieties of acacia furnish gum-arabic in the greatest profusion. The "cuapinol" (*catharto carpus*) is distinguished for the odorous gum which it distils. It is extensively used in the churches as incense, and the natives ascribe to it medicinal properties of the most miraculous character.

The *Sapindus Saponaria* grows throughout all the southern division, and forms an excellent substitute for soap; while the fibres of the plant (called by the Zapotecos *bequipe-bendi*) serve, from their intoxicating influence, a useful purpose in catching fish. The varieties of climbing-plants, especially those called "bejucos de agua," which encumber the foliage of the forests, are innumerable. They often serve, by the abundance of sweet cool water which they contain, to refresh, even more than the gushing streams that furrow the Isthmus, the Indian as he pants in the noon-day heat. The singular character of these plants seems sufficient to warrant a momentary trespass upon these pages, in order to describe one or two of the more important varieties. The "mondongo" or "tacalate-jaba" grows in all parts of the Isthmus, both upon low and high ground; it reaches a large size, sometimes more than a foot in diameter, and winds itself around trees in a grotesque manner like a huge serpent. This variety has a small leaf, and bears a bright-red flower in clusters with a single stamen. Another kind, "tachicon" (smaller than the preceding), grows nearly erect, is hard and durable, and bears a small white flower of delicious fragrance. A third kind, smaller still, called "parra," grows perfectly straight, has a light-colored, oval, serrated furzed leaf, and bears a white clustering flower, like the mondongo. A fourth variety, known as "chato," is also very erect; but, unlike the others, is flat. This furnishes a black fruit, growing in bunches like grapes, and ripens in October, November, and December.

The medicinal plants of the Isthmus present an innumerable variety, many of which have yet to find a name and place in the annals of botany. The *guaco*, celebrated for its astringent qualities, and as an antidote to the bites of serpents, is particularly abundant; as also the liquorice-root, the sarsaparilla, and vanilla; the *laurus-sassafras*, the *cubeba canina*, and a thousand other plants without names, and of a number not yet ascertained. The superior quality of the vanilla and sarsaparilla, found in almost every point of the Isthmus, and their incredible profusion of growth, cannot fail to prove a source of the most lucrative trade. Already the inhabitants cultivate them to some extent; but the amount under culture bears no comparison to that which grows wild in the dense forests.

In the production of fruits and leguminous plants, the Isthmus perhaps stands unrivalled; and it seems superfluous to enumerate, even incidentally, the different varieties which constitute either articles for food, or those deserving of especial culture and adapted for purposes of exportation. Yet many of them claim particular notice, either for their delicious flavor, abundant growth, or the nutritive qualities for which they are distinguished: among these we find the chico-zapote, lemoncillo, orange, chayote, cocoanut, lemon, pine-apple (sometimes reaching the enormous weight of fifteen pounds), melon, mamey, chiraymoya, citron, mango, banana, plantain, guava, and pomegranate.

At Tehuantepec, a native yam, very watery, but sweet and nutritious, grows in great abundance, and also an inferior variety of sweet potato, both of which might be raised in sufficient quantities to supply the place of the ordinary potato. On the Isthmus of Panama, a large yam of excellent quality (sometimes reaching forty and fifty pounds weight) is extensively raised. This might be introduced to great advantage on the Pacific plains;

and the esculents of Cuba would doubtless flourish in the fruitful soil of the Isthmus. Indeed, the country is capable of producing in the greatest profusion all kinds of native vegetable growth; but at present little more than enough is cultivated to supply the immediate wants of the inhabitants, whose agricultural pursuits are conducted in the most primitive manner, and who (singular as it may appear) are often driven, by their indolent habits, to the verge of famine and the extremes of suffering.

But when we reflect upon the productiveness of the soil, the salubrity of the climate, and the boundless character of the vegetation of the Isthmus, it is not difficult to see how great must be the reward which would crown the efforts of an industrious planter; nor is it inappropriate to conclude that a few energetic farmers, without much difficulty, could grow sufficient in a single year to supply the demands of a whole army of *employées*. To what extent the banana might be substituted as an article of food for the foreign laborers, is a consideration of no little importance, especially when it is known that on the same portion of land, and with the same quantity of labor, a much greater amount of nutritive substance can be produced than when planted with any kind of grain. Within eight months after planting, the banana begins to form clusters, and in the tenth or eleventh month of their growth, the fruit may be gathered. The green fruit is frequently cut in slices and dried in the sun, and being thus rendered friable, is reduced to powder, and serves the purposes of flour in many culinary preparations: it is also boiled, and cooked in a variety of ways. The facility with which this food is produced, gives it an advantage over every other alimentary substance in the same climate. The produce of the banana, as compared to that of wheat, is estimated as 133 to 1; and to potatoes, as 44 to 1.

A popular belief exists among foreigners, that the banana is unhealthy as an article of food, and that with persons not acclimated it is difficult of digestion. If the experience of the members of the survey (by whom it was indiscriminately used) may be considered as having any weight, this opinion with regard to the deleterious effects of the fruit would seem to need further confirmation.

VEGETABLE PRODUCTIONS.

The warm, humid valleys of the Gulf shore appear to be the natural position for the banana, where the fruit is occasionally eight inches in circumference, with a length of ten or twelve. Forty plants growing on a space of 1070 feet are calculated to furnish 4400 pounds of nutritive matter, a quantity above the acreable produce of any cereal crop. In other words, the same extent of ground under bananas, which will support fifty individuals, when under wheat, will only support two.

One of the peculiar productions of these latitudes is the treefern: its natural locality is at an elevation of 5000 feet, where the mean temperature is 66°. It is somewhat abundant between the Jaltepec and Sarabia rivers, and its trunk attains a diameter of between five and six inches. These arborescent ferns are singularly beautiful, from the depth of the green tint of the foliage and the graceful earing of the young fronds not yet unfolded, and which open out at the top of the tree. They are now confined within a narrow zone north and south of the equator on this hemisphere, and are the representatives of a large mass of fossil vegetation. Much of the woody matter of coal is made up of ancient tree-ferns.

In a country like Mexico, where the reproductions of nature are so rapid, it is but reasonable to suppose that there are corresponding elements of decay; nor is it affirmed that the Isthmus is entirely free from the destroying influences with which the regions of the tropics and the equator are usually so pregnant. But the effects arising from temperature, humidity, and the noxious character of the numerous insect tribes, are greatly modified by the abundance of such woods as are proof against their incursions. So far, therefore, as the immediate and necessary purposes of construction are concerned, there will be found no lack of durable timber on the Isthmus. Among these we may enumerate the guapaque, which may be considered first. In the Parroquia, at Tehuantepec, built by Cocijopi, last cacique of the Zapotecos, in 1530, the staircase is made of guapaque, which to this time exhibits no evidences of decay. Another instance of the durability of this valuable wood occurs at Boca del Monte, in the uprights of a little chapel, which have been buried in the ground for more than twenty-five years, and are still sound and perfect. In the construction of the Vera Cruz railroad, the cross-ties and sleepers are made of guapaque, and notwithstanding the exposed condition of the superstructure, the wood remains unchanged. Both mahogany and cedar are lasting timbers, as is satisfactorily proved by the age of the canoes, many of which are known to be more than forty years old. Of the value of the pine, oak, and cypress, it is, perhaps, sufficient to say that there are many of these trees (felled by the Spaniards) in a more or less perfect state of preservation, still lying in the Rio del Corte, where they serve to recall the faded glory of the naval arsenal at Havana. The castarica is also a valuable building timber, which possesses the merit of being indestructible by insects; and the macaya seems particularly adapted for the purposes of hydraulic construction. This latter tree is said to have the property of becoming petrified, in proof of which there are many now in that state, in the Arroyo de los Urgells', one of the tributaries of the Uspanapa, where they were felled in 1818, during the war of the Independencia, to obstruct the progress of the troops. The javicue, or jabi, also merits attention for its exceeding hardness and durability. This wood is incorruptible in water, and is useful for naval construction.

It is a matter of some regret that the limited time for the survey did not admit of any very accurate experiments to demonstrate the existence of the *teredo navalis* in the waters of the Pacific. But if the drift-wood on its shores (frequently imbedded in the sand, and submerged for months and years), without being attacked, be any criterion, there is reason to believe that the southern coast of the Isthmus is exempt from this scourge. In fact, no proof exists of their presence, and they are unknown to the natives. The *pholas dactylus* is, however, found in the waters of the Gulf shore.

Lastly, as the time of felling has an important influence on the durability of timber, it ought, of course, to be duly considered; but, without entering into the analysis of the rules observed, it is sufficient to state what those rules are, and the effects resulting from their non-observance. "The cutters proceed to fell the trees in the *wane* of the moon; for, however strange, it is a fact well known that the tree is then free from sap and sounder than when felled before the full." The rainy season is also regarded as an unfavorable time, on account of the migration of the insects, who then leave the soil and take refuge in drier places. In the report of Mr. W. H. Sidell to Colonel Hughes on the vegetation of the Isthmus of Panama, he says: "It is the universal opinion of the inhabitants of the country, that the quality of the timber is influenced by the time of cutting in regard to the age of the moon. It is a fact within my own observation, that no wood should be cut before the moon is full. I paid little attention to this popular belief until I found by experience that such is really the case. Insects will attack wood that will not be touched by them if cut after the full moon. This is very evident, if the wood is of a soft and spongy nature. Some vegetable productions will prove this in a most striking manner. If our common thatch be gathered under a new moon, it will rot in a few months, and be attacked by worms, while it will last from fifteen to twenty years if gathered at the full moon. Those who many years ago built houses in this country, are now most particular in selecting their woods after this manner."

In conclusion, it is utterly impossible, even at a momentary glance like this, not to be struck with the value of the boundless riches which nature has showered into the lap of the Isthmus; nor can we estimate the changes to be effected, or the benefits to result from their gathering, "when its soil shall become the emporium of commerce, and teem with wealth and abundance." Even the outline which we have traced presents but a feeble delineation of the golden harvest which is to be reaped in the future. Nevertheless, sufficient has doubtless been said to awaken attention to the natural resources of this favored region, and to show beyond question the present and prospective value of that which already exists.

BOTANICAL TABLES.

List of some of the most useful Trees and Plants found on the Isthmus of Tehuantepec.*

NO. I.—BUILDING, CONSTRUCTION, ETC.

Name.	No. of Varieties.	Average diameter in feet.	Location.
Almendrillo	1	$\frac{1}{2}$ to $\frac{5}{6}$	Pacific Plains. [north.
Brazil (*Cæsalpinia crista*)	2	1 to $1\frac{1}{2}$	" and sometimes on the
Caña-fistola (*Cassia-fistula*)	1	$\frac{1}{2}$ to $\frac{3}{4}$	Pacific Plains.
Caoba (*Swietenia mahogani*)	2	2 to 7	All parts of the Isthmus.
Caobilla (*Croton lucidum*)	1	1 to 5	Atlantic Plains.
Caracolillo (*Phascolus caracalla*)	1	1 to $1\frac{3}{4}$	Rio Tancochapa.
Cascalote	2	$\frac{3}{4}$ to 1	Borders of the Lagunas.
Castarica†	1	1 to 3	East of Coatzacoalcos.
Cedro fino (*Cedrela odorata*)	2	$1\frac{2}{3}$ to $2\frac{1}{2}$	Atlantic and Pacific Plains.
" blanco (*Cupressus thuyoides*)	1	$1\frac{1}{4}$ to 2	Chimalapas.
Ceiba (*Eriodendron anfractuosum*)	1	4 to 8	All parts of the Isthmus.
Céprés (*Cupressus sempervirens*)	1	$\frac{3}{4}$ to $1\frac{1}{4}$	Chimalapas.
Ebano (*Dyospyros lotus*)	2	1 to $1\frac{1}{2}$	Pacific Plains.
Encina blanca (*Quercus alba*)	1	$1\frac{1}{2}$ to $2\frac{1}{2}$	All parts.
" negro (*Q. virens*)	2	1 to 2	Atlantic Plains.
Fresno (*Fraxinus acuminata*)	1	$\frac{5}{6}$ to $1\frac{1}{4}$	Pacific Slope.
Gateado	1	1 to $1\frac{1}{2}$	"
Granadillo (*Brya ebanus*)	2	$\frac{5}{6}$ to $1\frac{1}{4}$	"
Guanacaste (*Lignum vitæ*)	2	1 to 3	Atlantic and Pacific Plains.
Guapaque† (*Ostrya mexicana*)	2	$1\frac{1}{2}$ to 3	" " "
Guayabo agrio (*Psidium pyriferum*)	1	1 to $1\frac{1}{4}$	All parts.
Guayacan (*Guaiacum sanctum*)	2	$\frac{5}{6}$ to $1\frac{1}{2}$	"
Guíra (*Crescentia cucurbitina*)	1	$\frac{1}{2}$ to 1	All parts.
Huacillo	1	$\frac{3}{4}$ to $1\frac{1}{2}$	East of Coatzacoalcos.
Jagua (*Genipa americana*)	2	1 to $1\frac{1}{2}$	" "
Javicue ó Jabi†	1	1 to 2	Atlantic Plains.
Jobo (*Spondias lutea?*)	2	1 to $1\frac{1}{2}$	" [Rivers.
Macaya‡ (*Arbor lapidescere?*)	1	1 to 3	Uspanapa and Tancochapa
Mesquite (*Acacia arabica*)	3	$\frac{3}{4}$ to $1\frac{1}{4}$	All parts.
Mangle (*Rhizophora mangle*)	2	1 to 2	Atlantic Plains.
Naranjo del monte (*Citrus vulgaris*)	2	$\frac{1}{2}$ to $\frac{3}{4}$	All parts.
Ocote, amarillo (*Pinus variabilis*)	2	1 to $2\frac{1}{2}$	Central Division.
" blanco (*P. strobus*)	1	1 to 3	Chimalapas.
Palma real (*Oresdoxa regia*)	1	$\frac{3}{4}$ to $1\frac{1}{4}$	Uspanapa River.
" yucateca (*Chamærops humilis*)	1	$\frac{1}{2}$ to 1	East of Coatzacoalcos.
" biscayol (Rattan)	2	$\frac{1}{12}$ to $\frac{1}{10}$	All parts.
Palo-baria (*Cordia gerascantoides*)	1	1 to 3	Atlantic Plains (east).
Palo-moro (*Morus tinctoria*)	2	$\frac{2}{3}$ to $\frac{5}{6}$	Atlantic and Pacific Plains.
Palo de rosa (*Pterocarpus santalinus*)	1	$\frac{1}{2}$ to $1\frac{1}{4}$	Pacific Plains.
Quiebra-hacha (*Hymenea*)	1	1 to $2\frac{1}{2}$	Atlantic Plains.
Roble-blanco (*Tecoma pentaphylla*)	3	1 to $1\frac{1}{2}$	All parts.
Sangre-draco (*Pterocarpus draco*)	2	$\frac{2}{3}$ to 1	"
Tamarindo (*Tamarindus occidentalis*)	2	1 to 2	Elevated sections.
Tepeguaje	1	$1\frac{1}{2}$ to 2	Pacific Plains.
Zapote (*Sapota mammosa*)	2	1 to $2\frac{1}{4}$	All parts.
Zapotillo (*Dyospyros obtusifolia*)	2	1 to $1\frac{1}{2}$	Pacific Plains.
Zopilote	1	1 to $1\frac{1}{2}$	"

* The names employed in this list are those most commonly in use on the Isthmus; and it has been deemed unnecessary to translate them into English.
† Indestructible by insects.   ‡ It is said to possess the property of becoming petrified.

VEGETABLE PRODUCTIONS.

NO. II.—DYES, ETC.

Name.	No. of Varieties.	Color.	Location.
Achote (*Bixa orellana*)	2	Scarlet.	All parts.
Añil cimarron (*Indigofera citisoydes*).	2	Indigo.	Pacific Plains.
" de Guatimala (*I. disperma*)	1	"	"
Azafron (*Carthamus tinctoria*)	1	Red & yel.	"
Brazil (*Cæsalpinia crista*)	2	Red.	Atlantic & Pacific Plains.
Campeche (*Hæmatoxylum campechianum*)	2	Blk. or purple.	Pacific Slope generally.
Cascalote	2	Black.	Borders of the Lagunas.
Ebano-verde (*Chloroxylum*)	1	Green.	Pacific Plains.
Güisache	1	Black.	Central Division.
Palo-amarillo (*Morus tinctoria*)	2	Yellow.	All parts.
Uale (*Genipa americana*)	1	Black.	Atlantic & Pacific Plains.
Vanilla (*Vanilla aromatica*)	1	Brown.	Central & northern parts.

NO. III.—TANNIN, ETC.

Name.	No. of Varieties.	Location.
Bejuco marillo	1	Pacific Plains.
Guamuchi	3	Central Division.
Guayabo (*Psidium pyriferum*)	2	All parts.
Mangle blanco (*Avicennia nitida*)	2	"

NO. IV.—GUMS, OILS, BALSAMS, ETC.

Name.	No. of Varieties.	Use.	Location.
Balsam del Peru quinquino (*Myrosperum peruiferum*).	1	Balsam Peru.	Central and southern portions.
Cedro blanco (*Cupressus thuyoides*)	1	Odorous gum.	Chimalapas.
Ciruela (*Spondias*)	1	Med. gum.	All parts.
Copalchi (*Hedwigia balsamifera*)	3	Varnish.	Pacific Plains. [tions.
Cuapinol (*Cathartocarpus*)	1	Frankincense.	Central & southern por-
Jaboncillo (*Sapindus saponaria*)	2	Soap.	Pacific Plains chiefly.
Liquidamber (*Styrax officinalis*)	1	Amber gum.	"
Mesquite (*Acacia arabica*)	2	Gum-arabic.	All parts.
Mulato	2	Med. gum.	"
Ocosote (*Arbor electrum ?*)	1	Amber.	Central Division.
Ocote, trementina (*Pinis religiosa?*)	2	Resin.	"
Palma corosa (*Cocos nucifera*)	1	Oil.	Atlantic Plains.
Palma crista (*Ricinus communis*).	2	"	"
Papaya (*Carica papaya*)	1	Cosmetic.	"
Palo-baria (*Cordia gerascantoides*)	1	Glue.	Atlantic Plains.
Sassafras (*Laurus sassafras*)	1	Balsam & oil.	Central Division.
Ule (*Siphonia elastica*)	1	India-rubber.	All parts.

VEGETABLE PRODUCTIONS. 199

NO. V.—CLOTH, CORDAGE, ETC.

Name.	No. of Varieties.	Quality.	Location.
Algodon (*Gossypium*)	2	Fine.	All parts.
Achote (*Bixa orellana*)	2	"	"
Ceibon (*Bombax pentandria*)	2	Excellent.	Southern parts.
Ixtle (*Bromelia sylvestris*)	3	"	All parts.
Masahua (*Hibiscus tiliaceus*)	2	"	"
Pita (*Furcræa fœtida*)	3	"	"
Maguey (*Agave americana*)	1	"	Central Division.
Palma sombrero (*Chamærops humilis*)	1	Fair.	Rio Sanapa.

NO. VI.—FRUITS, ETC.

Name.	No. of Varieties.	Location.
Anona (*Annona squamosa*)	2	Atlantic Plains chiefly.
Aguacate (*Persea gratissima*)	1	"
Chaymote	2	"
Chico-zapote (*Dyospyros obtusifolia*)	2	Atlantic and Pacific Plains.
Chayote (*Jatropha urens*)	1	Low lands, north side.
Chirimoya (*Annona cherimolia*)	1	East of Coatzacoalcos.
Chato-bejuco (*Coccoloba urifera*)	1	Forests on the Northern slope.
Cidra (*Citrus medica*)	2	All parts.
Ciruela coloradas y amarillas (*Spondias*)	1	
Coco (*Cocos nucifera*)	3	Atlantic and Pacific Plains.
Coroso (*C. crispa*)	2	"
Granado (*Punica granatum*)	2	"
Guayava (*Psidium pomiferum*)	1	Northern slope.
Higo-indios (*Opuntia var. es.*)	1	Pacific Plains.
Lima (*Citrus limeta*)	1	All parts.
Limon (*C. limonum*)	5	"
Lemoncillo (*Limonia trifoliatia*)	1	Gulf coast.
Mamey colorado (*Lucuma bomplandi*)	2	All parts.
Mamoncillo (*Melicocca bijuga*)	1	"
Mango (*Mangofera domestica*)	2	"
Melon (*Cucumis melo. var. es.*)		"
Nanche	1	Atlantic Plains.
Naranja de China (*C. aurantium*)	1	Santa M. Chimalapa.
" agria (*C. vulgario*)	1	All parts,
" del monte (*Id. var.*)	1	"
Name (*Discorea alata*)	1	East of Coatzacoalcos.
Papaw (*Asamina triloba*)	1	Atlantic Plains.
Papaya (*Carica papaya*)	1	"
Piña (*Bromelia ananas*)	3	All parts.
Plátano zapalot	1	"
" colorado (*Mus. rosacea*)	1	Uspanapa River.
" guineo (*M. sapientium*)	1	"
Platano dominico	1	Atlantic Plains.
Tamarindo (*Tamarindus occidentalis*)	2	All parts.
Tomato (*Lycopersicum*)	1	"
Toronja (*Malus citrus*)	1	Atlantic Plains.
Yucca (*Jatropha manihot*)	2	All parts.
Zapote, colorado (*Sap. mommosa*)	1	"
" negro (*Dyospyros obtusifolia*)	1	Pacific Plains.

VEGETABLE PRODUCTIONS.

NO. VII.—MISCELLANEOUS PRODUCTS.

Name.	No. of Varieties.	Quality.	Location.
Arroz (*Oryza sativa*)	1	Fair.	San Juan Guichicovi & Northern Division.
Cassia (*Cassia*)	2	Indifferent.	Pacific Plains.
Cacao (*Theobroma cacao*)	2	Excellent.	Atlantic Plains chiefly.
Café (*Coffea arabica*)	1	Fair.	Coatzacoalcos River.
Caña azucar (*Saccharum officinale*)	var. es.	Superior.	All parts.
Frijole (*Phaseolus vulgaris*)	2	"	Central Division.
Gengibre (*Amomum zingiber*)	1	Fair.	All parts.
Grana (*Cactus coccinelifer*)	var. es.	Superior.	Pacific slope (west).
Jicara (*Crescentia cujete*)	2	"	All parts.
Maize (*Zea mais*)	var. es.	Fair.	"
Pimienta (*Myrtus pimento*)	1	Excellent.	Southern part.
Tobaco corral (*Nicotiana tabacum*)	1	Superior.	East of Coatzacoalcos.
" del monte	var. es.	Coarse.	All parts.

ANIMALS.

The fauna of Mexico presents many of the characteristics of a district, where the natural distribution and locality of animals is less interfered with than in other places on this continent. The tropical exuberance of the vegetation, the uncleared condition of the ground, arising from the absence of agricultural operations, and the scattered population, leave the surface in the undisturbed possession of mammal, reptile, bird, and insect. There is here an abundance of reptile life, with the processes actively going on which diminish their excessive numbers. The countless myriads of insects threaten, by their prolific powers, to overrun the whole land, but the elevated hills of these districts afford the grand barrier to their distribution; they are confined to a zone of the air above which they do not travel, and into which they are pursued by the insectivora. Many of these animals will, no doubt, disappear upon clearing the ground; but still those useful will ever be retained, and serve to administer additional and peculiar aid to the wants of man, and add to the riches of the country by the exportation of the produce derived from their growth.

The domestic animals at present found on the Isthmus are, with rare exceptions, not indigenous, but were introduced from Europe in the sixteenth century, or at periods subsequent to the conquest of the country by the Spaniards. Some of these have since multiplied to a surprising extent, particularly horses, mules, and cattle, which are found in the greatest numbers throughout the inhabited parts.

The immense potreros which border all the principal streams on the northern division, furnish rich pastures of never-failing verdure for numerous herds. During the short season that these potreros are inundated, the cattle are driven to the more elevated savannas, remote from the river margins. The extensive table-lands in the central portions of the Isthmus, as well as the plains bordering the Pacific, also furnish abundance of excellent pasturage. Indeed, the whole country seems peculiarly well adapted to the raising of horned cattle. With little care on the part of their owners, they increase rapidly, grow to a large size, and have a remarkably sleek and well-favored appearance. Enjoying a range of the finest pastures in the world, they are usually in good condition, and make fair beef. But they seldom become very fat, especially on the Atlantic plains—a circumstance which may be reasonably attributed to the want of salt, and constant annoyance from the myriads of insects infesting the marsh and grazing lands. The inhabitants make very little use either of the flesh or the hides of their cattle; and milk is a luxury seldom enjoyed. This is a trait of the Indian character, to have forgotten, if it were ever known, the use of milk.

On some of the estates it is not uncommon to find five, ten, or even twenty thousand head of cattle, many of which roam over the prairies in a wild state, and when required for beef, or any other purpose, are secured by means of the *lasso*. The dexterity with which this instrument is used is truly astonishing—even women are familiar with the manner of throwing it, and children are early taught to lasso the chickens, dogs, and pigs, which, from their great numbers and perfect domestication, afford abundant sources for juvenile practice.

In slaughtering, the inhabitants are characterized by acts of the utmost cruelty. Sometimes a poor beast is permitted to remain for a week tied to a tree, without water or food, and often in such a manner as to prevent a recumbent posture: if in this position the animal becomes troublesome, quiet is enforced by severing the ham-strings with a *machéte*. Beef is cured by drying in the sun, being first cut into long, thin strips, which are rubbed with salt. This is called "carne seco."

No attention is paid to the breeding of cattle, as little value is set upon them; and the proprietor of the hacienda is often as poor amid his herds, as the peon whose life is spent in their care.

But, when the resources of the Isthmus shall have been developed by the establishment of proper roads, markets, and means of transport and communication, the immense droves which now roam wild in various localities will be found to constitute an important element of wealth.

The horses found in this portion of Mexico are of small size, and almost uniformly poor in flesh. They are, however, of great endurance, and possess much more spirit than is indicated in their looks. Comparatively, they are very intelligent, and under the guidance of the powerful Mexican bit are easily managed. The inhabitants employ them principally as saddle-beasts, though sometimes for draught, in which case the load is invariably attached to the animal's tail. As ridiculous and barbarous as this custom may appear, it is said to cause the horse no pain;* and if one may judge by the weight of the load, and the quiet manner in which the animal submits to the practice, this would seem to be the case. At all events, this primitive application of power is worth an engineer's remembrance, and may serve a useful purpose in some necessary contingency. But a small proportion of the horses are broke to use, the greater number being allowed to run untrained on the prairies. By attention to breeding, their size and quality could undoubtedly be much improved.

Nearly the entire transportation of the country is carried on by means of mules, which are small but very hardy, and peculiarly well adapted to the rough roads found in the more elevated sections. Their usual load is 225 lbs., but on the plains they often carry from 400 to 500. The sagacity manifested by them is truly surprising: in climbing the steep, rugged paths which traverse the mountain districts, often skirting the brink of precipices, where a single false step would be fatal, they not only tread with great caution, but also keep an eye to the load, which, from its bulky nature, is liable, by striking against a tree or other obstacle, to throw them off their balance. It matters not how much the burden projects on either side, the mule generally manages to keep clear of all obstructions, and will even stoop to pass under a jutting limb. The inhabitants employ but a

---

* It was one time the European mode to attach the plough to the tail of the beast.

small number of them for work; and the Mije Indians generally prefer transporting every thing on their own backs to burdening their beasts.

In the prosecution of such works as may be required for the opening of a line of communication across the Isthmus, the advantages accruing from the great number of horses, mules, and cattle can hardly be overrated. Good beeves may be had at prices ranging from four to six dollars per head; and for purposes of draught there is no lack of oxen. On the Pacific plains, where the surface of the country is sufficiently level to admit of wheeled vehicles, they are extensively employed—the yoke being secured by hide thongs to the horns.

On the less habitable portions of the Isthmus the numerous flies, ticks, and other vermin prove a serious annoyance to the larger domestic quadrupeds; and at some localities, especially Boca del Monte, the Vampyre bat (*Vampyrus spectrum*) exists in great numbers. Both men and animals are subject to its attacks, and nightly the latter suffer depletion from its fangs, frequently to such an extent as to be incapacitated for the next day's work. The Vampyre bleeds its victim with such extreme gentleness, and such is the noiseless flutter of its velvet wings, which stir the air to a soft and fanning breeze, that the sleeper is soothed into a calm, dream-like repose; while, unconscious of harm, he yields the vital fluid till he approaches the verge of delirium.

Goats are mostly confined to the southern division of the Isthmus, where they are found in considerable numbers. There are also a few sheep, which do not seem to thrive, partly from the want of care, but chiefly from the excessive elevation of temperature. The inhabitants, however, having no occasion for woollen garments, and the flesh being seldom eaten, sheep are a worthless possession. On the elevated spurs near San Juan Guichicovi there are a few Alpaca, or Peruvian sheep (*Auchenia*), notwithstanding it has been said that they are confined exclusively to portions of South America. Their existence on the Isthmus gives the appearance of truth to a tradition still preserved among the Mijes concerning the migration of their ancestry from Peru.

All the towns and villages literally swarm with dogs. These are generally small, wolfish-looking curs, totally devoid of courage, and only kept to alarm the inhabitants, by a series of the most piteous and cowardly yelps, on the approach of danger.

Among the more important quadrupeds found wild, is the Tapir, the Puma, or American Lion, the Jaguar, or Ounce (improperly called *tigre* by the inhabitants), the Ocelot, or small Tiger, the Wild-cat, Coyote, Peccary, or Wild-hog, Deer, Fox, Monkey, Coatimondi (*Nasua rufa*), Hare, Rabbit, Porcupine, Opossum, Armadillo, &c. In respect to size, the Tapir (*Tapirus americanus*), known also as the *Danta*, is most important, and is found chiefly in the central division of the Isthmus. This animal is not gregarious, and shuns the society of man—its chosen haunts being in the inmost recesses of the forest, and the inaccessible spots of the Cordillera. In color it is a deep brown, approaching to black, and the skin is so thick and tough as to resist a musket-ball; this, with a strong set of incisors, constitutes the animal's means of defence. The Tapir, however, being herbivorous, is of a peaceful disposition, and though possessed of great muscular strength, seldom attacks man or beast; but when closely cornered it defends itself vigorously.

The Jaguar, or "Tigre," is one of the most common, as also the most ferocious and destructive beasts of prey known to inhabit this portion of Mexico. Although considerably smaller than the African or Asiatic Tiger, its characteristics are identical with those species—preying upon all kinds of game, and not unfrequently on the larger domestic quadrupeds, as horses and cattle. It is, however, seldom known to attack a man, unless strongly impelled by hunger, or in self-defence. The Indians generally hold them in great dread, and will not traverse the forests alone where they are known to abound. The Juchitecos are in some respects an exception, as being more athletic and courageous than the other inhabitants of the Isthmus. They do not hesitate, even when alone, to attack a Tiger, and oftentimes with no other weapon than their machétes. On meeting, the Indian partially conceals his person by a blanket or cotton cloth pendent from the left arm, which is held horizontally before him. The Tiger, unable to distinguish between the "shadow and the substance," springs at the bulkiest part of the object, and as he passes, receives a dexterous blow across the neck from the machéte, which generally proves fatal. On some of the larger estates there is usually a "tigrero," or tiger-hunter, who is exclusively detailed to destroy the wild beasts that prey upon the herds of cattle. A number of dogs trained for the purpose are employed to worry the Tiger until he seeks refuge in a tree, where he is easily dispatched by a ball from the *escopéta* of the tigrero. A peculiarity which distinguishes these dogs is, that they never yelp on the scent, but follow as noiselessly as possible; otherwise the Tiger, being made aware of the approach, will leap from the trail for a great distance into a tree, and, concealing himself in the density of the foliage, escape. Some of their skins are exceedingly beautiful, the ground color being of a pale brownish yellow, variegated on the upper part of the body by dark oblong streaks, while the thighs and extremities are similarly marked with spots of black.

The Puma (*Felis discolor*) is also quite common. This animal is somewhat larger than the Tiger, but less destructive, generally preying upon smaller individuals. In the immense wilderness which intervenes between the settled portions of the country, both Tigers and Lions are surprisingly numerous, and roam un-molested throughout the dark, dense forest.

The Ocelote (*Felis pardalis*) differs but little from the Jaguar, except in point of size, and is found in great numbers. The same may be said of the Wild-cat.

The Coyoto, which seems to be peculiar to Mexico, and very numerous on the Isthmus, is thus quaintly described by the Abbé Clavigero: "It is a wild beast, voracious like the wolf, cunning like the fox, in form like the dog, and in some quali-ties like the jackal. It is less than the wolf, and almost the size of a mastiff, but slenderer. It has yellow, sparkling eyes, small ears, pointed and erect, a blackish snout, strong limbs, and its feet armed with large crooked nails. Its tail is thick and heavy, and its skin a mixture of black, brown, and white. Its voice hath both the howl of the wolf and the bark of the dog. The Coyoto is one of the most common quadrupeds of Mexico, and the most destructive to the flocks. It invades a sheepfold, and when it cannot find a lamb to carry off, it seizes a sheep by the neck with its teeth, and coupling with it, and beating it on the rump with its tail, conducts it where it pleases. It pursues the deer, and sometimes attacks even men. In flight it does nothing but trot; but its trot is so lively and swift, that a horse at the gallop can hardly overtake it."

Deer are found in great multitudes in all sections, and serve as an abundant source of prey for the numerous voracious animals which infest the country.

The Coatimondi somewhat resembles the racoon both in size and general appearance, but is easily distinguished from it by the elongation of its snout, with which it roots up the earth in search of ground-worms, &c. It is, however, sometimes known to prey upon smaller animals; and is generally found on the trees, where it has greater facilities for obtaining food and is less exposed to danger. Its flesh is much prized by the Indians, who represent it as being sweet and nutritious.

The Isthmus abounds in hares, rabbits, and squirrels, of almost every species; and on the elevated table-lands there is a large hare twice the size of the ordinary rabbit, which runs with incredible swiftness, and is said to be very fine eating.

The Peccary is very common in all parts, especially on the borders of the rivers, where the numerous varieties of palm furnish them with great quantities of food. They are also found in the uninhabited districts of the central division in great numbers; and, besides yielding a sweet and juicy meat, they serve a useful purpose by destroying the snakes which infest the forests. Ordinarily, the Peccary is as large as a well-grown pig of six months, very active, and apt to be dangerous when wounded. Its shape varies considerably from the domestic hog, having a very narrow head, small eyes and ears, high contracted withers, and the back sloping rapidly to the hind quarters, which are small and thin. The tail is exceedingly short, being nothing more in fact than a fleshy protuberance, concealed by long coarse hair, colored like the quills of the porcupine. A distinguishing feature in this animal is a gland on the back, from which a fetid secretion is exuded. Immediately after killing the

Peccary this gland should be completely removed, otherwise the whole flesh becomes infected with a poisonous putrescence, from which is supposed to originate many of the disgusting cutaneous diseases visible among the poorer classes.

The monkey tribes next claim attention, not only from their numerous varieties, but because they serve, by their droll mimicries and sportive gambols, to enliven the beauteous scenery of the mountains and river margins. Conspicuous among them are the Spider monkey (*Ateles paniscus*), the Preacher (*Mycetes beelzebub*), and the Howling monkey (*M. ursinus*). The cries of the latter kind resound throughout the forests, startling its echoes like the roar of some monstrous beast. The Spider monkeys generally associate together in great numbers, and assail those who disturb them in their haunts with a shower of dry or withered sticks broken from the trees: indeed, no one in passing a group of these singular creatures is entirely free from the danger of being struck by their missiles. The Preacher monkey (so called from its ludicrous imitation of a ranting orator, both in gesture and vehemence of expression) is somewhat interesting, and often serves to amuse the traveller in the loitering journeys of this portion of the republic.

The inhabitants make but little use either of the skins or furs of the wild animals found here, though many of them are of considerable value. That of the Tiger is particularly beautiful, and the hunter and trapper might realize amid the wilds of Tehuantepec a handsome return for their captures.

It has been truly observed, that as Africa is the country of beasts, so Mexico is the country of birds. This is especially true of the southern provinces; and among the almost endless varieties peculiar to the Isthmus, a large proportion of them are valuable either for the food they furnish, the beautiful plumage in which they are decked, or the sweet songs they pour forth in the sylvan bowers of the primeval forest.

Among the RAPTORES, or birds of prey, is the Eagle, Vulture, Hawk, Buzzard, Owl, &c. Of the former, there are several varieties, including the White-headed sea-eagle (*Haliætus leucocephalus*), which is very common on the Pacific coast. Of the VULTURIDÆ family we may mention the King-vulture (*Sarcoramphus papa*), the largest and most beautiful bird of its species, as also the Caracara of the genus *Polyborus*. The hawks and owls likewise reckon a numerous variety; but perhaps the most useful of all the Raptorial birds are the Buzzards, which are emphatically nature's scavengers, disposing of the putrid animal matter that would otherwise infect the atmosphere.

Of the PASSERINE class is the Crow, Blackbird, Bluejay, Kingbird, Scissor-tail (*Milvulus forficatus*), Mexican robin, Red-breasted thrush, Magpie, Mexican goldfinch, Shore-lark, Rice-bird, Cowbunting, Bullocks' hang-nests, Baltimore oriole, Peewee tyrant, Livid red-bird, Mexican red-bird, Worm-eating warbler, Humming-bird, Red-eyed fly-catcher, &c., &c. The Humming-birds are worthy of particular note on account of the transcendent beauty of some of the species. The genus of Orioles is also conspicuous among the beautiful birds of this region.

The SCANSORIAL birds constitute a very interesting class, among which is the Macaw, Paroquet, Lory, Carinated toucan, Woodpecker, Trogon, &c. With the former may be included the *Huacamaya* and the Blue and Yellow Macaw, celebrated for their brilliant and variegated plumage. There are also several species of both Paroquets and Lories; the latter associate in large flocks, often of many thousands, and, when perched upon the trees, their gorgeous plumage contrasting with the deep-green of the foliage, their appearance is extremely beautiful. The Toucans, which are quite numerous, are not the least interesting of this class of birds. Their enormous bills, which nearly equal in size the body itself, give them a most singular and uncouth appearance. They are easily tamed, and become exceedingly familiar and playful, practising a great variety of amusing feats.

But perhaps the most important class of birds in the Isthmus are the GALLINACÆ. The most numerous of this class are, the Wild turkey, Crested curassow, Partridge, *Chachalaca*, Tinamou, Quail, Pigeon, and Dove; all of which are found in great abundance through all parts of the country. The Crested curassow is a magnificent game-bird: it approaches the Turkey in size, and is easily domesticated, when it becomes very tame. Its plumage is of a deep, shining black color, reflecting purple and green shades; and the crest, which it can elevate or depress at pleasure, is composed of twisted black feathers, narrow at the base and broad at the tip. The females have a smaller crest, and their feathers are more dull. They associate in small flocks, build their nests in trees, and live on buds and fruits.

In the dense forests which skirt the Jaltepec River on the south, both the Wild Turkey and Curassow are surprisingly numerous, and have so little fear of man, that the Indians frequently kill them by means of stones or other missiles. The *Chachalaca* is about the size of a common fowl, and its flesh is even more delicate and nutritious. The cry of this bird is extremely harsh and disagreeable.

The GRALLATORIAL birds, though not the most useful, are by no means the least numerous class found here. On all the principal rivers, lakes, and marshes, we find immense flocks of these birds, including the Flamingo, Bittern, Heron, Jacana, Curlew, Teru-tero, Sand-piper, &c.; of most of which there are numerous species.

The PALMIPEDES also constitute a numerous class, embracing the Pelican, Duck, Gannet, *Torcaza*, *Pico real*, *Orilla*, Wild Goose, Frigate-bird, &c., &c. Ducks are very numerous in all the streams of any size, and present a number of species, including the Black Duck, Muscovy Duck, and Blue-winged Teal.

It will be seen from this hasty glance at the birds of the Isthmus, that this country presents a rich field for the investigations of the ornithologist; and it is to those professionally skilled in this branch of zoology that we must leave the enumeration and detailed description of the immense variety of birds inhabiting it.

Of REPTILES, we find the Tortoise, Alligator, Turtle, Lizard, Iguana, Rattlesnake, *Coralillo*, *Nojaca*, *Anchan*, *Jicotea*, *Colahuesa*, *Biber de sangre*, &c., &c. Alligators are numerous in all the principal streams on the Isthmus, even far up in the mountains, but are found in much greater numbers, and of a larger size, near the sea-coast. At daybreak these monsters emerge from the water and creep slowly to the shore, on which they compose themselves for a nap, by shutting their eyes and opening their huge jaws. As the sun rises the flies swarm into the inviting thorax, and revel for a while in undisturbed security, until the Alligator is satisfied that his "trap" is full, when he shuts the ponderous door, and opens his eyes as composedly as if nothing had happened.

Several species of Turtle are found both on the Gulf and Pacific coast, including the Green Turtle, whose flesh is so much esteemed as a wholesome and delicious food. There are also numerous species of Land Tortoises. A variety common in the lagoons bordering the Pacific coast are much valued for their shells; the combs manufactured from them by the natives are very beautiful. The Lizards present an almost endless variety. The species known as the Moloch Lizard (*Moloch horridus*), which are occasionally met with, are a foot in length, armed with two horns, and completely covered with small irregular scales, to which are attached large conical acute spines of a horny substance, altogether giving them a very ferocious appearance. The Iguana (*I. tuberculata*) is a genus of reptiles common on the Isthmus. It somewhat resembles in form and appearance the common lizard, being principally distinguished by a long flap or fold of skin under the throat, and a dentated crest along the back. It attains a great size, being from two to four feet in length. It is generally found in the trees bordering the streams, and when alarmed takes to the water, displaying on these occasions great activity. As an article of food, this animal is esteemed a great delicacy. It is the representative of a large class of fossils found in the upper secondary and tertiary beds, the species of which are now extinct.

The family of serpents constitutes a remarkable exception to the general fecundity which characterizes the developments of the animal kingdom in this country. Though there are numerous species of these reptiles, many of which are poisonous, yet the number belonging to each individual species is very limited, a fact which may be attributed to a variety of causes. In the central and southern divisions of the Isthmus an important agent in the destruction of reptiles of every description is fire, which annually sweeps over the prairies, burning every thing in its range. The numerous birds of prey also destroy many serpents; and on the Atlantic plains their numbers are reduced by the periodic overflow of extensive tracts of country. They are, perhaps, most numerous through that portion of the country lying immediately south of the Jaltepec River, where they are not exposed to the ravages of fire or water. The inhabitants of the country, though traversing it in every direction with their feet and limbs exposed, are seldom bitten.

Excellent fish are found in great profusion in all the rivers and arroyos that drain the slopes of the Cordillera, particularly in the smaller streams. In most of the larger ones there are many varieties of good size and fine quality; indeed, fish constitutes an important item of food for the inhabitants. Those living at Santa Maria Chimalapa, having but few domestic animals and no means of killing game, subsist almost entirely upon the fish obtained from the Rio del Corte. These are taken in such numbers, that they are salted and transported to supply the towns of the central division.

A species of vine known by botanists as the *Sapindus Saponaria* is used in catching fish. The fibres of this plant, when beaten and strewn on the water, exercise an intoxicating influence, which causes the fish to rise stupefied to the surface, where they are readily taken. This mode of fishing, although prohibited under severe penalties, is, nevertheless, extensively practised by the natives.

The great abundance of fish may be inferred from the immense numbers of aquatic birds which subsist upon them. Indeed there is, perhaps, no country in the world, situate within the same parallels of latitude, that produces an equivalent quantity and variety of fish and wild game as the Isthmus.

We must not, however, close this description of the animal productions of this region without glancing at the numerous insect tribes, some species of which, on account of their immense numbers and peculiarly blood-thirsty character, are deserving of particular notice. Of the more troublesome insects, bugs, spiders, &c., we may mention the Musquito or *Zancudo*, *Rodador*,* *Broca*, *Talaja*, *Tick*, *Garrapata*, *Pinolillo*, *Chigoe*, *Moyaquil*, Flea, Ant, Centipede, Scorpion, Tarantula, &c. Fortunately this formidable list of noxious insects is not fully represented at

---

* *Rodador* signifies "vagabond."

any one locality on the Isthmus. On the Atlantic plains Musquitos are very numerous, particularly on the low lands bordering the streams, where the dense foliage affords them protection from the winds and rains; but wherever the country is cleared up to any extent, so as to give the air free circulation, they are not reproduced so abundantly. The villages being uniformly located on elevated ground but partially sheltered by trees, the inhabitants experience very little inconvenience from these insects. Going southerly, the Musquitoes mostly disappear at the Jaltepec River, and in their place we have the Rodadors, or Buffalo Gnats, which are very numerous between this river and the plains of Xochiapa. South of these plains there are no Rodadors or Musquitoes, but more or less Garrapatas, Chigoes, Fleas, Centipedes, Scorpions, &c.

The Rodadors, though confined to less than one-third the breadth of the Isthmus, are exceedingly troublesome, their bites being more poisonous than that of the Musquito, and swarming in such immense numbers that it is very difficult guarding against their attacks. The inhabitants of the country, however, seem to disregard their bites altogether. This insect possesses one redeeming quality not exhibited by the Musquitoes, inasmuch as it suspends offensive operations during the night: it is a singular fact, that only the females exhibit these biting propensities. The Chaquiste is a species of gnat, smaller than the Rodador; and the *Gegin* is a still smaller variety, found only on the Gulf and Pacific coasts. The Garrapatas are a very large species of tick, which are particularly troublesome to horses, and are common on all parts of the Isthmus. The Pinolillo is a diminutive variety of the same species. The Chigoe (*Pulex penetrans*) is a very troublesome insect. It is an extremely small, black flea, which usually attacks the feet, insinuating itself under the skin so gently as not to be noticed, where, if not soon removed, it raises a numerous progeny, and if neglected for a long time, sometimes produces incurable ulcers. A most frightful case came under our notice while on the Isthmus in the person of a gray-headed Indian, who had been afflicted with it for more than twenty years; in him it was accompanied by Elephantiasis. His legs were swollen to more than three times their usual size, the skin leprous, the feet awfully distorted and looking like a sponge. There is little danger from the attacks of these insects if the feet are always covered.

The Moyaquil, commonly found on the leaves of a species of wild plantain growing in the country, is a worm which often proves a source of great annoyance to both men and animals. So minute are its dimensions, and such is the delicate nature of its operations, that it penetrates the flesh unperceived. There it gradually increases in size and vigor until it forms a protuberance which, if left to itself, becomes a painful ulcer: the worm in the mean time bedding itself more deeply until it penetrates the bone, from which it is exceedingly difficult of extraction without the aid of surgical instruments. They are, however, readily removed at an early stage by an external application of a little resin, derived from certain trees common in the forests. The oil of tobacco is also used as a remedy, and fire is sometimes employed to kill them. Fortunately the Moyaquil is confined to a few localities of small extent.

The *Broca* is a small insect which often does great mischief by boring into barrels and other wooden vessels containing sweets, thus allowing their contents to escape. The usual remedy against their incursions is to envelop the barrels with a tarred coat of paper.

The numerous well-beaten paths that traverse the country, bear testimony to the presence of ants, some of the larger species of which carry a kernel of corn with ease. A small variety of white ants deserve particular mention, as being the principal agents in the destruction of timber. Their nests are usually built of clay and leaves, adhering to the trunks and branches of trees. They always work under cover, and destroy the inner portions of the wood, leaving only a thin shell. In this manner their movements are unperceived, and it is difficult to detect the locality and extent of their depredations. They always travel under covered passages formed of clay, by which they are entirely shielded from observation. Several of the more valuable species of timber are exempt from the attacks of these insects (see Vegetable Productions, p. 194).

The Cochineal insect (*Coccus cacti*), so celebrated for the valuable and brilliant dye which it yields, is found on the Pacific coast, where the *Cactus coccinellifer*, from which it derives its nourishment, grows in great abundance. Formerly this insect was reared with care, and formed a valuable article of commerce until the discovery of French chemical dyes. Its culture was almost exclusively confined to the State of Oaxaca, and was a source of great profit. Lately, however, owing to the substitution of chemical equivalents, its value has been so much reduced as not to justify the great expenditure of time and labor required in its production. Indeed it may be well to mention, that in the year succeeding the discovery and use of the substitutes referred to, the price of cochineal in Oaxaca fell from three dollars to fifty cents per pound; the consequence was a universal bankruptcy, from the effects of which the State has not yet recovered.

The following is the method of cultivating the plant in the district of Oaxaca: The plantations are called *nopaleros*, and the female insects, which are wingless, are placed (when with young) in small numbers upon different parts of the cactus. This is called sowing. In this manner they increase rapidly in size and numbers for four or five months, when the harvest commences, and the insects are swept off with a soft brush (generally a deer's tail) by the Indian women, who often sit for hours under a single nopal plant, and kill them by scalding water, or by powerful vapors, which latter method, though more expensive and difficult, enhances their value, by preserving the powdery substance untouched. It requires about 70,000 of these insects to make the weight of a pound.

A species of honey-bee is found in some parts of the country in surprising numbers. They are smaller than the ordinary *Apis mellifica* of other countries, and stingless. Their nests are usually constructed in hollow trees, and such is the prolific result of their labors in the flowery fields of the Isthmus, that the Indians have been known to gather ten or twelve gallons of honey in a day. The quality of this honey is somewhat inferior to that of the domestic bee. The quantity of wax produced by this class of insects on the Isthmus is prodigiously great, and in connection with the honey gathered by them would doubtless prove a lucrative source of trade. At San Miguel Chimalapa, this branch already constitutes an important occupation of the people, who occasionally send to the large towns on the Pacific coast several hundred pounds of wax.

Among the numerous interesting *Mollusca* of this region is the *Aplysia depilans*, called by the ancients *lepus marinus*, and celebrated in history as furnishing the purple dye of vaunted Tyre. This shell-fish, from its limited distribution and extreme rarity, has been regarded by some naturalists as fabulous; but its existence on the shores of the Pacific coast is clearly beyond question. There the Mollusca is found in great numbers on the rocky points, and is extensively employed by the Indians to dye a kind of coarse thread, called *caracol*, from the local name of the animal. At the falling of the tide it is found adhering to the rocks, from which it is easily gathered. By blowing into the shell the animal contracts itself closely, and exudes an acrid liquid, extremely fetid, with which the skeins of thread are moistened to saturation, and subsequently washed with soap and water, when they become a permanent purple color. This operation of dyeing is said to strengthen the thread greatly, and to protect it from the effects of rot. It is manufactured to some extent by the Huave Indians, who find a ready sale for it in Tehuantepec. Besides the *Aplysia*, and the *murex purpura* (also found on the Pacific shores), there are a hundred objects of equal interest, the particular notice of which is necessarily precluded by the admission of more essential points. But it will scarcely be necessary to say as a concluding reference to this subject, that the fauna of the Isthmus, as a whole, presents a rich and boundless field either for the realization of pecuniary results, or for scientific investigation.

INHABITANTS.

The Isthmus of Tehuantepec comprises within its limits a mixed and heterogeneous population (as nearly as can be ascertained) of 61,000, consisting of *Europeans*, *Creoles*, *Mestizos*, *Indians*, *Mulattoes*, *Zambos*, and *Negroes*.

The *European* portion, numerically considered, is exceedingly insignificant; embracing only a small remnant of French colonists, with a few German adventurers, and some old Spanish settlers, dispersed over various localities. Their influence, however, is extensive; and to their energy is due the few evidences of civilization which exist. They control almost the entire trade of the Isthmus, and with few exceptions are the only mechanics and tradesmen to be found. Their houses are characterized by comfort and neatness, and the people themselves by the utmost hospitality to strangers.

The *Creoles* (the descendants of the Conquistadores and other Europeans) compose the native white population, and are somewhat more numerous. On the southern portion of the Isthmus, where they principally reside, they are found holding all the civil and military appointments; in the exercise of which, the power and prerogatives incident to official position are often abused to the exclusion of right and justice. Although the landed wealth of the country is mostly in their hands, they are far from being individually rich; and there is, perhaps, no social organization in which the extremes of wealth and the extremes of poverty so often meet. The difference in color is made the criterion of respectability; and a fair complexion is deemed a gift which makes honest labor a shame and a degradation. Under these circumstances, indolence and the gaming-table not unfrequently conspire to render the poverty of the creole greater than that of the peon. As a general rule, however, they are hospitable and kind, but effeminate in character, and live without much regard for the obligations of strict morality. With few exceptions, they exclusively possess the little amount of learning which is disseminated over the Isthmus—a circumstance that helps to define, with rigid accuracy, the boundaries of social distinction.

The *Mestizos*, in point of influence, may be justly considered next; the more especially "where rank depends more on the complexion than on endowments, and where almost every shade has its limits defined by terms which, though apparently only expressing the color, in reality express the rank of the individual." This division of the inhabitants has become, through the various attempts to colonize the Isthmus, an important part of its population, and constitute what may be appropriately denominated the middle class. As such, many of them are prominent men, and enjoy the advantages of comparative wealth and education. The Mestizos are scattered over almost all parts of the Isthmus, and comprise the *mayor domos*, the *mayorales* of the haciendas, the *arrieros* of the mule trains, and the under-officials of the custom-house, and of the municipal police. They are characterized by habits of industry, but not of strict sobriety. They are cruel and revengeful in their disposition, and exceedingly jealous of strangers. A peculiarity which marks this portion of the population is, that with few exceptions they are all of illegitimate birth; and the instance is exceedingly rare, where the Mestizo can point with certainty to the record of his father's marriage: still, for all this, he prides himself on the respectability of his ancestry, and reaps, as the reward of his "glory and shame," a fair and undisputed division of the paternal estate. This fact, coupled with the mutual affection always found subsisting between parents and their offspring, tends greatly to compensate for the wrongs of illicit love and the shame of an unchaste life.

The *Indians*, who are by far the most numerous portion of the inhabitants, comprehend the remnants of various once powerful tribes, which, notwithstanding the changes and vicissitudes that have marked their condition since the days of the Conquest, still exhibit distinctive characteristics sufficient to identify the sources from which they originally sprung. Among these are the *Aztecs*, *Agualulcos*, *Mijes*, *Zoques*, *Zapotecos*, and *Huaves*. These are distributed over the country in a manner which corresponds somewhat with its peculiar topographical divisions.

On the northern part of the Isthmus, within the intendancy of Vera Cruz, and extending as far south as Mt. Encantada (beyond which, to the Rio Sarabia, a broad belt of uninhabited country intervenes), are found the Aztecs and Agualulcos. The latter, however, are confined to the country east of the Coatzacoalcos, in the towns of Ishuatlan, Moloacan, Sanapa, Tecominoacan, and Mecatepec, with their neighboring ranchos. It is said that the Indians residing at Tesistepec, and in the villages in the vicinity of the sea-coast near San Martin, speak a language somewhat different from those mentioned above; but as their main characteristics are identical, it seems scarcely necessary to make a distinction. Indeed, whatever peculiarities may have existed in the idiomatic structure of the native languages of the Isthmus, it is certain that they are now little else than mere ill-spoken dialects, replete with corrupt and broken sentences of Spanish. Within a comparatively few years the priests have ceased to perform the offices of the church in the native tongue; and to this cause, together with that of the introduction of Christian names, of foreign habits, and of animals and plants not indigenous to the Isthmus (for which no corresponding terms were substituted), must be attributed the countless innovations that have been made.

In their persons the Indians are somewhat below the medium stature, but squarely built, and of great muscular strength, being often able to support a weight of from one hundred and fifty to two hundred and fifty pounds on their shoulders for several hours, exposed to the rays of the hottest summer sun. They are copper-colored, with smooth, coarse hair, small beard, diminutive eyes, prominent cheek-bones, low, narrow forehead, aquiline features, white teeth, thick lips, and a gentle expression of mouth, strongly contracted with a melancholic and severe look. The women, on the other hand, are less strongly built, and in some instances beautiful and well proportioned—a beauty which is enhanced by their devotion to home, and the natural grace of their carriage. Their movements are quick and mercurial, and their manners are characterized by shyness rather than modesty.

The *Abbé Clavigero*, in his excellent work on Mexico, says, in reference to the physical character of the Indians, that "there is scarcely a nation perhaps on earth in which there are fewer persons deformed; and it would be more difficult to find a single hump-backed, lame, or squint-eyed man amongst a thousand Mexicans, than among any hundred of any other nation." This assertion is literally true of the natives on the Isthmus. In their habits they are exceedingly simple, and their chief subsistence consists of vegetable food; but they are inveterate drunkards, and their passion for intoxicating liquors is carried to the greatest excess. When not under the influence of drink they are grave and thoughtful—a gravity which is particularly remarkable in Indian children. Their senses are exceedingly acute, especially that of sight, and their constitutions, notwithstanding habitual inebriation, sound, and their health robust. As a general rule, they are indifferent to advantages, and little inclined to work; but, from the natural docility of their character, it seems only reasonable to infer that under better and brighter circumstances they would become both useful and industrious. Every man and boy wears a *machéte*, and the facility and dexterity of its use is not a little surprising. It serves as a weapon for defence, an instrument for killing beef, an axe for cutting wood, and a knife for eating, &c. As axemen, to perform the grubbing and clearing on the route of the proposed railroad, their services will be found invaluable.

If the habits and manners of the Indians are simple, their mode of living is not less so; and their freedom from ordinary diseases is as much due to their abstemiousness as to the salubrity of the climate. Maize, which is the chief object of cultivation, is also a prominent article of food. This is manufactured by the women into cakes about eight inches in diameter, and of exceeding thinness, the grains being steeped in a weak solution of lime and water to render them soft and swollen; after which they are ground into paste on a coarse-grained stone for the purpose, called a *metate*. The cake is then beaten with the hand to make it thin, and when seasoned with a little salt, or colored with the viscous substance of the *Achote*, laid on a shallow plate of clay to bake. In this form they are eaten hot, and called *tortillas*. For distant journeys, &c., a more durable species, baked crisp and dry, called *tote-postle*, and somewhat analogous to sea-biscuit, is frequently made. On feast-days and such like occasions, these are sometimes made of the purple grains of the maize, and enriched by the addition of a few *frijoles*. Besides this primitive bread, they make from the maize a gruel called *atole*, which, when sweetened with wild honey, or *panela*, is an agreeable and salutary food. Next to maize, the vegetables most in use are the *cacao* and the *frijole;* of the former (especially from a kind called *petaste*, which has a full aromatic flavor) they make the delightful beverage of chocolate, while the latter, from its richness, serves in many instances the place of animal food. Indeed, in a comparative point of view, their consumption of flesh-meat is exceedingly limited; even eggs, of which they have an abundance, are seldom eaten, except those of the turtle and the *iguana*. In almost every case, a preference is given for wild game over every other kind of meat; and in some instances this predilection leads to the use of unwholesome food, which manifests itself in the form of cutaneous eruptions and leprous diseases of the most disgusting character. The endless variety of fruits peculiar to this portion of Mexico, also contributes largely to the subsistence of the Indians, and from them they make many refreshing beverages, while the trees themselves furnish either thatches, ropes, cords, thread, remedies, balsams, or dyes.

Little need be said of the dress of the natives, which is formed from the plainest and coarsest materials. The attire of the women consists of a simple cotton cloth, drawn tightly round the waist, and descending to the knees, leaving the breast and shoulders entirely exposed. The hair is either bound with gay-colored ribbons, and thrown in dark shining masses over the neck, or neatly looped up on the back of the head, where it is retained by a broad semicircular comb, and interspersed with wild-flowers; or, on the occasion of a *fiesta*, illuminated with the phosphorescent light of a shining beetle, called the *cucullo*. Utter nudity among the children of both sexes is of common occurrence.

Their amusements are scarcely worthy of note. In fact, an atmosphere of apathy seems to pervade every thing, and even their liveliest songs are sad, and their merriest music melancholy.

In religious matters they are reverential, but superstitious; and the ceremonies of the church, with its numerous *fiestas* and processions, are loved because they are gloomy and peculiar.

A striking but commendable feature in the character of the northern Indians is the respect paid by children to their parents; and the reverence accorded to aged people is no less worthy of remark. Between husband and wife cases of infidelity are rare; and whatever may have been the singular extremes of hospitality in times gone by, it is certain now that a regard is manifested for female virtue. To the credit of the Indians be it also said, that their progeny is legitimate, and that the vows of marriage are as faithfully cherished as in the most enlightened and favored lands. Youthful marriages are nevertheless of frequent occurrence: this is done to avoid a long and thankless probation in the military service of the Republic.

As agriculturists, the Indians are exceedingly primitive; and neither the accidents of foreign commerce, nor the contagion of example, have wrought any visible change in their ancient mode of cultivating the land. It is sufficient for them to know that "the soil nourishes him who tills it," and that no political or other contingency can destroy its overwhelming fertility. As a cultivator, the Indian is poor, but he is free; and he loves the solitude of his wretched *ranchito*, because it restores him, even as a peon, some of the long-lost liberty of his ancient race. This desire for solitude has given rise to that disposition among them to inhabit the elevated sections and summits, and to locate their *pueblas* on sites less convenient of access, and less advantageous to prosperity.

Under these circumstances, habituated to long slavery and oppression, it is not easy to judge of the intellectual developments of which they are susceptible; but there are abundant instances within the confines of the Isthmus, of those who have reached a comparatively high degree of mental culture, and who have evinced literary and military talent of no mean order. But to form a correct estimate of the indigenous people of the Isthmus in their present state of degradation and misery, it is necessary to turn back to the thrilling and dramatic incidents of their history, and to consider the evil influences to which they have long been subjected.

Everywhere on the Isthmus—even on the loftiest mountains, in the deepest dells, and in the most impenetrable forests—there are silent evidences of the history of a vast and powerful people, of which there scarcely remains now a tenth part, as the miserable consequence of their calamities. Indeed, throughout the whole record of their conquest and subjugation, their conversion to Christianity is the sole refreshing circumstance. This, though only nominal in some instances, has at all events released them from the bloody scenes of the sacrificial stone, and substituted for butchers and tyrants, priests of humanity and kindness, who, although not in all respects patterns of morality, and with whom the laws of nature have proved stronger than the obligations of celibacy, are, nevertheless, the friends and protectors of the Indians.

An elegant writer on Mexico has justly remarked, in reference to the moral faculties of the natives, that "it is difficult to appreciate them with justice. The better sort of Indians, among whom a certain degree of intellectual culture might be expected, perished in great numbers at the commencement of the Spanish conquest, the victims of European ferocity. The Christian fanaticism was particularly directed against the Aztec priests; and the *Teopixqui*, or ministers of the divinity, and of all those who inhabited Teocalli, who might be considered as the repositories of the historical, mythological, and astronomical knowledge of the country, were exterminated. The monks burned the hieroglyphical paintings, by which every kind of knowledge was transmitted from generation to generation. The people, deprived of these means of instruction, were plunged in an ignorance so much the deeper, as the missionaries were unskilled in the Mexican languages, and could substitute few new ideas in place of the old. The remaining natives then consisted only of the most indigent race—poor cultivators, artisans, among whom were a great number of weavers, porters, who were used like beasts of burden, and especially of those dregs of the people, who bore witness to the imperfection of the social institutions. How shall we judge, then, from these miserable remains of a powerful people, of the degree of cultivation to which it had arisen from the twelfth to the sixteenth century, and of the intellectual development of which it is susceptible?"

The Indians on the northern part of the Isthmus evince the greatest veneration for the memory of Doña Marina, the beautiful and well-favored mistress of Cortez. In her native village of Painalla, now called Jaltipan, a large circular mound of earth, known as the "Hill of Malinche," serves to recall the history of her imperishable deeds. Among the Indians, there is still preserved a tradition that her remains are buried beneath it, and that she promised to return from the captivity of death, to sweep from their thresholds the blight which she had involuntarily aided to bring. Who, then, can say that the traditionary dream of the Indian, as he veils the pangs of his heart under the deceitful guises of indifference and stupidity, is not already on the eve of realization, and that the ancient province of Coatzacoalcos, which through an humble captive slave exerted so powerful an influence over the commercial destinies of the world, may not again break forth from its sleep to effect changes far more lasting and glorious?

The *Mijes*, once a powerful tribe, inhabit the mountains to the west, in the central division of the Isthmus, and are now confined to the town of San Juan Guichicovi.* Physically speaking, they are similar to the Aztecs and Agualulcos, but more

---

* Hernan Cortez, in his Dispatches, says of these people: "They occupy a country so rough in its character, that it is impossible to penetrate it even on foot; nevertheless, I have made two attempts to conquer them, but without success. They are defended by strong fortresses, a mountainous region, and substantial weapons. In defending themselves, they killed a number of Spaniards; and they are constantly doing mischief to their neighbors, who are vassals of your majesty, attacking and burning their villages by night, and murdering the inhabitants.—*Let.* iv., p. 404.

repulsive in aspect; and, in a moral point of view, deeply degraded and grossly ignorant. Their language, too, is more harsh and less musical; and they are notorious in history as the most brutal and idolatrous of all the Isthmus tribes. Their conversion to Christianity is merely nominal, and religion is unknown to them, except in the exterior forms of worship. Even now, they secretly offer sacrifices of birds and animals to some unknown deity, and their minds are filled with dark and terrible superstitions. They pay little respect for age, and it is no uncommon thing to see old men and women bearing the burden of a beast. A singular object of their ambition, no less worthy of remark, is the desire to possess the greatest number of mules—a circumstance not easily accounted for, considering the little use they make of their animals, even in the carriage of their goods, which they seem to prefer to bear on their own shoulders. Indeed, this practice of carrying burdens is so common, that when they have no pack to carry, they have been known to put stones into their *tenates* in preference to travelling without any thing.

They are chiefly given to agricultural pursuits, and their crops of maize, beans, rice, and plantains are very considerable; but their *milpas* are often many miles from their habitations, in the rich bottom-lands that skirt the tributary streams of the Coatzacoalcos. As laborers, they possess great muscular strength and activity, and might, under rigid treatment, become exceedingly useful. They are, however, given to drink, and their lack of honesty is not the least objectionable feature in their character. Not more than a third part of these Indians speak Spanish.

The *Zoques* inhabit the mountainous region to the east, from the valley of the Chicapa on the south, to the Rio del Corte on the north. Originally occupying a small province lying on the confines of Tobasco, they were subjugated by the expedition to Chiapas under Luis Marin.* At present they are confined to the villages of San Miguel and Santa Maria Chimalapa. In some of their characteristics they are similar to the Mijes, but

---

* Vide *Lockhart's Trans. of Bernal Diaz*, Vol. II., p. 186.

more athletic, and easily distinguished by the prominence of their features and the singular custom they have of shaving the crown of the head. Their love of liquor is inordinate, and their manners are coarse and vulgar, but they are patient, enduring, and industrious. On the cleared portions of the Sierra, they cultivate large quantities of delicious oranges, maize, and tobacco; and their manufacture of articles from the *ixtle* and *pita* is justly celebrated over the Isthmus. Mentally, they are deplorably ignorant, and their conceptions of the Deity and of religion are vague and indefinite. Like the Guichicovi Indians, their knowledge of Spanish is limited.

The *Zapotecos* constitute the greater part of the population of the southern division of the Isthmus, and are incomparably superior to those of any other portion. The salubrity of the climate, the surpassing fertility of the soil, and the variety and richness of its productions, all minister to the prosperity of the inhabitants, who have from the most remote periods of their history been distinguished for their advances in civilization.* Their knowledge of the mechanic arts was not limited, even in the days of the Conquest, and their well-fortified towns did not fail to attract the admiration or excite the jealousies of the ancient kings of Anahuac. *Bernal Diaz*, in recounting the labors of the expedition in 1522, to Tehuantepec, says: "When Alvarado found what a quantity of gold the inhabitants possessed, he ordered them to make him a pair of stirrups of the finest gold, and gave them a couple of his own for a pattern; and, indeed, they were turned out very good."

Intellectually, the aborigines of Tehuantepec exhibit qualities of no mean order, and they are found intelligent, docile, and lively. In personal appearance, they are noted for the symme-

---

* *Clavigero* remarks that they "were civilized and industrious: they had their laws, exercised the arts of the Mexicans, and made use of the same method to compute time, and the same paintings to perpetuate the memory of events, in which they represented the creation of the world, the universal deluge, and the confusion of tongues, although the whole was intermixed with various fables. Since the Conquest the Zapotecos have been the most industrious people of New Spain. While the commerce of silk lasted, they were the feeders of the worms, and to their labors is owing all the cochineal which, for many years until the present time, has been imported from Mexico into Europe." Vol. I., Book II., p. 106.

try of their forms, the singularity of their features, and the vigor and sprightliness of their character. The women are delicately made, mercurial, voluptuous, and full of vivacity. They are particularly remarkable for the exquisite grace of their carriage, the winning softness of their manner of expression, and their love of gay costumes. In morals, they are loose and full of intrigue; but in habits, they are temperate and industrious. Many of them weave admirable fabrics from the wild silk and cotton, and their manufacture of conserves is unequalled in Mexico. The town of Tehuantepec gives employment to persons of various occupations, and its appearance is enlivened by the shops of carpenters, silversmiths, tanners, shoemakers, saddlers, and bakers. The manufacture of soap is very considerable, and the export of buckskins constitutes a lucrative trade.

The Indians of Juchitan, though numerically less than those of Tehuantepec, form an important part of the inhabitants of the Isthmus, as being superior in every respect. They are bold, independent, industrious, and temperate, possessing great muscular strength and a high degree of mental capacity. Of the value of their services, either as laborers in the construction of works, or as cultivators in the field, there can be no question. In aspect they are less pleasing than the Tehuantepecans, and in disposition less docile—a fact which may be attributable to their impatient character, and their keen sense of mental and physical degradation.

The *Huaves*, who according to their traditions came originally from Peru, and once a powerful race, have, from their successive struggles for supremacy with the Zapotecos and Mijes, dwindled down to a little more than three thousand, scattered over the sandy peninsulas formed by the lakes and the Pacific. At present they occupy the four villages of San Mateo, Santa Maria, San Dionisio, and San Francisco. Mr. Moro, in his report of his surveys, says: "These natives are easily distinguished by their aspect, which differs materially from that of the other inhabitants of the Isthmus. They are generally robust, and well formed; some of them evince a high degree of intelligence, but the majority are grossly ignorant. The Huaves of both sexes are habitually in a state of almost complete nudity.

Their industry consists of little else than fishing, and even this they can only do by means of sweep-nets; with the produce of their fisheries, however, they carry on an extensive trade, although not possessing proper vessels to venture into deep water, and being ignorant even of the use of the oar, they only frequent those spots which, from their shallowness, offer little danger, such as marshes, and the margin of the lakes and of the sea. It is a singular fact, that although the Huaves are chiefly fishermen, very few among them know how to swim."

The few *Mulattoes* who are scattered over the Isthmus, are the descendants of the native whites and the liberated slaves of the estates of the Marquesanas. They are generally robust and industrious, applying themselves to the cultivation of indigo and cochineal.

The *Zambos*, a half-cast between the Indian and the Negro, are found principally at El Barrio, Tarifa, and Niltepec. They inherit few good qualities, and are neither intelligent, industrious, or sober.

The *Negro* population is so insignificant that they scarcely claim attention. In some few instances, however, they are hard-working and deserving people.

In a retrospective view of the character and condition of the inhabitants of the Isthmus of Tehuantepec, there is little to excite our admiration, but much to pity and deplore; yet amid the atmosphere of degradation, ignorance, and depravity which overshadows the land, there are refreshing hopes that promise, under careful culture, to yield an abundant harvest. They seem to need only the example of activity to rekindle their dormant energies, and the neigh of the "iron horse" to awaken them from their indolent dream.

TOWNS, PRODUCTIVE INDUSTRY, ETC.

THE towns which are scattered over the Isthmus present so many interesting features, and are so intimately connected with the establishment of a great commercial route, that they deserve something more than a passing notice. Their situation—the character of their inhabitants—the nature of the lands within their jurisdiction—and the productive industry of various localities, are all matters of importance to the construction of a railroad, and to the future colonization and destinies of the Isthmus. Disregarding, however, the political and ecclesiastical departments to which the towns severally belong, it seems proper to consider them with exclusive reference to their geographical position, the order of their occurrence on the map, and their proximity to the proposed lines of communication. Beginning, then, on the Atlantic side, we have first the puebla of SAN CRISTOVAL ISHUATLAN, which enjoys a delightful and salubrious situation east of the Coatzacoalcos, three miles from the margin of that river, and within nine miles of the sea-coast. The town, which is accessible by a fair mule-road from Paso Nuevo (near the ancient site of Espiritu Santo), contains an Indian population of 680, and is scattered amid a grove of cocoa-trees over an elevation commanding an extensive view of the surrounding country. The precise date of its foundation is not known; but it is supposed to be in the early part of the seventeenth century, when the towns bordering the river were sacked and pillaged by the buccaneers. Ishuatlan contains ninety-seven houses and a neat church, with rude altar carvings and some obsidian tablets of exquisite beauty. The inhabitants, who are generally industrious, devote themselves to the raising of maize, sugar-cane, rice, and ixtle. Within a limited distance of the *puebla* are five small lakes, called respectively, El Potrero, Tierra Nueva, Guetascolapa, Jopalapa, and Los Pajaritos. The number of cattle, notwithstanding the rich potreros in the vicinity, is limited to between 3000 and 4000. The neighboring land is incomparably fertile, and the hills are studded with timber of great value. The town has a small primary school, and is governed by an alcalde, whose jurisdiction reaches over an extent of twelve leagues square; in ecclesiastical matters, it is subject to the district of Huimangillo. In a deep shady vale, a league from the town, in the direction of the Gulf, there is said to be a huge stone idol, which is held in great terror by the Indians, who believe that death will overwhelm any one who visits it. This absurd superstition proved an insuperable obstacle to our getting a guide to the place.

Three miles in an easterly direction from Ishuatlan, is the puebla of Santiago Moloacan, with an Indian population of 720. The location of this town, on the crest of an abrupt and narrow ridge that overlooks the broad potreros and rich vales that stretch themselves to the west as far as the eye can reach, is picturesque in the extreme. On either side of the single serpentine street that follows the summit of this rise, the descent to the valleys beneath is very precipitous. The town contains a church, 119 houses, and a wretched little school. The inhabitants are less hospitable than those of Ishuatlan, and given to many vices. Moloacan boasts of a great antiquity, and its settlement bears date anterior to the Conquest; but the landholders are without titles, and the immense plains of Gavilanes on the north, though cultivated to some extent, are still held by the government. The principal products are maize and ixtle, of which latter, more than 25,000 pounds are annually raised. Within eleven miles of this town, on the road to the Hacienda of San José, there is an extensive spring of petroleum, which covers an area of several acres. Of the value of this spontaneous product it is unnecessary to speak. No difficulty exists in the way of its transportation to the river; and the supply is said to be inexhaustible. Farther beyond, in the potrero of Ojapa, is a pool of sulphur-water; and near the western base of the Cerro Acalapa, is a mine of rock-salt, which, in times past, was extensively worked, but is now abandoned and grown over. The shale here is dark and very carboniferous, and the abundance of iron ore (red hæmatite) throughout all this locality deserves particular mention, and may eventually justify the establishment of furnaces for its reduction. At a distance of seven miles from Moloacan is the extensive *Hacienda of San Antonio*, which is irrigated by the river from whence it takes its name. The numerous valuable building sites on this estate—its proximity to the navigable rivers—the rich pasturage it affords—and the abundance of durable timber, vanilla, ixtle, &c., growing on it, all served to invest it with a degree of interest. The number of cattle, considering the immense extent of grazing-land, is, however, comparatively small, and 6000 head may be stated as the utmost range. To the north, in the potrero of Arenal, there are several springs of delicious water which supply the town. Notwithstanding the natural apathy of the inhabitants of Moloacan, they deserve credit for many enterprising works attempted by them. Among these is a bridge of sixty feet span across the Rio San Antonio, and a canal (cut in 1838), more than half a league in length, uniting the waters of the latter stream with those of the Uspanapa. By this the distance from Moloacan to Mina-titlan is shortened to four leagues.

SAN FRANCISCO SANAPA, on the northern bank of the river of that name, within eight Mexican leagues of its junction with the Tonala, was founded in 1808 by an old Spaniard named Fernando Moris y Virgil. It contains a population of 300, who are of the ancient race of Agualulcos. They are chiefly agriculturists, and raise maize, cacao, fruits, frijoles, coffee, tobacco, sugar-cane, and a small quantity of cotton. The country around Sanapa is exceedingly rich, and the climate is allowed to be of the most salubrious character. The cattle (which including the neighboring rancherias number about 10,000 head) are remarkable for their good condition; and every thing bears the impress of an industrious and intelligent people. Within eleven leagues of the puebla, on the road to Huimangillo (the head of the department on the east), are the villages of *Tecominoacan* and *Mecatepeque*, which contain together something more than

700 inhabitants, who are remarkably reserved in character, and who speak almost exclusively the old Mexican language. During the war of the Independencia, the commerce of Sanapa was very considerable; its products being carried in small vessels to Vera Cruz. Timber of all kinds is very plentiful, especially the *guapaque*, which, from its abundance, gives name to the neighboring Hacienda of *Guapacal*. All throughout this locality there are evidences of a population at one time numerically great; and the number of obsidian relics, as knives, razors, arrow-heads, beads, vessels, &c., with which the face of the country is literally covered, seem to indicate a degree of mechanical skill and an approach to civilization not usually exhibited among the remains of a barbarous people.

On the western bank of the Rio Tancochapa—the southern arm of the Tonala—thirteen miles above its confluence with that stream, is the magnificent Hacienda of *San José del Carmen*, the property of the late Don Juan Urgell, whose titles bear date of 1771. This embraces three *sitios*, or sites, and consists of pasture-lands and forests, which stretch on the north to the cerro of St. Vincente, and on the south to within a short distance of the spurs of the Cordillera. The location of this estate is most advantageous, lying between and bordering two navigable rivers, the Uspanapa and the Tancochapa, in the tributary streams of which (those irrigating the lands of the hacienda) are found fine pulverulent particles of gold; but to what extent these washings might prove lucrative further exploration must demonstrate. It seems important, however, to state, in connection with the finding of precious metal in these streams, that among the many remains of the indigenous people who formerly occupied this locality, there are a number of artificial wells on the west bank of the Tancochapa, which seem to be rather huge jars of earthenware, four or five feet high and three in diameter, buried in the ground, and which correspond precisely with those now existing in Sonora and other gold districts of Mexico. The peculiar construction and location of these receptacles, and the abundance of drinking-water in close proximity, justify the conclusion that they were formerly used for washing gold. This subject has been alluded to in the section on the Geology of the Isthmus.

The number and variety of mounds found near San José render it a place of considerable interest. These are scattered over various points, and are generally composed of chalky earth, alternated by various colored clay, beneath which are the fragments of ancient vessels. In excavating some of these mounds, several copper hatchets and other antiquities have been discovered. The banks of the arroyos exhibit great quantities of plumbic ochre, and usually intersect strata of variegated clay, suitable for purposes of pottery. The abundance of clay iron-stone is remarkable, and lead is also reported by the inhabitants as existing in certain localities. San José, however, derives its chief interest from the central position which it occupies, being midway between Acayucam and Tobasco, and the ferrying point for large quantities of cacao and tobacco, which annually pass by land to Vera Cruz, and thence to the towns of the interior. In the year of 1847, no less than 2000 heavily laden mules passed through this estate on their way to the capital. At present, considerable trade is carried on with Tobasco, and the family of Don Juan Urgell have the privilege of collecting tolls, the legal rate of which is two reals for a mule and cargo, and one real for each arriero, or passenger; this includes ferriage across the river. The woods and forests present an innumerable variety of valuable building timber, dye-woods, gum-trees, &c., &c.; and the land appears admirably adapted to the cultivation of cacao, cotton, tobacco, sugar, rice, and maize. The *potreros* are incomparably rich, and the cattle (numbering upwards of 8000) are unequalled on the Isthmus. The limits of this estate are, however, not very clearly defined, and at present the greater part of it is a wilderness. The Hacienda proper, which contains a population of 100, is accessible on the west through the Arroyo de los Urgells, one of the tributaries of the Uspanapa, by which canoes ascend to El Paso, from whence a tolerable road exists to the settlement. The *camino real*, from Tobasco, via Huimangillo, Moloacan, and Ishuatlan, also passes through San José.

MINA-TITLAN next claims attention, not only from its being the present head of ship navigation on the Coatzacoalcos, but also as the only existing outlet on the north for the surplus productions of the Isthmus. The village is located on the western bank of the river, twenty miles from its mouth, and contains some 70 habitations, with a mixed population of 460, who are variously occupied as boatmen, agriculturists, and carpenters. The houses are generally built to face a single street, crossing at right angles a sloping gravelly ridge, which runs parallel with the Coatzacoalcos. Back of the village, the land continues moderately high and undulating for some distance, but the river margins in the immediate proximity are low and subject to periodic inundation. Timber of all kinds grows in great abundance, and the profusion of fruit, as guavas, oranges, mangoes, melons, lemons, &c., is not the least interesting feature of the place. The people generally are more intelligent than in other towns of the Isthmus, a fact which is doubtless due to their intercourse with foreigners. Little attention is however paid to agriculture, and the productive industry of Mina-titlan is correspondingly limited. Cattle and other live stock constitute the principal wealth of the people, who, notwithstanding their mental superiority over those of other parts, are indolent and apathetic. The landed property of those who reside within the precincts of the town is limited, with few exceptions, to certain shares in the immense tract called the Potrero de la Isla, lying on the east bank of the Coatzacoalcos. The climate is generally salubrious and healthy; and the advantageous position of the village, its limited distance from the sea, and the capacity of the river at that point for ship navigation, cannot fail, under any circumstances, to make it hereafter a place of considerable importance.

COSULIACAQUE, irregularly built on an elevated broken ridge, shaded by a grove of trees, seven and a half miles west from Mina-titlan, is an Indian village, settled in 1717. It contains several *adobie* houses and a venerable-looking church, on a beam in the centre of which is inscribed the names of certain priests, by whom it was built, and the date "1796." In the vicinity of this place is a broad strip of level country, well adapted for cultivation or pasturage, and irrigated by three rivulets abounding in excellent fish. The productions of Cosuliacaque consist of Indian corn, sugar, and bananas. The degree of salubrity here may be inferred from the fact, that there are twenty old men in the village whose individual ages reach beyond 81 years ; and there are the same number of women, whose joint longevity equals the sum of 1780. According to Señor Iglesias, the wife of Don Juan Martin died in 1830, at the extraordinary age of 136 years. The inhabitants, who number 2000, are quiet, inoffensive, and industrious.

About two miles westward of Cosuliacaque is the small village of OTIAPA, built on an elevated table, gradually sloping to the east, and overlooking a range of country to the right and north, in which direction San Martin and Mount Pelon are distinctly visible, presenting a strong contrast to the general uniformity of the surrounding land. The inhabitants, numbering about 900, cultivate considerable quantities of ixtle, as also maize and sugar-cane. The village is watered by three small streams, that empty into the Tierra Nueva and Huasuntan rivers. Otiapa is about eight Mexican leagues from the bar of the Coatzacoalcos, and five from La Barrilla, to which it descends by an imperceptible declivity. In its vicinity there are excellent grazing-lands, which contain many fine cattle. Something more than a league from the debouche of the Coatzacoalcos, a portion of its waters, under the name of Rio de las Calzadas, takes a westerly direction until reaching the settlement of Tierra Nueva, where, forming an extensive marsh, it bends towards the coast, and leads to the grazing-lands of Rancho Nuevo. Leaving this, the river resumes its western direction until its confluence with the Huasuntan, which is navigable to the Lake of Ostion.

One and a half miles northerly from Otiapa, is the neat village of SAN JUAN CHINAMECA, beautifully located on an abrupt alluvial spur, the sides of which slope to the north, east, and south. It contains several well-constructed houses, with balconies supported by arches of stone. The principal object of interest in the village is the church, built in the centre of a beautiful common, surrounded by lofty cocoanut-trees running parallel to the sides of the building, which is an oblong stone structure with arched door-ways and tiled roof. The interior decorations, though rudely made, are nevertheless valuable, especially the candlesticks and altar service, which are formed of silver said to have been brought from the head-waters of the Uspanapa. Chinameca contains about 1400 inhabitants, who are characterized by industrious habits and hospitality. The houses, which are chiefly *adobie*, are ranged to face the sides of a long winding street, form quite a contrast with the mud ranchos of neighboring villages. To the south is an extensive strata of calcareous earth, through which runs a small river of cool refreshing water. In the vicinity are several fine estates, containing in the aggregate some 5000 head of horned cattle, and upwards of 1200 horses and mules. At a distance of two leagues from Chinameca is a coffee plantation, growing 7000 trees, and within six miles of the village, in the direction of San Martin, is a spring of thermal water.

JALTIPAN, reached by an excellent mule-road five miles southwesterly from the last mentioned village, is somewhat celebrated as being the birth-place of the romantic and seductive *Malinche*, or *Doña Marina*, the favored mistress of Hernan Cortes. The town, which has a population of 2300, and some 400 houses huddled together without reference to order or regularity, with the exception of one or two principal streets, is laid on a slightly elevated plain, which overlooks the contiguous country. At the southern end of the town is an extensive artificial mound, about 40 feet in height by 100 in diameter at the base, known as the " Hill of Malinche," from the summit of which the view is magnificent, embracing San Martin, Cerro Tecuanapa, Mt. Encantada, and the sharp peaks which jut up from the range of the Cordillera on the south. The soil about Jaltipan is sandy, and intersected by strata of calcareous earth. Within a league of the place is an old salt mine, which, according to the statements of Padre Mota, formerly yielded upwards of 1000 mule-loads per year. The inhabitants raise considerable indian-corn, sugarcane, tobacco, and ixtle. The island of Tacamichapa is reputed to belong to the town, and is claimed on the ground that it was conceded to Malinche by the crown of Spain, in consideration of the invaluable services rendered by her to the great conqueror. The women of this place are not undeservedly famed as the fairest and most beautiful throughout the district; and in times past are said to have carried their ideas of hospitality and entertainment to a very singular degree.

Mr. Moro says: "A singular circumstance, deserving the attention of the ethnologist, is the existence of a race of *dumb* people, of which there are numerous families in Jaltipan. However strange this may appear, it is nevertheless certain, and the *Rancho de los Mudos*, established a few years since, near the lower part of the island of Tacamichapa, owes its designation to the fact that the individuals are all dumb who inhabit the three or four houses which form this settlement."

Jaltipan enjoys a great salubrity; fevers are seldom known to occur, and the musquitoes and other annoying insects are exceedingly few. There are several stores in the town, and some half a dozen well-built houses of stone. The church is a rectangular structure, so similar in all respects to those already noted, that a particular description would be only useless repetition.

Nine miles southwest from Jaltipan is TESISTEPEC, built on the summit of a broken sandstone ridge, and contains a population of 2200, who are almost entirely Indians. The town is supplied with water from wells, sunk in the rock to depths varying from 20 to 40 feet. The soil in this vicinity is remarkably fertile, and tobacco, rice, maize, sugar-cane, and ixtle are produced in large quantities. The principal manufactures of Tesistepec are shoes and cigars.

The town contains a tolerably well-built church and a primary school. Some of the neighboring estates are rich and valuable, especially the Hacienda of *Almagro, Casas Viejas*, and *Correa*, all of which abound with excellent cattle. Almagro alone contains no less than 16,000 head, with a proportionate number of horses and mules. The numerous metallic indications of this locality invest it with peculiar interest.

HIDALGO-TITLAN (so called in honor of the celebrated Mexican general, Hidalgo), but more frequently known as *Almagres*, from the banks of red clay in the vicinity, is situated on a verge of green and sloping hills on the eastern shore of the Coatzacoalcos, seven and a half miles above the junction of the Brazo Mistan, and eighteen miles above Mina-titlan. This puebla, founded in 1821 by a French colonist, is the only inhabited point between the head of ship navigation and the upper waters of the Coatzacoalcos. It contains 60 houses and 370 inhabitants, who possess some 4000 head of cattle, part of which are pastured on the island of Tacamichapa. Oranges are grown here in great numbers, and the rich fruits which flourish in the vicinity load the air with their fragrance. Above and around the village the soil is exceedingly fertile, and in a good state of cultivation, producing corn, coffee, and tobacco in great abundance. Some distance further up, on the Tacamichapa side, are perpendicular cliffs of light, porous, decomposed sandstone, from sixty to one hundred feet high, from which issue numerous delightful springs of clear pure water. These cliffs are overlaid by strata of red and blue clay of remarkable tenacity, extensively used by the natives for various purposes of pottery.

SAN MARTIN ACAYUCAM is by far the most important town in the northern division of the Isthmus, and the capital of the district of the same name. Located on a ridge which extends from the mountains of Tuxtla, its climate is cool, salubrious, and healthy. It is the residence of the *gefe politico*, and a place of considerable trade, containing some 5200 inhabitants, a parroquia, two or three primary schools, several stores, a cotton-gin, and one or two sugar-presses. Latterly, however, Acayucam has greatly diminished in wealth and importance. At the period of the Conquest it was the court and residence of one of the most powerful caciques of the great empire of the Aztecs; but unfortunately the old archives have perished with its greatness, and a few incomplete documents recording the events of the years 1600 and 1658 are all that now remain; these contain nothing of interest. In the vicinity the soil is remarkably fertile, producing maize, sugar-cane, coffee, cacao, ixtle, and a great variety of esculents. The surrounding forests also abound with valuable trees, and afford frequent bowers of rare and picturesque beauty. Most of the trade of Acayucam is carried on through the Paso San Juan, on the river of that name, which serves as an outlet for the productions of all the northern division, except such as find a market by sea from Mina-titlan. In times of prosperity the annual exports of cotton and ixtle alone, through the Paso, to

Vera Cruz are said to have reached beyond $1,256,000. Now they scarcely average one-twentieth of that sum.

Within the jurisdiction of the town are numerous haciendas and settlements, abounding in cattle, horses, and mules, and presenting many features of interest to the agriculturist by the fecundity of the soil; to the machinist, by the abundant sources of water-power; to the sportsman, by the myriads of game; to the geologist, by the nature and variety of the formations; to the botanist, by the rich and varied character of the vegetation; to the antiquarian, by the number of ancient idols and relics; and to the ethnologist, by the heterogeneous condition of the people. The neighboring towns also merit attention; among these are *San Juan Oluta* (a favorite resort of the Acayucaños), *San Andres Sayultepec, Santa Ana Soconusco, San Pedro Joteapa, Santiago Mecayapa,* and *Santa Maria Minsapa.* The date of these settlements is now lost among the "dim traditions" of the Aztec race, and their inhabitants are but the shadows of the past—poor, degraded, and often living in a state of nature.

According to the statements of Señor Iglesias, the canton of Acayucam contained, in 1831, 20,421 inhabitants, who have increased considerably since that time. At the close of his report he says:

"This canton has 14 towns, 11 settlements, 12 haciendas, 27 grazing farms, 6 rivers, 28 rivulets, 14 lakes, 6 marshes, 1 vein of chalk, 3 of alabaster, 4 of petroleum, 2 springs of sulphurous water, 2 metallic veins, 2 thermal springs, 1221 ixtle plants, 6720 trees of coffee, 71,113 head of cattle, 12,126 horses, and 594 mules." It is scarcely necessary to say, in conclusion, that this statement of its wealth is far short of the truth now.

After leaving Almagres, there are not any settlements met with throughout all the broad belt of country lying contiguous to the Coatzacoalcos, until reaching MAL PASO, otherwise called the *Paso del Sarabia*,* situated at the forks of the Coatzacoalcos and Sarabia rivers, and the present general head of canoe navigation for all travel to and from the northern and

---

* So called after Don Pedro Sarabia, who settled near San Juan Guichicovi, at the close of the Conquest.

southern division of the Isthmus. The products of the Pacific side, destined for the Gulf coast, are first brought down to this place for embarkation; and occasional cargoes of goods from Vera Cruz ascend the river to this point, from whence they are carried to the Pacific plains on mules. Opposite the mouth of the Sarabia River, on the right bank of the Coatzacoalcos, is the site of a French settler, now abandoned. The rancho has rotted down, and the luxuriant forest has grown over the cleared portion, leaving no traces of the place ever having been inhabited, save a few orange and cocoanut trees which struggle with the pressure of the vines and foliage. At Mal Paso are two small ranchos which are untenanted, except by an occasional custom-house official on the arrival of a cargo of goods. They however serve as shelter for travellers, and prove a welcome resting-place after a slow and toilsome ascent of the river.

It would be a fruitless task to attempt a description of the scenery between the habitable points of this vast wilderness. Everywhere clustering lilies bathe their fragrant heads in the shining river, and thousands of creeping plants, decked with blossoms, bend downward from the overarching growth above, forming strange and fantastic bowers, while a hundred little streams pour their bright tributaries into the bosom of the great "Father of Waters." Beyond Mal Paso is SAN GABRIEL BOCA DEL MONTE (entrance to the forest). This is an extensive hacienda, between the Sarabia and Malatengo rivers, and is traversed by the road which connects the more interior towns with Mal Paso and the Coatzacoalcos. As a permanent settlement it bears date of 1824, when the present proprietor, D. Bartolo Roderiguez, obtained a concession of four and a quarter leagues square of land from the government. This colony now contains thirteen ranchos, and sixty-eight inhabitants, who are chiefly employed in raising cattle, and cultivating tobacco, maize, coffee, and vanilla. The road from Mal Paso to Boca del Monte traverses, for three or four miles, the summit of a high, narrow ridge, which divides the waters of the Sarabia from the Coatzacoalcos. It then follows the immediate margin of the former stream, occasionally diverging when the banks become rocky and precipitous, and crossing a succession of high spurs and intervening valleys. The road for the whole distance (to within a mile of the hacienda) lies through a dense forest, that scarcely permits the rays of the sun to penetrate; but the immense growth of the timber, the varied character of the foliage, the grotesque windings of the *bejucos*, the beauty of the orchidacæ, the exquisite hues of the flowers, and the delicate fragrance of the vanilla, added to the melodies of birds, and the murmuring sounds of the rapids, all conspire to render the scenery of this road most enchanting. On emerging from the forest, the view of the surrounding country is extremely beautiful; and by ascending a small eminence, immense prairies, clothed with luxuriant grass, are seen stretching to the bases of the distant mountains. Looking south, one sees the low depression formed by the passes through the dividing ridge which separates the waters of the two oceans; and to the right and left the main chain of the great Cordillera, rising in sublime grandeur. The soil, with the exception of that in the valley, and on the margins of the streams, is coarse, gravelly, and unproductive: this refers especially to the country south and west of the Hacienda. To the north the vegetation is more rank, and the character of the land superior. The number of cattle about Boca del Monte is limited to less than 3000, but they are remarkably well conditioned, and generally a larger breed than are found on the Atlantic plains.

Southwesterly, nine miles from this Hacienda, is the extensive Indian puebla of SAN JUAN GUICHICOVI, accessible by a narrow mule-road, which crosses the Mogañe (one of the tributaries of the Malatengo) five miles from Boca del Monte, and soon after is rugged and steep. Within a mile of San Juan it intersects the Pachine, and extends through a shady grove, leaving which it suddenly becomes rocky, and for the rest of the way winds along ravines and overhanging precipices. The situation of Guichicovi is remarkable, being built on an elevated table-land, which constitutes the summit of an abrupt spur of the great Cordillera, and overlooks a broad range of country to the east and south, variously diversified by hills, dales, and rolling prairies. The site of the town comprises an area of about thirty acres, over which the houses are scattered without reference to order or regularity; and the streets are narrow, tortuous, and contracted. The inhabitants, who constitute the remnant of the old Mije tribe, are generally an idle, worthless set, half civilized, and poor amid abundant sources of wealth. Their number is about 5200, who cultivate the rich valley and bottom-lands to some extent, raising maize, sugar-cane, ixtle, rice, frijoles, and plantains. The number of cattle is comparatively small, but the inhabitants pride themselves on the possession of their mules, which are said to amount to several thousand. The chief object of interest at San Juan Guichicovi is its venerable church, which is an unfinished stone structure, oblong, with broken arches, roofless, and in ruins. Of the date of its foundation nothing is now known. On one of the old bells, supported by scaffolding, and bearing the insignia of the Order of Santiago, is the following inscription:

<blockquote>
PIE PATER DOMINICE ORA PRO NOBIS.
ROQVE GALLARDO—GOVERNADOR.
A
1767.
Fray JOSE MARIANO PALANO.
CURA Y PRESIDENTE.
Sancte Joannes Baptista ora pro nobis.
</blockquote>

A vulgar tradition exists among the natives of Guichic*,* with regard to the building of this church, which is said to have been erected by Cortes in a single night—who quarried the stone, and mixed the mortar with the white of eggs. But, as the time for its completion was limited to the crow of the cock, the great conqueror broke his contract, and no hand has since been raised to undertake what so valiant a man failed to accomplish.

The veins of iron ore in the immediate vicinity of this place are the richest and most extensive known to exist on the Isthmus. Tin is also found some distance beyond, in the Cerro de los Mijes.

The road south from San Juan Guichicovi to the interior towns lies through the *Hacienda of Santissima*, across the Malatengo and Citune rivers, sometimes passing along precipices of considerable height, from whose summits the caps of Masahua, Petapa, and the dividing ridge between the eastern boundaries of the Isthmus and Chiapas, are often visible.

With the exception of Espiritu Santo, SANTA MARIA PETAPA is the oldest Spanish settlement on the Isthmus, and is prettily located on a plain, bounded on the north and west by an amphitheatre of lofty mountains. This town, which once contained a population of 5000, and embraced within its limits both EL BARRIO and SANTO DOMINGO, is now reduced to a little more than 1300, who raise maize, frijoles, indigo, calabashes, limes, &c. The church, still in a very perfect state, is said to be upwards of 300 years old. This is a rectangular building, about 200 feet by 50, with a low dome, and constructed after the style of the sixteenth century. It contains a tolerable organ and some very good paintings, among which that of the "Annunciation" and the "Prayer in the Garden" are best. The walls are indifferently painted in stucco, and the images present some rude specimens of carving. Within the last half century, Petapa has dwindled to an insignificant village; and a few agricultural products, and some manufactured articles, as shoes and buckskins, constitute the only resources of the people.

SANTO DOMINGO, a mile and a half westerly from Petapa, once constituted a part of the old city; at present it contains 900 inhabitants, who annually produce a considerable quantity of vanilla, indigo, and sarsaparilla. The chief attractive features of this vicinity are the mountain caves, which merit some attention, from their connection with the past history of the indigenous people. The entrance to the principal cave, called that of Santo Domingo, is elevated about 700 feet above the base of a limestone mountain, a mile north from the village, and is accessible only by a steep path. The mouth to this cave has an arch spanning 80 feet by 20 in height, and the plane of its floor cuts the horizon at an angle of thirty degrees, until reaching a depth of 100 feet below the entrance. At the foot of this slope is a magnificent apartment some 300 feet in diameter and 50 in height, with its sides ornamented with stalactites and stalagmites of every conceivable form and variety. The floor is quite level; and at one extremity is a sparkling pool of clear, cold water.

Beyond this antechamber, the cave extends into the mountain for a distance of more than 2000 feet, sometimes expanding into large halls, or forming regular arched passage-ways several hundred feet in length, alternately ascending and descending into ridges and valleys. On the walls, at the extreme end of the cave, are several circular paintings, rudely executed with red ochre, and probably intended to represent the sun and moon. There are also several representations of the human hand, done in black. Immediately fronting these drawings, in the floor of the cave, is a small aperture through which, by means of ropes, access is obtained to an apartment beneath. In this are fragments of arrow-heads, human bones, and antique pottery.

EL BARRIO DE LA SOLEDAD, on the road to Tehuantepec, nine leagues from Boca del Monte, and within two miles of Petapa, by which it is separated by a small arroyo, contains a mixed population of 1200, consisting of Indians and Zambos, who are chiefly agriculturists. The production of sugar, fruits, vanilla, and common lime constitute their principal occupation. The town has one or two small stores, a *posada*, and a well-built church, erected in 1834. During the last year, El Barrio lost thirty inhabitants by cholera. In the neighborhood there are one or two fine estates, especially the *Rancho de Calderon*, upon which a considerable quantity of sugar-cane is annually grown. The proprietors of this hacienda are the principal business men of El Barrio.

Immediately east and south of El Barrio are a number of small settlements embraced within the limits of the estates of Marquesanas: these include *La Chivela*, *Tarifa*, *Santiago*, and *Agua Escondida*. The hacienda of *La Chivela*, situated on the plains, at the entrance of the pass of the same name, 780 feet above the Pacific Ocean, and twelve miles southeasterly from El Barrio, has a population of about seventy-five persons, and some fifteen or twenty ranchos. As a settlement, it is only important as being the residence of the chief *guarda de ganado* of the "Marquesanas," the property of Don Estavan Maqueo, and the principal place for the sale of cattle belonging to the estate.

Santiago, beautifully located on a level plain, seven miles from La Chivela, and three miles from the Pass of West

Piedra Parada, is surrounded by an amphitheatre of hills, and contains a population of sixty inhabitants, who are the *employées* of the estate. Its elevation is 800 feet above the Pacific, and the *Wine-palm* grows in great abundance all throughout its vicinity.

Tarifa, built on the plains of that name, derives some interest from its being the point selected by Señor Moro for the western termination of his ship-canal feeder, which was to conduct the waters of the Chicapa and Ostuta rivers along the southern slope of the Albricia range to the summit-level of these plains. It is possible that the waters of the Rio del Corte might be brought to Tarifa on a shorter distance, at a much less cost, and a more abundant supply obtained. But little doubt, however, exists that from either of these sources a sufficiency of water for the summit-level of a ship-canal, with capacity to pass 100 ships per day, might be brought. The item of *cost* would, therefore, determine the source and the route of the feeder. The hacienda contains 18 houses and 100 inhabitants, who are occupied in taking care of the cattle of the estate, which number, including those of Santiago and La Chivela, upwards of 15,000 head.

The Rancho of *Agua Escondida*, four miles from the Portillo of Tarifa, and immediately at the eastern base of the Cerro Rincon Chapa, forms one of the numerous settlements belonging to the immense estates of the Marquesanas. This point contains about a half dozen houses, and some twenty inhabitants: its elevation is 300 feet above the Pacific. In this neighborhood is a number of indigo vats, located on the Arroyo de Agua Escondida, which takes its name from the fact that the stream loses itself in the sands of the plains—hence the term of " concealed water."

SAN MIGUEL CHIMALAPA is built in the valley of the Chicapa River at its confluence with the Monetza, five miles easterly from the plains of Las Tablas. This town, which is inhabited exclusively by Indians of the Zoque tribe (of whom only about three-fourths speak Spanish), has a population of 460, who are chiefly occupied in raising *ixtle*, from the manufactures of which considerable trade is carried on with Juchitan and Tehuantepec.

Timber of all kinds is particularly abundant about this vicinity; and there are many valuable sites for mills on the Chicapa.

A singular custom exists among the Zoque Indians of "waking the dead." When one of their number dies, the whole populace assemble round the body with musical instruments, and an ample supply of *aguardiente*. This gathering is generally succeeded by a dance and a night's debauch, accompanied by yells and shouts of the most diabolical character. At other times, the people are industrious, and comport themselves well, producing calabashes, fruits, wax, tallow, chocolate, and frijoles.

Between San Miguel and Santa Maria Chimalapa the road is perhaps the most rugged on the Isthmus, and for the greater part of the distance (nine leagues) lies through a dense and almost impenetrable forest, traversed by innumerable small streams, which, during the rainy months, are so swollen as to be impassable. In the dry season these are nicely bridged by hewn logs placed side by side. At the distance of two leagues north from San Miguel is the *Rancho of La Cofradia*, a small cluster of huts on a green knoll in a secluded vale. Two leagues beyond this is the beautiful Cerro *Jacal de Ocotal*, so called from the ocote (or pine) forest which covers its summit. From this point the view of the country is magnificent, and the hues of the foliage in the valleys beneath surpass in richness the most brilliant tints of our northern Indian summer. Descending from this eminence into a dark and shadowy ravine, studded with every conceivable form and variety of tree, a ride for a league and a half further brings you to the base of a gentle cerro of bright-red clay, upon the summit of which is a ruined rancho, called *El Chocolate*. Leaving this the road becomes better until reaching the Rio Milagro within a mile of SANTA MARIA CHIMALAPA. All along this valley the maize and tobacco plantations are very numerous and productive. Fording the stream, the ascent to the puebla, by means of a foot-path deeply worn in the limestone rock, of which the whole mountain is composed, is steep, winding, and slippery.

The town is built with some regularity on an elevated ridge, within a mile of the Rio del Corte, and contains 2 churches, 104 houses, and a population of 680, of whom no more than three-fourths speak Spanish. Distant from the shores of the Pacific, and approachable only by a wretched road, the inhabitants have comparatively little social intercourse with other settlements. Their products are nevertheless much more numerous than those of more favored places, and considerable quantities of oranges, maize, tobacco, and ixtle are annually transported by means of *balsas* down the Rio del Corte, for the supply of El Barrio, Petapa, &c. The dexterity with which the Indians manage these balsas (often heavily laden), in passing over terrible rapids and through narrow passages filled with rugged rocks, where even a canoe could not possibly live, is truly surprising. These rafts are rudely constructed from the *jonote*, an exceedingly light wood, which grows in great quantities. The river abounds in excellent fish, and the inhabitants, whose cattle, from the want of grazing lands, are very limited, eat scarcely any other animal food. The scenery on the Rio del Corte is unequalled in beauty, and the abundance of valuable timber, as the pine, live-oak, and cypress, invest this part with peculiar interest, and cannot fail to attract a share of the future timber trade of the Isthmus.

Of the date of the original settlement of the Chimalapas, nothing is now preserved, except a vague tradition that they were built by a remnant of the Zoque tribe, who escaped from the malady which depopulated Chimalapilla, a large and thriving town on the river of that name, more than a hundred years ago. The ruins of this ancient place are still visible within sixteen miles of Santa Maria; and as the dead were left unburied, the ground is said to be strewn with bones and skulls. This has given rise to the belief that the spot is haunted, and no reward would be deemed sufficiently great to induce the Indians to visit it.

At Santa Maria Chimalapa there is a family of *Albinos*, whose appearance forms a striking contrast with the sombre color of the Zoques. The quality of oranges raised here are superior to those of any part of the Isthmus, and constitute an important part of the trade of the town. * * * *

Returning again to the central division of the Isthmus, the road from El Barrio to Tehuantepec takes a direction nearly south, by way of the Cerro Guiévixia, and through the Pass of Guichilona. In ascending to this part of the dividing ridge the road is steep and winding, and on reaching the summit the declivities increase. At this point, however, the scenery is of a shadowy and sylvan character. To the north are the table-lands, with the glistening church spires of El Barrio and Petapa; and to the south, beyond the great chain, the plains, dotted with cheerful towns and haciendas, shrouded in a misty haze, which skirts the lagoons and marks the bounds of the broad Pacific. Descending by a slippery road, which at some points slopes at an angle of 15°, we reach the estate of *Guichilona*, formerly a large and valuable hacienda, but now abandoned, and only used as a stopping-place for the mule-trains on their way to and from the Pacific. Here are extensive corrals and several indigo vats, but the buildings are almost roofless and in ruins—the pictures of desertion and neglect. A league beyond this is the vast ridge of the Cordillera, from which the plains are again clearly perceptible; and not least conspicuous among the objects that arrest the eye, is the white dome of the little church at Chihuitan, shining in the sun-light above the masses of foliage which obscure the village. Near here is a branch road leading to SAN GERONIMO, a league from the mountain-bases, on the margin of the Rio Juchitan. This town, founded by the Spaniards soon after the Conquest, contains a population of 500 Zapotecos, whose chief occupation is the raising of indigo. With the exception of its admirable situation and healthy climate, the only attraction is the church, built by the Dominican friars in the sixteenth century. This is an oblong edifice, in the Moorish style of architecture, and in very good repair, considering the carelessness of the natives and the long period of years that have intervened since its erection. Above the altar there are some tolerable *basso relievo* carvings of the patron-saint of the puebla—of San Miguel, San Pablo, and San Elias. Altogether, the village is neat and picturesque. The railroad will probably pass through it or in its vicinity.

Leading to San Geronimo is a road from Chivela Pass, a portion of which was built by the engineers of Don José de Garay. In some places this is quite steep, and presents many difficulties for wheeled vehicles; but by blasting at one or two points it may be rendered almost immediately serviceable. All along the line through the Pass the scenery is beautifully varied, and within a short distance of the plains are several mineral springs, which with so many attractive features, are doubtless destined to become places of frequent resort. Indeed, it is not unlikely that the Springs of Chivela may become, in the course of time, as well known and as fashionably frequented as those of *Saratoga* and the *White Sulphur*. After reaching the base of the mountains in the vicinity of the Rio Verde, the road finally comes on to the plains through the Portillo de la Martar.

Two miles northwest from San Geronimo is the neat settlement of SANTO DOMINGO CHIHUITAN, through the centre of which courses the clear, silvery stream of Los Perros. Beyond a picturesque location and its beautiful church, Chihuitan is an unimportant place, numbering some 600 inhabitants, who are remarkable for their hospitality; it is, however, the chosen resort of thousands who congregate from all portions of the Isthmus to attend a fair annually held there. This generally lasts for a week—during which time the roads in every direction are thronged by the Indians, who hail the occasion to expose for sale at so grand a market the trifling results of their industry.

Half a league nearly north from Chihuitan, over a beautifully level road, on either hand of which are luxuriant hedges, is the extensive sugar-mill and plantation of *Santa Cruz*, the largest in this portion of Mexico, and the property of Don Antonio Mass. The machinery used is remarkably imperfect and old-fashioned, but the establishment is maintained in excellent order, and the quality of sugar, rum, and molasses manufactured here very fair. The rollers and presses are driven by water-power, of which the Rio de los Perros furnishes an abundant source, and the refinery gives employment to more than 150 men, who seem to understand very well the production of sugar. With few exceptions, this mill supplies nearly the whole southern division, and indeed a great portion of the State of Oaxaca. During the year 1850, the amount of sugar manufactured at Santa Cruz alone, exceeded 160,000 pounds.

Almost directly south from San Geronimo, at a distance of five miles, is the town of ITZTALTEPEC, signifying in the Zapoteco language "the Hill of Salt." The Rio de los Perros, which passes to the east, in the immediate vicinity, becomes almost entirely dry during the summer months on account of the absorbing nature of the soil. The town contains an industrious and quiet population of 1500; and the number of well-built houses, cisterns, indigo-vats, and other stone structures, attest the vanished thrift and prosperity of the place. Diagonally opposite from Itztaltepec, within half a mile, on the road to Juchitan, is the village of EL ESPINAL, with some 300 inhabitants, who cultivate tobacco, indigo, and fruits. An old time-worn church is the only attraction, and even this is fast crumbling to decay.

With the exception of Tehuantepec, JUCHITAN is the largest town on the southern division of the Isthmus, and contains a population of nearly 6000, among whom are many Europeans. Of the foundation of this place little or nothing is now known, although tradition imputes to it a very great antiquity. Its appearance from the plains on the north is that of a large city, and the contrast between the white of its buildings and the deep brilliant hues of the surrounding foliage is pleasing to the utmost. Somewhat conspicuous, in the central part of the town, is the Parroquia, built by the Dominican friars in the early part of 1600: this is an antique-looking structure with arched roof and massive walls, supported at the corners by strong buttresses, which are surmounted by columned towers and pinnacles. The building is entirely without windows and the only light admitted is through a system of loop-holes, which seem to indicate that the church was designed as much for defence as for religious worship. The chancel consists of massive carvings in gilt, and the interior walls are variously painted in stucco. On each side, above the altar-table, are very well-executed pictures of the apostles Peter and Paul, and in the centre is an excellent painting of San Vincente, the patron saint of the town. The whole structure is inclosed by a brick wall several feet in thickness, with high-arched gateways opening on the south and east.

The inhabitants of Juchitan are characterized by habits of industry, and their numerous manufactures of hats, shoes, cotton cloth, hides, buckskins, mats, hammocks, &c., bear ample testimony to their mental superiority over the other settlements of the Isthmus. Among the articles raised are maize, indigo, and fruits. In addition, considerable valuable wood is annually gathered, and the inhabitants export large quantities of tallow and gum-arabic. Altogether, and in spite of many severe obstacles imposed by the government, Juchitan is the most industrious and thrifty town on the Pacific plains. Its appearance is enlivened by bustling shops, and the streets are more or less filled with ponderous carts drawn by oxen, and laden either with salt from the lagoons, or goods brought from Guatimala.

TEHUANTEPEC is the second town in the State of Oaxaca in point of numbers, manufacturing and commercial importance. It is situated eleven miles from the Bay of Ventosa, and about the same distance from Salina Cruz. It contains a population of about 13,000 inhabitants, mostly Indians, some half-breeds, and a few Castilians.* The better class are very aristocratic, the half-breeds civil and polite, the poor Indians humble and thankful for the smallest favor. Tehuantepec boasts of sixteen churches, among which is the venerable Parroquia built by Cocijopi, last cacique of the Zapotecos, in the year 1530, when it was dedicated to the purposes of Christian worship by the Dominican friars, to whom it was left as a legacy by the ill-used and dying cacique. This church is an extensive rectangular building, constructed somewhat Saracenic in its style of architecture. Its massive walls, arched gateways, and ruined dome, though fast crumbling to decay, speak in voiceless eloquence of the greatness of a people whose dust is mingled with its own. In the western end is a large chapel containing three altars and many rich ornaments in silver, with a due proportion of rude statuary in wood. A doorway on the left leads to a long corridor, the walls of which are hung with musty pictures of saints, and scenes now long forgotten. Some of the apartments on this floor are appropriated for the students of a college established in Tehuantepec in 1850, and supported by the funds of the

---

* This includes both San Blas and San Sebastian, which are separated from Tehuantepec by the river of that name.

ayuntamento. Already it numbers sixty students, who are taught Latin, French, drawing, and philosophy. Ascending a broad staircase, at the head of which are long aisles crossing each other at right angles, and divided into gloomy little cells, we reach that part of the building which was at one time the convent of "Santo Domingo," now vacant, and its archives and inmates long since transferred to the city of Oaxaca.

The next place of attraction is the market-place, bounding the northern side of the *plaza* or public square. Here is to be seen a motley group of women of all ages, sizes, and complexions. Indeed, all the marketing business may be said to be controlled by the weaker sex, who throng the long tiled shed (for such it is only) by hundreds at earliest dawn, startling the echoes of the overhanging Cerro del Tigre with their shrill and merry chatter. Here is ever a motley group of venders and buyers, duly besprinkled with hogs, dogs, and donkeys, the shouts, and grunts, and barks, and brays of which ring on the morning air all through the broad plaza. Here is a girl vending cheese — there a *donçilla*, with a calabash of jonquils and poppies — there again a withered old woman with *iguanas*, with dislocated shoulders and broken backs, panting for a purchaser — another with *sillas* and *frénos ;* a fifth with chicozapotes and tamarind water; a sixth with *huevas* and *chile ;* a seventh with corn and *sandillas ;* an eighth with *carne* and *ajos ;* and here and there an Indian maid with *tabacos* and *dulces.*

The manufactured articles of Tehuantepec are leather, cotton cloth, silken sashes, shoes, hats, mats, silver-ware, saddles, horse-appointments, and pottery, besides a considerable quantity of buckskins and soap. The town is governed by an ayuntamento, or town council, composed of the first, second, and third *alcaldes*, with an under magistrate elected from each of the sixteen *barrios*, or wards, into which the town is divided. The three first-named officers hold their courts daily in the town-house, and are assisted by a judge of the first instance, in the disposition of appeals and the trial of larger causes. The department of Tehuantepec is controlled by a governor, who exercises jurisdiction over all the alcaldes of all the towns and barrios, and who is directly responsible to the State government at Oaxaca. Police duty is performed by the soldiers of the National Guard, whose quarters command the entrance to the plaza. The cleaning of streets, repairs of pavements, &c., is executed by the prisoners in the public jail. The trade with Oaxaca consists of cochineal, cacao, fish, *camarones*, saddles, shoes, and leather; with Guatimala (which is *contraband*, and conducted chiefly by the Juchitecos), it is mostly manufactured English and French goods, as calicoes, linen, muslin, silk and cotton handkerchiefs.

The *coup d'œil* from the summit of the Cerro del Tigre is pleasing and picturesque in the greatest degree. But age, decay, war, and a hundred untold calamities have swept away the city's greatness, and every thing now wears the gray and grief-worn aspect of olden days. The houses are of massive structure, like antique fortresses, and of a style that might have rivalled those of more classic lands. But where once was wealth, and hope, and comfort, the spider now weaves his web. Westward the Tehuantepec River is visible, clear, and winding through many a league, its banks margined with fields of grain and the houses of old aristocratic landholders. Westward, further still, is the mountain of Guiéngola, with its ruined city, its broken arches and crumbling columns. Looking south, lies Ventosa and the granite hills of the Morro dividing it from Salina Cruz. There are plains here, there, and everywhere, watered by many a stream, clothed with luxuriant woods, decked with fields, ripe and in blossom, and smiling with an eternal spring-like beauty. On the opposite shore is San Sebastian and San Blas, the pictures of quietude, ruin, and decay; and beneath, noisy men, marching soldiers, beseeching beggars, ladened mules, braying asses, and dark, voluptuous women. But, besides all these, Tehuantepec has her public schools, play-grounds, flower-gardens, and places of amusement, stores, cabinet shops, shoemakers' shops, and workers in silver, brass, iron, and other metals. There are also several hotels and *posadas* for the accommodation of travellers.

One of the most interesting features near Tehuantepec is *Mount Guiéngola*, some five leagues distant in a northwesterly direction. This mountain is celebrated for having once been inhabited by a very large population, the evidences of which are palpable to this day, from the immense heaps of ruins which are now found in various parts of it. Among these is a massive wall, said to be several leagues in extent, built on the verge of a precipice, and reaching across a deep ravine which separates Guiéngola from the main chain. Within the inclosure of this wall are the ruins of several houses built of small ledge-stone, and above these a bold, precipitous spur of perforated limestone. Near the summit of this, is a cave of small entrance and above seventy-five feet deep. From the roof of this cave are pendent stalactites of a brilliant snow-white color. These stalactites, when struck by a hard substance, make a musical sound similar to that of an organ, and are capable of producing as many different tones.

A gentleman who explored this cave and the ruins, thus describes his visit:

"The general direction of the cave is downward at an angle of about forty-five degrees. As far as we went there were several large openings, or rooms, with a level floor, and passages from one to the other, varying from three to eight feet in diameter. It has evidently at some period been inhabited, for we found several pieces of earthenware, some of which were in a perfect state of preservation. At sundown we arrived at the top of this precipice of limestone, and came to a valley running horizontally, one-fourth of a mile wide and about two miles in length, which ended in a deep rocky ravine to the left. In this valley we found a large temple built of small flat stone, solid throughout, and in quite a perfect state, with the exception of the lime with which it was originally plastered. Time has worn off the principal part of this. Here we camped for the night upon the top of the temple. Early in the morning I sent the guide and 'moza' for water, and we commenced our exploration of the valley.

"The form of this temple is oblong, 33 feet high, at the base 105 feet long, 90 feet wide; at the top, 75 feet long, and 60 feet broad. There are four terraces surrounding the work, making each terrace six and a quarter feet high, one above the other. There are steps fronting the valley 25 feet long, extending to the top, also narrow steps at each end. The temple is at the side of a square inclosure which covers about two acres of ground, and surrounded by a wall 8 feet high and 12 feet broad. It is supposed that this structure was used for offering up sacrifices. Directly opposite, on the other side of the valley, we discovered another temple resembling this in form and material, but more than one-third larger. This had on the top the ruins of several houses built of brick. As far as we explored in this valley we found ruins of houses in every direction, even extending up on the steep side of the mountain. This valley we judged to be 1000 feet above the plain.

"Being determined to reach the summit, if possible, I took water and provisions for two days, and started with no one but the guide to accompany me. Before we got out of the valley I discovered a heap of ruins covering a quarter of an acre of ground, but the stone was so much broken down, that I could form no idea of its original shape. We proceeded on with much difficulty, and at dark arrived nearly at the summit of the mountain, where we made a large fire and camped for the night. At sunrise we renewed our attempt to reach the highest point, which occupied us until ten o'clock A. M. This summit is crowned with lofty pines so closely foliaged, that in order to get a view of the country beneath, I was obliged to climb one of the tallest of the trees, which well repaid my efforts. Indeed, it has never been my fortune to behold a scene so magnificent. In the distance was the broad Gulf of Tehuantepec—the silver lake of Telema—the immense plains, with here and there a small angular hillock rising out of it like an island from the sea—the waving fields of ripening grain—the shining spires of the distant city, and the green winding hedges which mark its suburbs.

"About mid-day we started to return, retracing our steps by the same path until reaching the valley where we bore off to the south, and came into it again some distance from where we crossed it on our way up. Here I found a large mass of ruins, some ten acres in extent, partially inclosed by a wall ten feet high and four feet thick. Within this inclosure the ground was paved with stones, which are in excellent preservation. In the centre there are two monuments, one square and the other round, each about twenty feet in diameter at the base. These are broken down to within ten feet of the pavement, and are surrounded by steps. * * * These ruins which I have described are but a small portion of what exist in other parts of the mountain.

"The Indians have a superstition that there was a church on the top of this mountain, over the ruins of which the devil is supposed to preside; and when they saw my fire, various speculations and opinions were advanced as to the manner his Satanic majesty would dispose of me. Indeed, so current is this superstition, that while among the ruins I could not get my guide ten steps in advance of me, and he even climbed the tree after me for protection. * * * In the archives of Juchitan there is still a traditionary document which makes the depopulation of Guiéngola three hundred years ago. How long anterior to that period its works were constructed, is a matter of grave or fanciful conjecture."

Between the southern slope of the dividing ridge and the ocean there are several minor settlements, among which are *La Cienega, Tlacotepec, Comitancillo, Mistequilla, Huilotepec, Huazontlan*, and *Zuleta*. In addition, there are also the Huave towns of *San Mateo, Santa Maria, San Dionisio*, and *San Francisco*, located on the sandy peninsula separating the lagoons from the Pacific, all of which have so little of interesting detail that one may be readily pardoned for passing them over in silence. Huilotepec, from its peculiar situation, is, however, somewhat of an exception, and may in time become an important point in the establishment of the proposed railroad. At present it is an insignificant village, located on the eastern shore of the Tehuantepec River, within four miles of the sea, at the base of a sharp angular cerro, called, in the language of the Zapotecos, the "Hill of Crystals," and which gives name to the settlement. It contains a few scattered houses and a population of two hundred and eighty, whose only animal stock consists of dogs, of which there are several hundred.

Immediately north and in close proximity to Ventosa, is a broad rich plain, which offers incomparable advantages for the location of a city. Free from overflow, or the presence of miasmatic marshes, and with abundant sources of delightful water on either side, it is but reasonable to conclude that before many years, the dense forest which now studs the plain will give place to cheerful habitations, and that where now only is the abode of the bird and the insect, will be heard the hum and the bustle of life's business.

No. 1. Statistical Table—Northern Division.

Names of Towns.	Population.	No. Horned Cattle.	No. Horses and Mules.	Remarks.
San Cristoval Ishuatlan..	680	4,000	80	
Santiago Maloacan......	740	6,000	120	Including San Antonio.
San Fran. Sanapa.......	330	10,000	250	Incl'g neighboring ranchos.
Tecaminoacan and Mecatepeque	700	?	?	
Hacienda of San José....	100	8,000	160	
Mina-titlan	530	1,500	250	Incl'g neighboring ranchos.
Cosuliacaque..........	2,000	900	468	
Otiapa................	900	160	148	
Jaltipan...............	2,300	700	240	
San Juan Chinameca....	1,400	5,000	1,250	[jas, &c.
Tesistepec.............	2,300	16,500	580	Incl'g Almagro, Casas Ve-
Almagres	370	4,000	100	
San Martin Acayucam...	8,940	56,630	10,055	Incl'g neighboring estates.
San Juan Oluta........	700			
Santa Ana Soconusco....	1,650			
San Pedro Joteapa	1,700	1,400	460	
San Andres Sayultepec..	1,240			
Santiago Mecayapa.....	750			
Santa Maria Minsapa....	800			
	28,130	114,790	14,161	

No. 2. Statistical Table—Southern Division.

Names of Towns.	Population.	No. Horned Cattle.	No. Horses and Mules.	Remarks.
Boca del Monte........	68	2,860	75	
San Juan Guichicovi....	5,200	400	3,000	
Santa Maria Petapa.....	1,300	?	?	
Santo Domingo.........	900	?	?	
El Barrio..............	1,200	2,000	290	
La Chivela	75			
Tarifa.................	60	15,000	700	Estate of Marquesanas.
Santiago	100			
Agua Escondida........	20			
San Miguel Chimalapa...	460	200	60	
Santa M. Chimalapa.....	680	100	20	
San Gerónimo..........	500			
Santo Domingo Chihuitan	580			
Itztaltepec............	1,600	18,180	?	Incl'g neighboring estates.
El Espinal.............	540			
Juchitan	6,400			
Tlacotepec	300			
Tehuantepec...........	13,000	11,805	3,600	Incl'g neighboring estates.
Huilotepec	280	800	90	
Total South. Div.	33,263	51,345	7,835	
" North. "	28,130	114,790	14,161	
Total on the Isthmus	61,393	166,135	21,996	

17

APPENDIX.

APPENDIX.

DOCUMENTS.

(No. 1.)

Memorial of Don José de Garay, soliciting of his Excellency, the President of the Mexican Republic, the Privilege of opening a Communication between the Atlantic and Pacific Oceans through the Isthmus of Tehuantepec, and Decree granting the same.

SIR—Your Excellency has caused the Mexican public to look forward to the present epoch as one of improvement and gigantic advancement in the career of national aggrandizement.

No measure can be more fruitful in prosperous results, none more memorable or more glorious, than that which shall form a junction between the two oceans, without the necessity of doubling that stormy cape which forms the southernmost extremity of the American Continent.

Thousands of ships yearly perform this difficult and tedious voyage, passing twice through the tropics, in the midst of innumerable and imminent dangers.

The mind is bewildered with the difficulty of embracing, in one comprehensive view, the astonishing consequences that would result from a communication between the two oceans, by means of which ships sailing from Europe will save two thousand leagues, and those from North America three thousand one hundred leagues, in their voyages to the coasts of China. What an economy of time and money! And how far will these advantages extend, now that the lines of steamboats established upon the high seas have so prodigiously shortened distances!

A great revolution will take place in the commercial, and even in the political affairs of all nations, the instant America shall open the passage through any of her isthmuses. The epoch which shall see this effected will be more memorable than that of the discovery of this Continent, and the name of him to whom the world shall owe this event will be at least as glorious as that of Columbus.

If your Excellency is ambitious of this glory for yourself and your country, you should now dedicate your attention, and the powerful mind with which you are endowed, to the execution of the enterprise contained in the present representation, and to which is annexed the project I have conceived for forming a communication between the two oceans.

By this your Excellency will see that I propose to execute this grand work in a very short time, considering the magnitude of the enterprise; that I ask not the least pecuniary assistance from the government; and that from the commencement I offer to the national treasury a considerable revenue, viz., one fourth of the net profits which may arise from the dues and imposts to be collected on the line of the route, and which dues and imposts will, after the term of fifty years, belong wholly to the Republic.

What I ask as an indemnification of expenses is certainly not much, when it is recollected that it will be necessary to form ports, raise fortifications and various other edifices, and open roads and canals; and when it is borne in mind that the indemnification does not consist in any valuable property of which the government is at present possessed, but in property to which I must create a value.

Should the lands of which I solicit a grant come to have a value hereafter, my exertions will have caused this effect, for at the present day they have none whatever.

The enterprise could not be undertaken for less than what I have solicited, because the magnitude of the works will be such as probably to absorb the resources arising from what I ask.

Your Excellency cannot fail to remark two very striking features in my project. First, the establishment of the lands to be conceded for the enterprise into a neutral territory: this is a point worthy of the magnanimity of government, and necessary to interest all nations, in order that the communication may not be seized by any foreign power, but be ever preserved as the property of the Republic. Secondly, that I have not proposed to open immediately a ship canal across the Isthmus; because I have seen this project abandoned in other parts of Central America and Columbia, for it had to encounter invincible difficulties on account of its magnitude. Desirous of carrying into execution a very gigantic undertaking, a lesser, but still a grand one, has been neglected.

Convinced that it has been well and truly said that, "*By grasping at too much, we often lose what is in our power,*" I have resolved to carry the latter into effect, without, however, renouncing my hopes of accomplishing the former. Although a communication by water will not be attempted for the present, this will infallibly take place when the Isthmus shall be well known to all nations as forming a convenient centre for carrying on the commerce of the whole world; when the advantage of giving to this grand work all the perfection of which it is capable shall be duly appreciated; and when both sides of the line of transport shall be dotted with rich and populous cities, as will certainly happen in a few years.

Let this be enumerated among the acts of your Excellency's public life, and your name will not only belong to the glory of your country, but will be identified with the best interests of mankind, and immortalized by the most imperishable of monuments. The whole world will receive incalculable benefits; and what advantages will not accrue to America in particular, when the accomplishment of this undertaking shall make her the centre of universal commerce, giving a vast impulse to the elements of her territorial wealth and greatness, dormant as yet, and incapable of being developed from the little intercourse she at present enjoys with the splendor and industry of Europe!

I beg leave, sir, to repeat, that the mind is bewildered, and loses itself, when it attempts to grasp the beneficial results that must accrue to Mexico on the completion of this project, from the facility with which her native products will be exported, and from her becoming the emporium of the commerce of the world, as also from the immense sums arising from duties and other contributions, paid, not by the inhabitants of her soil, but by foreigners, and from the great influx of population and capital to which it will inevitably lead.

May your Excellency, therefore, become the author of these great and numerous benefits to your country, by adopting the articles of my memorial, and thus acquire the most memorable and well-founded of titles to an illustrious and patriotic career.

Jos. de Garay.

Mexico, *February* 25, 1842.

(No. 2.)

Decree ordering the opening of the Isthmus, with the Grants therein specified; and Contract between the Supreme Government and Don José de Garay.

(stamp.)

In the City of Mexico, on the second day of March, in the year one thousand eight hundred and forty-three, I, the undersigned Notary national and public, being in the office of the Secretary of State for Foreign

Affairs of the supreme Government of the nation, and in the presence of the said Secretary of State, Don José Maria Bocanegra, also Magistrate of the Supreme Court of Justice, he said : that his Excellency the President of the Republic, General of Division, Benemeritus of the Country, Don Antonio Lopez de Santa Anna, in the exercise of the authority conferred upon him by the seventh clause of the Convention of Tacubaya, sworn to by the Nation, and by the Representatives of the several Departments of the Republic, was pleased to issue, and cause to be published with due solemnity, the following :

(DECREE.)

" Antonio Lopez de Santa Anna, General of Division, Benemeritus of the Country, and Provisional President of the Republic of Mexico, to all the inhabitants thereof,

Know ye, That firm to my purpose of aggrandizing the nation and of rendering the people happy, having before me the propositions which Don José de Garay has presented, and considering that no means are so sure and effectual for promoting the national prosperity as that of making the Republic the centre of the commerce and navigation of all countries, and that this must be the consequence of the establishment of an easy and short mode of transporting effects from one ocean to the other : As nature offers the means of accomplishing this, without opposing any great obstacles in the way of it, and without the necessity of incurring any vast expenses, in the Isthmus of Tehuantepec ; inasmuch as there the Cordillera dips or lowers itself to such a degree that it may almost be said to disappear, and that there are two harbors in these parts, one towards the north and the other towards the south, at a short distance from each other, a considerable portion of the space between them being easily transitable by means of a navigable river and lake, and the nature of the intermediate surface being very favorable to carrying on the works which it may be necessary to undertake, as it abounds in materials for construction : And considering that if up to this moment public attention has not been properly called to this enterprise (which alone is capable of aggrandizing the Republic), it has, perhaps, originated in not having duly calculated the important consequences which must result from it, either because its execution has been deemed impossible, or that a prejudice existing in favor of making a cut through the Isthmus to join the two oceans, the advantages of a railroad or canal destined for the transhipment of goods, by which the same results might be approximately obtained, has been entirely lost sight of : And furthermore desiring, if more cannot be done, to accomplish what is practicable when it is of importance to the Republic and to the world in general; and seeking, by promoting the execution of what is at present attainable, to give an impulse to future attempts on a larger scale (for the opening of a line of communication, by tending to show that it is not difficult to cut across the continent, may hereafter conduce to the undertaking of this great work): Feeling, besides, that in order to encourage the spirit of speculation, it is necessary to make concessions and confer privileges, by which alone enterprise has ever been fostered, and that by this enterprise in particular the nation will obtain revenues with which it cannot reckon at present, paid by the commercial interests of other nations, and immediately reap the advantages which must result from universal intercourse, when its soil shall become the emporium of commerce, and, consequently, teem with wealth and abundance, when its various products shall become articles of exportation: *Therefore,* by virtue of the powers and faculties vested in me by the seventh article of the Convention signed at Tacubaya, and sworn to by the Representatives of the Departments, I have determined to issue the following:

(DECREE.)

ARTICLE 1.—A line of communication shall be opened between the Pacific and Atlantic Oceans, through the Isthmus of Tehuantepec.

ART. 2.—This shall be performed by water, except where it is impracticable, when railroads and steam-carriages shall be used.

ART. 3.—The passage across the Isthmus having been opened, it is hereby declared neutral and common to all nations at peace with the Mexican Republic.

ART. 4.—The execution of this work shall be confided to Don José de Garay, to whom is hereby granted an exclusive privilege to this effect. His obligations and indemnifications shall be as follow:

FIRST.—Don José de Garay shall cause to be made, at his own expense, a survey of the ground and direction which the route should follow, and also of the ports which may be deemed most commodious. All which shall be concluded at furthest within the space of eighteen months from the date hereof, and the works shall be commenced within the space of ten months next hereafter; and, in case this should not be performed within the time specified, the exclusive privilege hereby conceded to him shall cease.

SECOND.—The said Don José de Garay shall cause to be made in the ports which he shall select all kinds of works that may be necessary for shelter and utility. He shall construct in each of them fortresses and warehouses: he shall carry into effect the line of communication between the two ports by means of water-carriage or railroads, in both cases by means of steam; and he shall establish as many steamboats and trains of steam-cars as shall be deemed necessary.

THIRD.—The grantee shall pay at a just valuation for any private property through which the route shall pass; but he shall not occupy, on account of public utility, more than a quarter of a league on either side of the line, which is all he can require the proprietors to sell.

ART. 5.—The indemnifications which are hereby accorded to the grantee, and to those who may acquire his rights, or any part thereof, are the following: He shall have the right of collecting the passage dues for the term of fifty years, at the expiration of which time they shall revert to the Government of the Republic; and for sixty years the exclusive privilege of carrying on the transport by steam-vessels and railroad-cars, with the right of determining an equitable rate of freight. But he shall give to the Government, from the time that the line of communication shall be opened for the transport of effects, the fourth part of the net produce of the receipts for this purpose, deducting the expenses of administration, preservation, and repair thereof. The Government shall also give a fourth part of the net profits to the Negotiation during a like term of fifty years, when it shall enter into possession of its before-mentioned rights over the line of communication. The Government and the Negotiation may each name their agents to look into the receipts and expenditures, during the whole of the time that each respectively shall be entitled to the before-mentioned fourth part of the profits. All the unoccupied lands for a distance of ten leagues on either side of the line of communication are hereby conceded in fee simple to the Negotiation.

ART. 6.—All foreigners are permitted to acquire real property, and to exercise any trade or calling, not even excepting that of mining, within the distance of fifty leagues on either side of the line of transit. That territory shall be the country of all who may come to establish themselves there, subject, however, to the laws of the Republic.

ART. 7.—The Government engages to give to the Negotiation every protection and assistance, as well for effecting the survey as for carrying on the works, but the remuneration of the services of the inhabitants of these parts shall be at the expense of the Negotiation. The Government also engages not to impose any contributions or taxes upon travellers or effects *in transitu*, until the expiration of the aforesaid term of fifty years, and not to levy upon the Negotiation or its funds any imposts or forced loans.

ART. 8.—The Government shall have the right of appointing the custom-house officers which it may see fit, in the ports and in any other points it may choose on the line of communication; but only for the purpose of recovering the duties of importation and exportation upon articles which do not come and go merely for the purposes of transport, and for preventing smuggling; and in no case shall they interfere in the collection of transport dues, nor in the collection of freights, lighterage, or tonnage, or of any other class of dues; for none shall be payable by vessels loading or unloading for the transport of effects as long as the communication shall belong to the Negotiation. The measures which the Government shall take for the prevention of smuggling shall be such as to cause no embarrassment or delay in the transport of effects across the Isthmus, and particular regulations will be adopted and issued to this effect.

ART. 9.—When the works shall be completed, they shall be examined by two surveyors, one to be named by the Government and the other by the Negotiation, in order that they may declare whether it has fulfilled the terms of the contract; and, in case these shall disagree, they shall nominate an umpire, who shall have the casting vote; but no kind of question or difference shall prevent the line of communication from coming into operation as soon as it shall be ready; and the Negotiation is always bound to fulfil the contract in every particular.

ART. 10.—In case it should hereafter be found practicable to join the two seas by a cut, and that propositions to this effect shall be made by any individual or any company, they shall not be admitted during the period of fifty years, for which the privilege is granted to Don José de Garay, without his previous consent, or that of those who may have acquired his rights.

ART. 11.—The contract between the Government and Don José de Garay shall be drawn out in writing, according to the tenor of the articles forming the basis of this decree, with all the formalities required by law.

Therefore I command that it be printed, published, and circulated, and duly carried into effect. Given at the Palace of the National Government this 1st day of March, 1842.

ANTONIO LOPEZ DE SANTA ANNA.

JOSÉ MARIA BOCANEGRA.

(CONTINUATION.)

"That for the fulfilment of the preceding decree, and in accordance with the enactments of the Supreme Government, it was determined to draw up and execute the title deeds to which it refers, effecting them in the best and most binding form; and, therefore, he declares that in the name and with the power of the Supreme Government fully and extraordinarily authorized by the before-mentioned seventh clause, and by its especial tenor, he grants to Don José de Garay the exclusive power of opening and constructing in the Isthmus of Tehuantepec a communication between the Pacific and Atlantic oceans, with the obligations, rights, and advantages contained in the preinserted decree dated the 1st instant, conceding to him in full right of property and dominion all the waste lands in the Isthmus within ten leagues on either side of the projected communication, granting him also the same right possessed by the nation of making use of the private property for objects of public utility, that he may acquire the grounds necessary for the transit, including a space of one fourth of a league on either side, with due and previous remuneration to the proprietors according to valuation, and without regard to the increased value which the grounds may afterwards acquire in consequence of the projected works and the expenses incurred by the parties effecting the communication; and under no excuse whatever will the Government lay any tax or impost upon any of the articles passing through the Isthmus during the period in which the proprietors of the transit shall have the exclusive enjoyment of its proceeds, as well as the regulation of its tariff rates, as mentioned in the seventh and eighth clauses. That in the name of the Supreme Government, and under the most solemn protests, he declares and promises that all and every one of the concessions mentioned in the preinserted decree shall be honorably fulfilled, now and at all times, pledging the honor and public faith of the nation to maintain the projector, Don José de Garay, as well as any private individual or company succeeding or representing him, either natives or foreigners, in the undisturbed enjoyment of all the concessions granted, holding the National Administration responsible for any acts of its own or its agents, which, from want of proper fulfilment of the covenant, might injure the interest of the proprietors—all, of course, subject to the exact tenor of the inserted decree. And Don José de Garay being also present, and whom I hereby certify I know, said that he had accepted, and again accepts, the above-mentioned contract, and solemnly submitted to all and every one of the conditions therein expressed, ac-

APPENDIX. 269

cording to the tenor of the preinserted decree of the Supreme Government; and he willingly consents to forfeit the privileges granted to him, and whatever sums he or those who might succeed him should have advanced, if by any unforeseen event the line of communication shall not be established; and he is also willing that the enterprise should be held bound to fulfil all that is here agreed upon. And his Excellency the authorized Minister of State, and the same Don José de Garay, in their respective capacities, renounce any laws in their favor, and hold this as the most binding obligation, accepting and taking for granted any additional clause which might make it still more so.

It was so declared and signed by his Excellency the Minister, and also by Don José de Garay, and witnessed by Don Manuel Madariaga, Don Manuel Rojo, and Don José Mendoza of this city: which I certify.

J. M. DE BOCANEGRA,
JOSÉ DE GARAY.

FRANCISCO DE MADARIAGA,
Notary Public and National.

Engrossed duplicate, at the request of Señor Garay, this 19th day of December, one thousand eight hundred and forty-three, in seven sheets, the first bearing the first stamp and the other the fourth.

Corrected, the same parties being witnesses, which I certify.

(Signed) FRANCISCO DE MADARIAGA,
Notary Public and National.

(No. 3.)

Communication from Don José de Garay to his Excellency the Minister of Foreign Affairs and Home Department, showing the progress of the work of exploration in the Isthmus, and soliciting to be put in possession of the waste lands granted to him by the decree, dated the 1st March, 1842, the Supreme Government being pleased also to declare included in them all the concessions previously made of any part of the said grounds which may have been forfeited in consequence of the parties not fulfilling their contracts.

MOST EXCELLENT SIR—I, Don José de Garay, projector of the line of communication between the two seas intended to be established in the Isthmus of Tehuantepec, with due respect beg to submit to your Excellency, that in the fulfilment of my engagements to execute that undertaking, and in accordance with that which I made in the first part of Article 4 of the decree of the 1st March, 1842, since then committed to writing, I appointed and provided with every necessary means the Commissioners who investigated the locality, without sparing either labor or expense, which latter amounts already to a considerable sum. The results of this investigation are perfectly satisfactory, as your Excellency will see in the accompanying copy of the note which the Secretary of the Commission addressed to me privately from the Venta de Chicapa on the 11th January last. The possibility of opening the projected communication is by these proceedings ascertained, a fact which cannot but be highly gratifying to the Supreme Government, so deeply interested in the execution of a work of the greatest importance to the aggrandizement of the Republic. My first engagement is, therefore, fulfilled. To fulfil the second, which must begin by marking out and opening the line of communication, levelling the ground, giving a different course to rivers, lakes, and creeks, and performing whatever is needful to realize the undertaking, the Supreme Government ought without delay to direct the civil authorities to place at my disposal the lands through which the road must pass, from the bar of San Francisco in the south to that of the Coatzacoalcos in the north, as well as of the uncultivated or unclaimed lands mentioned in the 5th Article of the said decree. This last clause is essential to the realization of the third part of the 4th Article, since, without being able to commence immediate operations on hills, plains, and rivers, it will be impossible to fulfil the second part of my duties relative to the execution of the works.

The Supreme Government has seen the zeal with which I have attended to my engagements in the very fact of the investigations for which eighteen months were allowed having been performed in nine, notwithstanding the difficulties and drawbacks which the Commission had to encounter. It is the same spirit of activity and solicitude that urges me to make the above demand, especially as if, from want of the necessary orders, the Commission be needlessly detained a month longer, my expenses will be materially increased. According, then, to the above statement, and to the claims which my agreement gives me, I beg that the Supreme Government may be pleased to issue orders to put me in possession of the territory through which the works must be carried on, as well as for the fulfilment of the 7th Article of the above-mentioned decree of the 1st of March. I must, besides, call the attention of the Supreme Government to the circumstance that various portions of land on both shores of the River Coatzacoalcos, through which the line of communication must pass, having been granted to colonists, it is natural that they will allege their rights as proprietors against those I have acquired by my engagements. These colonists, however, having neither cultivated nor peopled the lands which had been ceded to them for such purposes, have, according to the laws of the country, lost their right to the property—a fact which I request the Supreme Government, in justice to myself, will make public by a decree, lest I be involved in disputes and litigations after the outlay of large sums.

Jos. DE GARAY.

MEXICO, *February* 9, 1843.
To his EXCELLENCY THE MINISTER FOR FOREIGN AFFAIRS.

(No. 4.)

Official communication from his Excellency the Minister of Foreign Affairs to Don José de Garay, inclosing a copy of the orders given to the Governors of Oaxaca and Vera Cruz, to place the untenanted lands at his disposal, and that every measure be taken to prevent his agents from suffering any obstacle in their operations.

OFFICE OF FOREIGN AFFAIRS.

SIR—I subjoin a copy of the communications addressed this day to their Excellencies, the Governors of the Departments of Oaxaca and Vera Cruz: "Most Excellent Sir—On the first of May of last year, the Provisional President published a decree granting to Don José de Garay an exclusive privilege to open a communication between the Pacific and Atlantic Oceans, in the Isthmus of Tehuantepec; ceding to him, by Article the 5th, the possession of the untenanted lands that lay within ten leagues on each side of the projected road, and promising, by Article 7th, to render him every assistance in carrying on both the survey and the works. The survey is so far advanced as to allow the commencement of the works and other operations, without which a project of such magnitude would be thrown into jeopardy, greatly to the detriment of the Republic. His Excellency the Provisional President, having present these considerations, and others which spring from the same decree, and wishing to render effectual the solemn promises made, has been pleased to direct me to inform your Excellency of the above, that your Excellency may give the necessary orders for the fulfilment of the 5th Article of the decree, by which Don José de Garay is to be put in possession of the untenanted lands that lie within ten leagues of both sides of the line of road, requesting, at the same time, that your Excellency will do all in your power not only to render effective the grant of lands as far as your Department is concerned, but also to give the assistance and protection promised by the Supreme Government to Don José de Garay, so as to remove every obstacle likely to prevent or retard the execution of the plan.

"It is essential that the Commissioners and other agents employed in the opening of this road, which must extend from the bar of the Coatzacoalcos on the north to that of San Francisco on the south, should be protected against every thing that may prevent the performance of their duties, and in case any claims to ownership of lands should be put forth by private individuals, your Excellency will regulate your proceedings according to the obligation which the 4th Article of the decree imposes upon Don José de Garay. Full liberty must also be allowed him to give a different course to the River Coatzacoalcos and its tributaries, or any other rivers, lakes, or creeks, to clear their borders, and use the timber when not required to be felled on private ground.

"To know how far it will be necessary to make use of private property, as well as to mark out the limits of the grant of territory awarded to Don José de Garay in the above-mentioned decree, that gentleman is authorized to appoint land surveyors, who will be subject to no control but that of the officer whom your Excellency may be pleased to appoint, and intrust with instructions agreeably to this order, and the attendance of the adjoining land-owners, whose measurement will fix and determine his right of claim to possession. In case any proprietor of land refuses to give up his property in conformity with this decree, a valuation will immediately be set on foot, and according to it the land purchased for the undertaking.

"The greatness of this enterprise merits every effort to promote its realization; and it is with this object that I have the honor to transmit this communication from his Excellency, the Provisional President, availing myself of the opportunity to assure your Excellency of my deep respect and consideration."

God and Liberty, Mexico, 9 February, 1843.

BOCANEGRA.

Señor Don José de Garay.

(No. 5.)

Decree by which the Government declares that all the Lands granted previous to the Decree of the 1st March, both to Natives and Foreigners, and which are neither tenanted nor cultivated, belong to Don José de Garay.

OFFICE OF FOREIGN AFFAIRS.

To their Excellencies, the Governors of Oaxaca and Vera Cruz.

(COPY.) His Excellency, the Provisional President, has been pleased to publish the following decree:

Nicolas Bravo, General of Division, Benemeritus of the Country, and Provisional President of the Republic of Mexico, to all the inhabitants be it known: That a grant having been made in favor of the undertaking to open a communication between the two oceans, through the Isthmus of Tehuantepec, of the untenanted lands lying within ten leagues on both sides of the line of communication, which, according to the surveys already made, must pass through the River Coatzacoalcos, and, wishing to remove every obstacle which might prevent or retard the realization of the undertaking, I have deemed it necessary, in right of the faculties which the 7th Article of the Convention signed at Tacubaya, and sworn to by the Representatives of the various Departments, awards to the Supreme Government, to declare the following:

All the grants of land made either to natives or foreigners previous to the decree of the 1st March, 1842, from among the untenanted lands mentioned in the 3d Article of the said decree, and which actually remain uninhabited and uncultivated, are comprehended in the concessions made in behalf of the undertaking for the communication of the two seas; therefore I do order this to be printed, published, and circulated, for the purpose of being fulfilled.

Palace of the Government of Mexico, February 9, 1843.

NICOLAS BRAVO.

J. M. de Bocanegra, Minister for Foreign Affairs.

A true copy of the original document transmitted to the Governors of Vera Cruz and Oaxaca, which I inclose to you for your intelligence.

God and Liberty, Mexico, February 9, 1843.

Decree ordering 300 Convicts to be placed under the direction of Don José de Garay, to work in the projected Canal.

OFFICE OF FOREIGN AFFAIRS.

His Excellency the President has been pleased to issue the following decree:

"Antonio Lopez de Santa Anna, General of Division, Benemeritus of the Country, and Provisional President of the Republic of Mexico, to all the inhabitants be it known: That whereas the survey of the Isthmus of Tehuantepec has been concluded, and the works to open a communication between the two oceans about to be begun, and it being my wish to assist the director by every means in the power of the Supreme Government, I, by virtue of the prerogatives allowed me by the nation, decree as follows:

"ART. 1.—A convict station shall be established with 300 convicts, to be employed in the works of the canal.

"ART. 2.—The judicial authorities of Vera Cruz and Oaxaca shall send to the said station all criminals sentenced to public works, until the number be completed.

"ART. 3.—The director of the undertaking will clothe and victual those 300 convicts, and provide them with tools on his own account.

"ART. 4.—The troops necessary to guard the station shall be provided by the military force of the Department where the said station may be established, and paid by the director of the undertaking."

And that this decree may be known, circulated, and fulfilled, I hereby order it to be printed.

National Palace of Tacubaya, October 4, 1843.

ANTONIO LOPEZ DE SANTA ANNA.

J. M. de Bocanegra, Minister for Foreign Affairs.

I have the honor to communicate this decree to you for your information and guidance.

God and Liberty, Mexico, October 6, 1843.

BOCANEGRA.

Señor Don José de Garay.

Decree granting to Don José de Garay the term of a year, according to his request, for the commencement of the Works.

(STAMP.)

I, the citizen Francisco de Madariaga, Public Notary of this Capitol,

APPENDIX. 275

do hereby certify and bear witness that a decree, signed by his Excellency the Minister for Foreign Affairs, Don José Maria Bocanegra, was presented to me by order of Señor Don José de Garay, which is exactly as follows:

(SUPREME ORDER.)

OFFICE OF FOREIGN AFFAIRS.

SIR—His Excellency the President *ad interim*, whom I acquainted with your request that the period prescribed in the decree of March, 1842, for the commencement of the works in the Isthmus of Tehuantepec, should be postponed for the term of a year, has been pleased to determine in Council, this day, that the same shall be granted.

God and Liberty, Mexico, December 28, 1843.

BOCANEGRA.

Señor Don José de Garay.

This copy of the supreme order agrees with the original, which I have returned to the person who, in the name of Don José de Garay, presented it to me, which I hereby witness. And that it may be known to all whom it may concern, I give this in the city of Mexico, on the 29th December, 1843.

Witnesses.—Don Manuel Madariaga,
   Don Manuel Rojo,
   Don José Mendoza.
   (Signed)   FRANCISCO DE MADARIAGA,
              Public Notary.

Extract from a Decree of General Don José Mariano de Salas, at the time exercising Supreme Executive Power, and dated at the Palace of the National Government, Mexico, 5th November, 1846.

ARTICLE 1.—The decree of 1st March, 1842, of the Provisional Government, which concedes to Don José de Garay the exclusive privilege of opening a line of communication across the Isthmus of Tehuantepec, so as to connect the Atlantic and Pacific Oceans, is hereby confirmed.

ART. 2.—The decree of 9th February, which grants to the projector all the waste lands within ten leagues on either side of the line of the canal, is hereby confirmed.

ART. 3.—The decree of 6th October, 1843, which establishes a convict station to assist in the works to be carried on by the enterprise for effecting a communication between the two oceans, is hereby confirmed, with the understanding that it is not to be considered obligatory that the precise number of convicts shall be 300.

Art. 4.—The term for the commencement of the works allowed to Don José de Garay shall be further extended for two years more, to be reckoned from the date of the publication of this decree.*

Art. 5.—The rates for lighthouses, pilotage, and for the transmission of letters shall be fixed by a special law, analogous to the provisions of that of 1st March, 1842.

Art. 6.—A compensation for all lands belonging to individuals, communities, or corporations, which may be found within the ten leagues on either side of the transit, shall be made to the enterprise in other waste lands it shall select in districts nearest to the Isthmus.

Art. 7.—All colonists making settlements under the enterprise to carry out the project, shall be exempt from military service for the term of twenty years, excepting only in the case of a foreign invasion of the Isthmus.

Art. 8.—They shall be similarly exempt, for the same period, from all contributions not in the nature of municipal taxes.

Art. 9.—All implements intended for agricultural purposes, and instruments for the arts, shall be exempt from all duty for a similar term.

Art. 10.—All articles of subsistence, clothing, furniture, and other things useful for the construction and embellishment of houses, shall be exempt from all duties for the term of six years, to be computed from the establishment of the colony; but in case such articles should be intended for consumption in the interior, then they shall be subject to the general existing laws of the Republic.

Art. 11.—All articles intended for the construction and repair of the line of communication shall be admitted free of duty, it being required, however, that they shall be subject to a previous examination.

Art. 12.—No colonists shall be allowed to settle who are at the time citizens of a State at war with the Republic.

Art. 13.—It shall be an express condition in all contracts with colonists, that they shall renounce the privileges of their original domicil so long as they reside in the country, subjecting themselves to all the existing colonial regulations which are not in conflict with the present law.

Art. 14.—The enterprise shall submit for the approval of Government all contracts which it shall make for the introduction of families and la-

---

* It is proper here to observe that the works on the Isthmus were commenced within the time prescribed by the decree, and have since been continued.

borers, and it shall keep a public and authentic register of all its transactions in respect to all matters of colonization.

Art. 15.—The waters of all rivers and streams which empty into the canal, and serve to feed it, shall not be disturbed nor turned away in any part of their course, nor in their sources, so as to deprive the enterprise of the use of them. In case any person has a right to the use of the said waters at the present time, the enterprise shall indemnify such parties in the manner prescribed by the existing laws which regulate the appropriation of private property for public uses.

30th Congress,   [SENATE.]   Miscellaneous.
2d Session.   No. 50.

PETITION OF P. A. HARGOUS,

Offering to the consideration of Congress the advantages of a Railroad across the Isthmus of Tehuantepec, and praying that Congress, before its final action on the subject, will allow time for establishing the facts therein stated.

[February 6, 1849.—*Ordered to be printed.*]

To the Honorable the Senate and House of Representatives of the United States in Congress assembled:

The petition of Peter A. Hargous, of the city of New York, for himself and in behalf of others interested with him, respectfully represents, that they are invested with full authority from the Mexican Republic, under the most solemn guarantees from that Government, to open a communication between the Gulf of Mexico and the Pacific Ocean, across the Isthmus of Tehuantepec.

Your petitioner respectfully represents the following facts, which he has derived from the authentic and published report of the engineer who made the surveys in relation to this route, in order that your honorable body may possess all the necessary information on this highly important subject.

The grant from the Mexican Government, by which the privilege is secured to your petitioner of opening a communication across the Isthmus, is of the most liberal character, and offers the strongest inducements for undertaking the enterprise. The privileges of the grant are secured to your petitioner and those associated with him for the period of fifty years; and during this time the Government of Mexico has pledged itself "not to impose any contributions or taxes upon travellers or their effects in transitu, and not to levy any imposts or forced loans on the grantees." The grant also secures the right to "all foreigners to acquire real property, and to exercise any trade or calling, not even excepting that of mining, within the distance of fifty leagues on either side of the line of transit."

Finally, "in the name of the Supreme Government, and under the most solemn assurances, it is declared and promised that all and every one of the concessions mentioned shall be honorably fulfilled now and at all times, pledging the honor and public faith of the nation to maintain the projector, Don José de Garay, as well as any private individual or company succeeding or representing him, either natives or foreigners, in the undisturbed enjoyment of all the concessions granted, holding the national administration responsible for any acts of its own or its agents, which, from want of proper fulfilment of the covenant, might injure the interests of the proprietor."

Under this grant topographical, geological, and hydrographical surveys of the line of a communication across the Isthmus have been made. They were made under the direction of Mr. Moro, an Italian engineer of high distinction, assisted by two other scientific gentlemen. "The entire line of country was carefully surveyed and mapped; the face of the land, its productions and capabilities, were examined with untiring perseverance," and a very full report was subsequently drawn up, which has been published, with accompanying maps; all of which are now in the possession of your petitioner.

"From these surveys it is established that the entire distance from sea to sea is 135 miles in a straight line, and presents a wide plain from the mouth of the Coatzacoalcos to the port of the Mesa de Tarifa, a table or elevated plain on the line of the Andes, which rises to the height of 650 feet above the level of the sea, and at the distance of 5 miles again descends to a plain which reaches the Pacific. The summit level to be overcome is only 650 feet; 30 miles of the River Coatzacoalcos are navigable for ships of the largest class, and 15 miles beyond this for vessels of light draught, leaving only about 115 miles of railroad to be made. It would occupy too much space to enumerate all the details of these surveys, and which go to show so strongly how easily a railroad can be constructed across the Isthmus of Tehuantepec. It is sufficient to say that the absolute practicability has been clearly ascertained."

In other respects it affords great facilities for construction. "The entire course of the Coatzacoalcos is bounded by forests, which can supply immense quantities of the proper kind of timber suitable for the construction of a railroad, and all of which is, by the terms of the grant, the property of the company undertaking the construction of the road. Limestone, strong clay, asphaltum, and building stone of the best quality, suitable for bridges, where necessary, are placed, as if purposely by nature, all along the direction of this route. The Zapotecos and other Indians can be found in quite sufficient numbers to carry on the work, and at those points where foreign labor is indispensable, the temperature is such as to allow them to pursue their labor without either inconvenience or injury to their health. The climate, though warm, is healthy. The natives are mild, submissive, and tractable. There are ample sources whence to obtain a stock of domestic animals and beasts of burden. Throughout the whole line secured by the grant as well for the purposes of a communication across the Isthmus as for the settlement of the country by foreigners, all the productions of the equatorial and temperate regions are found in the greatest abundance; for the valley of the Isthmus produces the former, and, on ascending the more elevated country bordering on the valley, the climate of the temperate zone is found there as well as its productions. At each end of the railroad are suitable places for fine harbors, as well as to depth, size, and security from storms. It is true, there is a bar at the mouth of the Coatzacoalcos. By different navigators the water has been sounded, and from twelve to eighteen feet have been found on it at low water. Commodore Perry, in his survey in 1847, found twelve feet. At a small pass at the entrance of the ocean on the Pacific side there is at low water seven feet.

Your petitioner, however, is convinced, from the character of the obstructions, that they can, at a small expense of time and money, be easily removed, and will then open an entrance for vessels of large size into ports equal to any in the world. He is prepared to show this to the satisfaction of your honorable body.

Such are some of the physical advantages connected with this route. There are others, however, no less important. The distance from the mouth of the Mississippi to San Francisco, by the Isthmus of Tehuantepec, is 3294 miles; by the Isthmus of Panama, 5000—thus showing that the route by the Isthmus of Tehuantepec is 1706 miles shorter than by Panama. The distance from New York, by the Isthmus of Tehuantepec, is 4744 miles; by the Isthmus of Panama, 5858 miles—making the route by Tehuantepec from New York to San Francisco 1104 miles shorter than by the Isthmus of Panama.

The mere statement of these facts carries with it its own importance; for it is an axiom that in all human operations the saving of time is the saving of labor and money. This fact is already exercising its influence;

for enterprising men are at this very moment turning their attention to this route without the advantages of an artificial communication across it.

In time of war, too, the route by the Caribbean Sea would bring us under the guns of hostile forts and fleets, without any port of our own to resort to either for shelter or repairs; whereas, by the Tehuantepec route, we would be all the time within the limits of our own sea—for such, in truth, the Gulf of Mexico may be considered in relation to us.

Your petitioner has already adverted to the fact that, under the grant from Mexico, 150 miles on each side of the route of the proposed road across the Isthmus are open to the emigration of foreigners, who are entitled to the privileges of holding lands in fee. From the inducements of climate and production throughout this region, and more from its great water-power, which is abundant on all the table-land, your petitioner is firmly convinced that in the course of a few years this whole country will be settled by people from the United States and Europe; and thus, while all these rights will be in our hands, the blessings of our civilization will silently but powerfully extend themselves.

Besides these civil and moral advantages, which of themselves are sufficient to show the important character of this route, there is a consideration of a political kind not less important than all of them. The policy of cultivating the most friendly relations, and of cementing the good understanding which now so happily exists between the United States and Mexico, must be strikingly obvious to every American statesman. Political friendships are best secured through the interests of nations, and especially where they can be made mutual and identical. The broadest foundation is laid for an extensive and lucrative commerce between the two countries, from the fact that we are neighbors, both by land and sea, with ports facing, and almost within sight of each other, and each possessing what the other wants. It is, therefore, clearly for our interests to take all the necessary steps to promote this desirable end. Nothing could be more opportune than a communication across the Isthmus of Tehuantepec under the guidance and capital of the United States; for the advantages will incidentally be so great to Mexico, that her interests, as well as a wise policy on her part, will induce that Republic to cherish the most friendly relations with us; and hence, through the harmonizing influence of reciprocal commercial interests, we will secure a firm ally in our neighbor. All other routes carry us into the land of strangers, far from our own shores, with interests dissimilar if not adverse to ours, and where, from the nature of the climate and the character of the people, no affiliation of either political or commercial relations can ever be advantageously established.

At the present moment every thing conspires to aid the undertaking, and to insure for it a successful result, and nothing more so than the fact that the inhabitants of the Isthmus have testified the greatest interest in the project, have given to it in all the forms required of them their hearty approbation, and are ready to afford all the facilities for the construction of a road.

In addition, your petitioner will forthwith take the necessary steps to obtain all proper guarantees from the Government of Mexico for the security of the rights of the company which he proposes to form, in which he has entire confidence that he will succeed, as he knows that the Mexican people are not only favorably disposed to the projected road, and have a full perception of its importance to their country, but are anxious for its completion. If such guarantees are obtained, he will immediately organize an American company for the construction of the road, and he has not the slightest doubt that the requisite amount of stock will be subscribed, and the road forthwith commenced. In the mean time he does not desire to precipitate the Government of the United States into any contract until full assurance is given of the completion of the road; but he only asks that the Government will not hastily commit itself, without a full knowledge of all the advantages of the road which he proposes to construct in comparison with any and all others.

As to the practicability of the route, it may be well to give the very words of the distinguished engineer who surveyed it, and all of which has the confident conviction of your petitioner as to its truth. He says: "The careful survey of the line of transit over the Isthmus demonstrates the practicability of the project, since it presents no one serious difficulty which may not be readily conquered by means of capital and science, the gigantic developments of which at this auspicious period seem to have placed at the disposal of the engineer inexhaustible and unlimited power."

Your petitioner has brought these principal facts to the notice of your honorable body, in the hope further steps may be adopted, which will insure a full examination of the results of the survey, in the firm conviction on his part that such an examination will establish the value of this route to the United States in a communication with its possessions on the Pacific shore.

P. A. HARGOUS.

In the early part of 1850, when the New Orleans Company first contemplated making the survey of the Isthmus of Tehuantepec, application was made to the Mexican Government, through the State Department at Washington, for permission to that effect. This permission was granted, and a letter written by Mr. Lacunzu, Mexican Secretary of Foreign Affairs, to the Governor of Oaxaca, informing him that Major Barnard, with sundry engineers, were coming to make the survey of the Isthmus for the purpose of opening the inter-oceanic communication, and directing the said Governor to give aid and hospitality. A copy of this letter was furnished Major Barnard, but was left among his papers either in New Orleans or in Mexico. This was a virtual passport to the whole Commission, for the express purpose of making a survey. In addition, each member was furnished with a passport at New Orleans, of which the following is a verbatim copy:

[MEXICAN COAT-OF-ARMS.]

Vice-Consulado de la Republica Mejicana
EN NUEVA-ORLEANS.

ORTHON LORENZO DABELSTEEN,
VICE-CÓNSUL DE LA REPÚBLICA MEJICANA

EN NUEVA-ORLEANS.

No.

[SEAL.]

Firma del interesado.

J. J. WILLIAMS,
Principal Assist. Eng.

CONCEDO libre y seguro pasaporte al Sor. J. J. WILLIAMS, de la compª. de reconocimiento natural del estado de Massachusetts, ciudadano de los Estados Unidos, de edad de treinte uno años, y de profesion Ayudante Engeniero para que pase al puerto de Vera Cruz, en el vapor Americano "Alabama," segun ha solicitado.

Por tanto ruego á las Autoridades de los países estranjeros por donde transitare, no le pongan impedimento alguno en su viaje, y á las de la República recomiendo su persona para, que le dispensen la proteccion que conceden las leyes.

Dado en la ciudad de Nueva-Orleans, á diez de Diciembre de mil ochocientos cincuenta.

O. L. DABELSTEEN, *Vta.*

Derechos dos pesos.

APPENDIX. 283

[Copy of Translation.]

MINISTRY OF FOREIGN RELATIONS.
MEXICO, *December* 10, 1850.

HONORED SIR—The Minister of Relations has received the letter in which his Excellency, Mr. Letcher, communicates the sailing from New Orleans of the American steamship Alabama for Coatzacoalcos, and, obeying the desires of his Excellency, has given the necessary orders to the governments of Vera Cruz and Oaxaca, that they may place no obstacles to the voyage of the Alabama, or any other vessel which has the same object, providing they subject themselves to the laws of navigation.

The Minister of Relations, on giving these orders, has done it under the intelligence that the engineers who accompany Major Barnard form no military body, as Governor Letcher knows that, forming such a body, they would not be permitted to disembark.

The Minister of Relations reiterates to his Excellency, Governor Letcher, the assurances of his very distinguished consideration.

To his Excellency, Gov. R. P. LETCHER, Envoy Extraordinary and Minister Plenipotentiary of the United States at Mexico.

Copy of the Letter addressed to Major Barnard by the Governor of Tehuantepec.

SIR—The Secretary of dispatches of the Supreme Government of the State, in a supreme order of 23d May, among other things says what follows:

"His Excellency, the Minister of Relations, in an official document of the 22d of last month, says the following to the Governor of the State:

"SIR—In a separate note I communicate to you the decree passed to-day by the National Congress, annulling that of the 5th November, 1846, which prorogued the privilege conceded to Mr. José Garay to open an inter-oceanic communication across the Isthmus of Tehuantepec. The President, deeply appreciating the constitutional duty by which he has to enforce the orders of Congress, orders you to publish immediately said decree, and that you suspend immediately all scientific works going on either at Tehuantepec or at Coatzacoalcos, causing all the Americans employed on said works to leave the country, or permitting them to remain as long as they desire, it being understood by them that for no motive will they be allowed to continue said work, and that they will be subject, as all other strangers, to the laws of the nation. You will communicate to me the result of this resolution, accepting the assurance of my appreciation."

I transcribe for you the orders of the Governor for your intelligence. I have the honor to insert for your information, and so that, complying with it exactly, you may suspend immediately all the secondary parties working under your orders in the Isthmus of Tehuantepec, be they either scientific or hydrographic operations. You may return speedily to the United States, for which be so kind as to send me a list of the individuals, so that it may be proved and they obtain their passports from the supreme authorities, informing those who wish to remain longer in this Republic as private individuals, and like all other strangers, they will be under the Mexican laws and the vigilance of the authorities, taking care to take out letters of security to legalize their residence. Before concluding this note, I should inform you that for no motive or pretext your works can or ought to be prosecuted by the commission of which you are chief; on the contrary, I shall order them to be suspended according to the order inserted in the supreme note.

I offer you, this time, my distinguished consideration. God and Liberty. Tehuantepec, 3d June, 1851.

MAXIMO R. ORTIZ.

To the Chief of the American Commission, MAJOR J. G. BARNARD, United States Army.

Copy of the Reply of Major Barnard.

To his Excellency, Señor Don Maximo R. Ortiz, Governor of Tehuantepec:

SIR—I have the honor to acknowledge the receipt of the letter of your Excellency, and the papers inclosed, announcing the act of the Congress of Mexico, by which the grant under which the Commission, of which I am the head, is acting, is declared as forfeited and null; also informing me that the works of the Survey must cease, and the members of the party return to the United States, excepting such as may choose to remain with letters of security under the general protection of the laws of the Republic. While deeply regretting the course of the Government, and protesting against the action under it, as involving in deep injury those in whose service the members of the Company are engaged, I have, nevertheless, no other course than to comply with your orders, so positively expressed, and have in consequence of them caused the labors of

APPENDIX. 285

the Survey to cease, and the members of the Commission to return with all dispatch to the United States, except a few, who will remain, under the present conditions, in charge of such property as cannot now be disposed of, until final orders on the subject be received from the officers of the Company in the United States. I send, as you have been pleased to order, the names of those who will leave the country, as well as of those who will remain.

I have the honor to be your Excellency's obedient servant,

J. G. BARNARD,
Chief Engineer of Tehuantepec Survey.

EL BARRIO, *June* 9, 1851.

CONSULATE OF THE UNITED STATES OF AMERICA,
CITY OF TEHUANTEPEC, REPUBLIC OF MEXICO.

By this public instrument of protest be it known to all persons, that J. G. Barnard, Major U. S. Army, and William H. Sidell, Civil Engineer, citizens of the United States, agents of whom it may concern, did, on this eleventh day of June, A.D. 1851, personally appear before me, Charles R. Webster, Consul for the United States of America, at this place, and enter their ·solemn protest against the Government of the Republic of Mexico, the agents and officers of said Government. The said Major J. G. Barnard and William H. Sidell, agents as aforesaid, hereby protesting against the said Government of Mexico, its officers and agents, declare and say, that on the 1st of March, A.D. 1842, a grant was made by the Mexican Government to one of its citizens, having for its object the construction of a road or canal across the Isthmus of Tehuantepec, and that the privileges of said concession were from time to time extended by the legal acts of said Government, until, in the year (A.D.) 1850, all the duties having been complied with by the said citizen or his assignees, and the rights under the concession remaining in full force, "*and the honor and public faith of the nation having been pledged under the most solemn protests to the grantee or his assignees—whether natives or foreigners—that all the conditions on the part of the Government should be honorably fulfilled,*" it was resolved by them to obtain a thorough survey of the route, with a view to the immediate construction of the works necessary to its being properly opened; that, in pursuance of this, the said Barnard, one of the protestants, with a party of engineers, came to the Isthmus of Tehuantepec in the month of December, A.D. 1850, and entered upon the duties with the greatest activity, his party being large and efficient, and the funds ample; that, from the date of his arrival until a few days since, these labors were continued and prosecuted with success, when they were suddenly brought to a close by an order of the Mexican Government—as unexpected as unjust—whereby the operations of the survey were required to be discontinued, and the members of the surveying parties were compelled to leave the country, or obtain other sanctions for their protection, while remaining, than those which had from the first been sufficient, and a portion of the work of the greatest importance left incomplete, thereby detracting materially from the value of the whole survey; that the said order by which the works were stopped, and the engineers required to leave, was in the form of a letter from the Governor of Tehuantepec, dated 3d June, A.D. 1851, transmitting from the Governor of the State of Oaxaca an order from the Minister of Relations of the Supreme Government of Mexico, requiring the discontinuance of the works in consequence of a law, which was inclosed, passed by the Mexican Congress, and signed by the President of the Republic, the 22d May, A.D. 1851, which said law declared the grant under which the survey was being conducted, forfeited and null, on the ground that the Provisional President of the Republic, Salas, in the year A.D. 1846, transcended his powers in extending the time for the commencement of the work, whereby, as it is asserted (the works not having been commenced), the rights under the concession were forfeited. And the said Barnard and Sidell, agents as aforesaid, declare and say that the said law under which the order prohibiting the further prosecution of the work was issued, is, in their view, unconstitutional and unjust, for the reason that the said President, Salas, was, by the decree of his appointment, fully invested with the necessary power to extend the privileges under said grant, and his acts were subsequently legitimated by the regularly constituted authorities of the Republic, and the legality of the said extension fully recognized on divers important occasions by the Government under different administrations; and that if even these reasons did not exist, *no judicial decision* has been given against the validity of the concession, by which alone, and not by Legislative or Executive action, can the rights accorded under the grant be invalidated. And the said Barnard and Sidell, further protesting, say that the survey having been undertaken on the faith of the most solemn and public recognition of the rights under the concession, and with the especial favor and good-will of the Government, and with orders from the said Government to the local authorities to give every aid, protection, and assistance, it was right to assume that the works would not be violently interrupted before completion; and, acting under this assumption of the good faith of the Mexican Government, the work was projected and undertaken; but, by the recent action of the said Government, the projectors have been disappointed in their reasonable expectations, and the benefit anticipated cannot be realized, and the vast expenditure of time, toil, and anxiety, and the outlay of capital, have been made without the possibility of an adequate return. And for these, and all other injuries resulting from the action of the Government, not only to the projectors, but to the individuals acting under or with them, the said Barnard and Sidell, agents as aforesaid, in their own names and in the name of the Company under which they act, enter this as their formal and solemn protest against the said Mexican Government and its officers aforesaid, reserving for themselves, and all connected with them, or for whom they may be acting, the right to claim and receive from the said Government of Mexico, its officers and agents as aforesaid, full indemnity for the said acts of the said Government, its officers and agents, and for all other and further damages and injury as may in this matter be made to appear as resulting from the aforesaid unconstitutional, unjust, and injurious conduct of the said Government of Mexico, its officers and agents as aforesaid.

J. G. BARNARD,
Chief Engineer Tehuantepec Railroad Company.
W. H. SIDELL,
Associate Engineer Tehuantepec Railroad Company.

Duly attested by the certificate and seal of office of Charles R. Webster, Esq., U. S. Consul at the city of Tehuantepec, on the 11th day of June, 1851.

CARD.

As the attention of the people of the United States has been recently directed to the present aspect of our relations with Mexico, and to the difficulties growing out of the Tehuantepec grant, and as many erroneous impressions as to the facts of the case have become prevalent, the Tehuantepec Company deem it their duty to place before the public, in as succinct a manner as possible, the history of the grant, and the nature of the title which is vested in them.

On the 1st March, 1842, Santa Anna, then President of the Republic of Mexico, and invested with the supreme dictatorship, granted a concession to Don José Garay, a Mexican citizen. In it he says, that "in the name of the Supreme Government, and under the most solemn protests, he declares and promises that all and every one of the concessions mentioned in the preinserted decree shall be honorably fulfilled, now and at all times, pledging the honor and public faith of the nation to maintain the projector, Don José de Garay, *as well as any private individual or company succeeding or representing him, either natives or* FOREIGNERS, in the undisturbed enjoyment of all the concessions granted."

By the terms of the decree of this date, the Government of Mexico gave numerous important privileges, and a large grant of land, comprising all that was vacant for ten leagues on each side of the line of communication, to José Garay, for the purpose of enabling him to establish a connection by steam between the two seas, across the Isthmus of Tehuantepec, either by railroad or water.

On the 9th February, 1843, the Government of Mexico issued orders to the Governors of the Departments of Oaxaca and Vera Cruz (within whose limits the Isthmus is comprised), directing that Garay should be put in possession of the vacant land conceded to him by the first decree, and that every facility should be granted for the prosecution of the enterprise. These orders were issued by Nicholas Bravo, then President of the Republic; and on the same day another decree was issued by the same President, declaring that in the grant of vacant lands were comprehended all lands which had been previously granted by the Government to natives or foreigners, and which remained uninhabited and uncultivated.

These decrees were executed by the local authorities, and Garay was put in actual possession of the lands.

On the 6th October, 1843, Santa Anna, who was again President, issued a decree, stating that the surveys by Garay had been concluded, and the works about to be begun; and ordering the Governors of Oaxaca and Vera Cruz to furnish convicts, to the number of three hundred, to be employed on the work.

On the 28th December, 1843, by another decree of Santa Anna, the period for commencing the works on the Isthmus, which, under the original grant, was to expire on the 1st July, 1844, was extended to the 1st July, 1845.

In the fall or winter of 1844, Santa Anna was no longer in power; the country was exposed to constant internal convulsions, resulting from the struggles for power of different leaders, who rapidly succeeded each other in the Presidency; and in the beginning of 1845 the difficulties with the United States had already assumed a menacing character. Garay became satisfied that the time allowed him was insufficient for organizing an enterprise of such magnitude, and in June, 1845, he made application to the Mexican Congress, asking a further delay, soliciting additional privileges and facilities for the introduction of the necessary materials and supplies, and praying that further inducements, in the way of exemption from taxes and imposts, might be accorded to persons disposed to settle as colonists on the Isthmus.

A law was introduced in the Mexican House of Representatives in accordance with the tenor of this application, and was passed by that body. It was sent to the Senate, there referred to a committee, who reported favorably, and was on the eve of being submitted to the vote of the Senate, when there occurred one of those events unfortunately too frequent in the history of our neighboring Republic.

The administration of Paredes was attacked and subverted by Mariano de Salas, at the head of an armed force; the Congress was dissolved, and Salas took possession, as dictator, of the supreme executive power. This advent of Salas was marked by consequences much more important than those which usually accompany the numberless *pronunciamentos* which have occurred in that country. The entire system of government was revolutionized; the form was changed from a central, or a consolidated, into a federative one; the quotas of contribution of the several States of the Republic were fixed; the most important administrative measures organized; the liberty of the press established, &c., &c. All these measures which now exist in Mexico, and this form of government now established there, derive their origin from decrees of Salas, no one of which has ever been brought for one moment into doubt or question, except in the single instance which will presently be noticed.

While Salas was thus exercising, *de facto*, the supreme power of the Government—while his dictatorship was thus unquestioned—his attention was called to the law which was on the eve of being passed when the Congress was dissolved; and, after examination of the subject, he promulgated his decree of the 5th of November, 1846, *which is a copy of the law that had passed the Mexican House of Representatives* and *the committee of the Mexican Senate.*

By the terms of this decree the delay of commencing the works on the Isthmus was prolonged to the 5th November, 1848. The work was actually commenced prior to that date, as is established by the official reports of the Mexican authorities on the Isthmus.

The simple narration of the foregoing facts seems amply sufficient to establish, in the most conclusive manner, the validity of the grant in question, and to preclude the Mexican Government, at this late date, from raising a question on this subject. All these decrees, however, formed a contract, to which the only parties in interest were the Mexican Government and one of its own citizens, and in which no foreign nation would have a right to interfere; and however scandalous might be the violation of public faith committed by a confiscation of the grant, neither the Government nor people of the United States would have the slightest ground for interference.

It becomes necessary, therefore, to consider in what manner our Government and people have acquired an interest in this matter, and the extent of their right to enforce the execution of the grant.

It will be recollected that, by the terms of the concession, Garay was authorized to assign his rights to any *private individual or company, natives or foreigners.* He availed himself of this privilege, and made transfers of all his rights, in the years 1846 and 1847, to Messrs. Manning and Mackintosh, English subjects residing in Mexico. This transfer was duly notified to the Mexican Government. It was fully recognized and approved, and, on the complaint of Manning and Mackintosh, President Herrera, on the 6th and 10th August, 1848, issued orders to the Governors of Vera Cruz and Oaxaca to prevent the cutting of mahogany on the Isthmus by any other than the *English* company.

In 1847, Mr. Trist, by virtue of instructions from Mr. Polk, when negotiating the treaty of Guadalupe Hidalgo, tendered fifteen millions of dollars to the Government of Mexico for a right of way in favor of the United States across the Isthmus of Tehuantepec. The commissioners empowered by Mexico to treat with him replied, "that Mexico could not treat on this subject, because she had several years before made a grant to one of her own citizens, who had transferred his rights, by the authorization of the Mexican Government, to English subjects, *of whose rights Mexico could not dispose.*"

A declaration so important as this could not fail to awaken the attention and excite the interest of every American citizen. Mexico had declared, on the most solemn occasion of public intercourse between nations, that the grant, in her estimation, was beyond question; that its validity admitted of no doubt. Fifteen millions of dollars are offered for the sale, and she replies, "I cannot sell, because what you want to buy belongs to others—to English subjects." Accordingly, Mr. P. A. Hargous, a native of Pennsylvania, but whose long experience in the trade with Mexico had enabled him to appreciate the immense value of this grant, became its purchaser from Manning and Mackintosh, and subsequently associated with

APPENDIX. 291

him in the prosecution of the enterprise a company of citizens of New Orleans.

Before commencing their works, these American citizens were, however, desirous of ascertaining beyond a doubt the honest intention of Mexico to forward this great enterprise, and also of shielding themselves, under the protection of their own Government, against the dangers arising from the constant change of rulers and forms of government in that country. They therefore applied to their Government for this two-fold object, and met with every encouragement and assistance that a subject so deeply interesting to the nation was calculated to elicit. Mr. Letcher was instructed to inform the Mexican Government of the desire of the holders of the grant to commence their work by a thorough re-survey of the Isthmus, as full confidence was not reposed in that which had been made by the engineers employed in 1842 and 1843; and to make overtures for a treaty of joint protection of the work. The Mexican Government made not the *slightest objection, did not suggest a doubt of the rights of the company*, forwarded passports for their engineers and officers, and issued orders to the Departments of Oaxaca and Vera Cruz to avoid interposing any obstacles to their work, but, on the contrary, to afford them aid and hospitality. This occurred in April, 1850. The engineers were accordingly sent, the ports thrown open for their supplies, and more than one hundred thousand dollars have already been expended in the surveys, and in opening and cutting roads through the most broken parts of the country.

On the application for a treaty, the Mexican President and Cabinet desired that a modification should be made in the terms of the grant, and especially that the company should give up its right to fix its own rates of toll for goods and passengers, and should consent to admit the joint control of the two Governments on that subject. They therefore introduced a clause to that effect in the treaty, and as it was perfectly understood that the rights of the grantees could not be affected without their own consent, another clause of the treaty provided "that the actual holders of the grant should file their assent to the treaty before its ratification by the two Governments." And in this form the treaty was concluded in Mexico between Mr. Letcher and the Mexican President and Cabinet.

It is difficult to conceive how, after such action as this, the Mexican Government can now pretend that there exists no grant! that the concession is utterly null and void!

This is not all, however. On the arrival of the treaty in this country, the holders of the grant were invited, by the Secretary of State, to examine it, in accordance with its terms, and to signify their approval or dissent. On examination, although satisfied with the provisions of the treaty, they were fearful of future difficulties that might arise from the ambiguity of certain passages, and declined to approve it, stating the clauses to which amendments were solicited.

The treaty was sent back to Mexico. In the mean time a new election for the Presidency of that Republic had been held; a new President inaugurated; a new Cabinet formed. On the application for amendment of the treaty, the requests of the grantees, through their Government, were favorably considered, many of them accorded, and a new treaty negotiated. During this entire negotiation not a hint was thrown out, not a suggestion made, indicating on the part of either of the two Presidents of Mexico, or any member of the two successive Cabinets, a doubt as to the entire validity and binding force of the grants and decrees above related, nor as to the titles of the present holders. And it is, perhaps, worthy of remark, that they were both negotiated in the city of Mexico, by Manuel G. Pedraza, an ex-President of that Republic, and at that time President of the Mexican Senate.

The second treaty was sent to this country for approval and ratification, and on the 18th February, 1851, the following letter was written, viz.:

DEPARTMENT OF STATE,
Washington, 18*th February*, 1851.

To P. A. HARGOUS, ESQ., Washington:

SIR—I have to inform you that a convention between the United States and the Mexican Republic, relative to a transit way across the Isthmus of Tehuantepec, was signed in the city of Mexico on the 25th ultimo. As its twelfth article requires that the holder of the grant conferred by the Mexican Government, pursuant to its decree of the 1st March, 1842, shall file his assent to the convention in the office of the Mexican Minister at Washington, before the instrument shall be submitted to the Senate of the United States, you are requested to call at this Department for the purpose of examining the convention.

I am, sir, very respectfully, your obedient servant,

DANIEL WEBSTER.

In compliance with this invitation, the treaty was examined by Mr. Hargous, and approved for himself and in behalf of the company. The treaty, *together with the titles to the grant*, were submitted to the Senate, unanimously approved and ratified, and the treaty was engrossed, signed, and returned.

In the mean time, and before the treaty had been sent back to Mexico,

APPENDIX. 293

Pedraza had died, and a sudden change seems to have occurred in the views, opinions, and feelings of the leading men of that country. It would not be proper, at this time, to state the nature of the influences brought to bear on the subject, nor the parties most actively engaged in exciting a feeling of hostility towards the people of this country, with the view of defeating the enterprise. It suffices to state, that a law was introduced into the Mexican Congress and passed, whereby the Congress declared, "that the decree of General Salas, of November, 1846, was null and void, because he had no power to make such decree."

This is the only action of the Mexican Congress on the subject, and, although the evident intention is to annul the original grant made by Santa Anna in 1842; yet, as no pretext could be invented for attacking it, the committees of the Mexican Congress were driven, in their reports to the two houses, to rely *solely* on the ground that Salas was without the power to grant to Garay a delay of two years for commencing his work, feeling certain that if they could succeed in this point, they would be able afterwards to attack the original grant, on the ground that the work had not been commenced in sufficient time.

Let this fact, however, be borne in mind, *Mexico has neither annulled the original grant nor rejected the treaty.* The rights of the company are precisely such as they were prior to the law of the Mexican Congress, with this single exception, that the law just passed affords a pretext on which the Government *might bring suit against the company* to annul its grant.

Whether the pretext thus sought by the Mexican Congress can be made available for the intended purpose, is the next subject for consideration.

It might be sufficient on this point to say, that the Government of Salas was a Government *de facto*, and that the universal principle on which all civilized nations act, is to consider that the Government actually exercising supreme power in a country is entitled to represent that country in all foreign relations; and that even if its powers are usurped, its acts are as binding as would be those of a regularly constituted government. Our country, in its relations with others, never undertakes to determine whether the parties found in possession of the sovereignty are rightfully entitled to it, but treats with them as having the undoubted authority to act, and to bind the country whose destinies are at the moment under their control.

But the application of this general principle is not required in the present case, and a plain recital of the history of Salas's administration affords the amplest refutation of the position now, for the first time, assumed by Mexico.

In his *pronunciamento*, when he came into power, he declared that "the cessation of all anterior pacts is indispensable, because they are all either affected with nullity or repugnant to a portion of society; but the common law which is in full force, and *those which this provisional Government will publish*, will, to a certain extent, fill the void created by the present state of things."

So that, on assuming power, he declared himself authorized to make and publish laws; or, in other words, declared himself dictator.

After having accomplished his purpose of creating a federal system of government; after causing to be held an election for President, which resulted in the choice of Santa Anna; and after convoking the Congress in order to surrender his dictatorship, he proceeded, through his minister of foreign relations, to render an account to Congress of what he had done.

This minister reported to Congress, "that the provisional Government of Salas had exercised, as the nature of the case required, a real and very ample dictatorship, which lasted till the publication of the new constitution." The minister then set forth, with great minuteness, in a report printed and submitted to Congress, all the decrees rendered by Salas. Amóngst them are the following:

A decree organizing the bureau of general archives.

A decree relative to the liberty of the press.

A decree relative to colonization.

A decree relative to literary property.

The decree of November, 1846, *extending for two years to Garay the period for commencing the work on the Isthmus of Tehuantepec.*

A decree authorizing popular meetings.

A decree concerning naturalization.

And, in closing, he stated "that he had called the Congress together at the earliest possible moment, in order *to put an end to the dictatorial period.*"

When this account was thus rendered by a dictator laying down his temporary power in the face of the constitutional authorities, not one voice was heard in Mexico, in her counsels, nor in her press, breathing a suspicion of the purity of his motives, the validity of his acts, or the extent and nature of the power which he declared he had just exercised. Ever since then the Mexican Congress, executive, courts of justice, and public functionaries of all classes, have been in the habit of citing the decrees of Salas as a part of the fundamental law of Mexico; nay, it will scarcely be credited, that the very Congress which declared that Salas had no power to pass a decree in favor of the Tehuantepec grant, *annulled a law of the State of Sonora on the ground that it violated the decree of Salas on the subject of colonization.*

Comment on facts like these could not aid in a proper appreciation of them. Six successive Mexican administrations have, directly or indirectly, declared the validity of the grant now held by the citizens of the United States. Three different administrations, in negotiating with this Government, have, in the most solemn manner, recognized its binding force. Whence now springs the difficulty or the doubt? There can be but one answer. Mexico had avowedly no control over this concession, when it belonged to *English* subjects. Her views of her rights were only changed when a transfer had been made to citizens of the United States.

That this is not a gratuitous assertion is apparent from the report of the committee of the Mexican Senate, of the 22d March last, in which it is asserted that "the fact has now become apparent which was before only suspected, and *had been the object of serious fears—the enterprise has taken root in the United States,* and the privilege is now, as has been announced in public documents, in the hands of inhabitants of that nation, who are using every effort to obtain the protection of their Government, in order to secure the success of the work and the removal of all obstacles to its completion."

It is in this same spirit that the officers engaged in the survey, whose conduct, in conformity with the instructions of the company, has been such as to secure the friendship and sympathy of the entire population of the Isthmus, have been exposed to wanton insults and outrages from the very Government which had promised them aid and hospitality, and invited their presence by its passports; that, in fine, a proclamation has been published directing their expulsion from the country, and ordering troops to be sent to the Isthmus for the enforcement of this decree.

There is, however, yet reason to hope that better and wiser counsels will prevail in that unhappy country, and that a returning sense of justice will induce such action as is due to the plighted faith of the nation.

J. P. BENJAMIN,
Chairman of the Tehuantepec Railroad Company.

ERRATA.

Page 9, (Illustrations,) for "MAPS," *read* MAP.
Page 77, line 16 from bottom, for "$954,155 78," *read* $5,954,165 73.
Page 126, line 20 from bottom, for "work," *read* business.
Page 193, Table III., for "Bejuco marillo," *read* Bejuco amarillo.

Printed in Dunstable, United Kingdom